The Daddies

Social Fictions Series

Series Editor

Patricia Leavy (*USA*)

Scope

The *Social Fictions* series emerges out of the arts-based research movement. The series includes full-length fiction books that are informed by social research but written in a literary/artistic form (novels, plays, and short story collections). Believing there is much to learn through fiction, the series only includes works written entirely in the literary medium adapted. Each book includes an academic introduction that explains the research and teaching that informs the book as well as how the book can be used in college courses. The books are underscored with social science or other scholarly perspectives and intended to be relevant to the lives of college students—to tap into important issues in the unique ways that artistic or literary forms can.

Please consult www.patricialeavy.com for submission requirements (click the book series tab).

VOLUME 28

The titles published in this series are listed at *brill.com/soci*

The Daddies

By

Kimberly Dark

BRILL

SENSE

LEIDEN | BOSTON

All chapters in this book have undergone peer review.

The Library of Congress Cataloging-in-Publication Data is available online at
http://catalog.loc.gov

ISSN 2542-8799
ISBN 978-90-04-38354-8 (paperback)
ISBN 978-90-04-38355-5 (hardback)
ISBN 978-90-04-38356-2 (e-book)

This book is printed on acid-free paper and produced in a sustainable manner.

ADVANCE PRAISE FOR
THE DADDIES

"No one anywhere writes all the way through eros, power exchange, and sexuality more fiercely than Kimberly Dark. In *The Daddies,* Kimberly risks what most writers will not, opening up and asking how masculinity has woven through every realm of our existence, how it has seduced us, betrayed us, protected us, violated us, how it lives in men and women and every other gender and sexuality, how we are facing a reckoning. Kimberly Dark asks us to embrace and reimagine masculinity from the inside out and hold the embrace long enough to change the world."
Lidia Yuknavitch, author of *Small Backs of Children and Chronology of Water*

"To say that *The Daddies* is an intensely textured, kaleidoscopic take on masculinity, Daddy-dom, and the pleasures, perils, and politics of femininity is only partly true. More accurately it is a hypersaturated, unrelenting *Willy Wonka* boat ride through a pulsating circulatory system of patriarchy, pain, and desire. Kimberly Dark has done something brave and difficult here, and I do not refer merely to the text."
Hanne Blank, author of *Straight: The Surprisingly Short History of Heterosexuality*

"About time someone wrote this book! And what good news that a writer and researcher as skilled as Kimberly Dark has taken it on."
Laurel Richardson, author of *Why I Love Ernest*

"Daddy is a person with the kind of power that asks to be misused. This is an honest, disturbing, difficult confrontation with the uncontainable. A labor of truth-telling."
Sarah Schulman, author of *The Cosmopolitans* and *Conflict is Not Abuse*

"Dark's work is a multi-layered hybrid of fiction, poetry, non-fiction, autoethnography, biomythography, and collage, which explores the concepts of 'Daddy' through social critique of news and pop culture. This is the very best of Dark – storytelling that highlights gendered interactions and what they tell us about erotic love and masculinity. This book caresses important things in social science that need focus and attention – sexual abuse, gendered expectations, and figuring out identity and desire in a patriarchal world. Dark's panache for nuanced cultural analysis and story-telling makes this book the kind of medicine you can't wait to take; you will want to buy a copy for all the people in your life."

Sandra L. Faulkner, Director Women's, Gender, and Sexuality Studies, Bowling Green State University, author of *Writing the Personal* and *Knit Four, Frog One*

"Feminist in its worldmaking, intellectual in its erotic poetry, and razor sharp in its depictions of contemporary American gender ideology, Kimberly Dark's *The Daddies* is a complex and genre-bending contribution to the archive of queer feeling and to theorizing through storytelling. In this autoethnography of Daddy's Worlds, the girls who inhabit and work in them are allowed to examine pleasures and pains of power and contradiction. Taking a range of positions, Dark's writing dares to interrogate the psychic structures and deep ambivalences of a queer desire and kinship form in ways that move us beyond simplistic ideas of perversion and subversion. *The Daddies* is a welcome addition to fem(me)inist sexual theory and a portrait of contemporary patriarchy by and for Daddy's girls, by an author who has lived and survived and dared to tell. Plus we learn more about what is at the root of #metoo and its perpetual reproductions from this book than many other contemporary sources."

Ulrika Dahl, Professor of Gender Studies at Uppsala University, co-author of *Femmes of Power: Exploding Queer Femininities*

"In this intricate and robust account, Kimberly Dark explores the world of Daddies who repel and compel us. Dark reveals in story after story a masculine culture that garners consent and insists on resistance. For readers who think this is not their world, they may be surprised to find themselves. For readers who already live there, they will see themselves rendered with sensitivity, intelligence, and compassion. For all readers, they will feel they are in the trusted hands of a careful scholar and skilled writer. Pleasure waits for those who will allow Kimberly Dark to take charge from page one to the very last word."
Ronald J. Pelias, University of Louisiana

"*The Daddies* is an unforgettable book. Beautifully written, brutally honest, poignant – essential reading for anyone interested in the complexity of gender identity, relationships and sexuality, the forever affect of incest between daddy and daughter, as well as the importance of sharing our stories as part of the journey toward transformation and healing."
Mary E. Weems, author of *Blackeyed: Plays and Monologues*

"What a deep and moving work, with plenty of meat for the erotic imagination *and* our inner culture spelunker. Kimberly Dark's strong, nimble writing dances complexly – but so, so readably – through the mythic, the erotic, the sociopolitical, the pop-cultural. It invites us to take an insight-provoking journey through many kinds of gender, many kinds of sex, many kinds of love. Thank you, Kimberly, for refusing to whittle all this down to make it seem simple."
Carol Queen, PhD, author of *The Leather Daddy & the Femme and Real Live Nude Girl*

For Jim, Chuck, Kim, Bowen ...
and every good father everywhere

CONTENTS

PREFACE

The Daddies is a love letter to masculinity, a kaleidoscope of its pleasures and horrors.

***

I hold masculinity in all the gentle forms I can find. I hold it in men and in women, I vote for it in politicians. I held my father's hand while he was dying. I learned to adapt, as all who love will do.

I am constantly looking and it is no small task because Daddy has truly run amok. Daddy is the man in the charge, the guy making the rules, he is father and stepfather and overlord and big brother. He is she and he and we, so many places at once. Daddy is in the sky looking down on us and in the government and in the military. Daddy wants to keep us safe and give us love and more than anything Daddy wants power.

I have learned to adapt and because I have fallen hard for possibility, I am still in love with masculinity, but I am no longer in love with Daddy.

***

I'm supposed to call this a novel. I know that. A novel is a work of fiction but the lines between fiction and fact have blurred these days. A work of fiction can contain true stories, whatever "true" means in an era when memory is questioned (rightfully) as collective re-membering and memoir is really "wemoir" – the story of who we are as a culture. My students in a memoir class a few years back decided to use this word, "wemoir." I don't think they were wrong. So yes, if you want to call this a novel, you have my permission. It's a novel in the way that Eileen Myles' *Chelsea Girls* or Deb Busman's *Like a Woman* is a novel, which is to say that it's not, except when it is.

I'm worried about calling this book autoethnography in the same ways I'm worried about calling it a novel. Literary terms like "novel" create a certain type of distance from material – like the reality of the "characters" can be dismissed. Terms like auto-ethnography, grounded in process, method and theory seek to legitimize personal storytelling with a different kind of distance still. I recall a literature professor's comment, back in 1998 when I was first touring my solo-performance *The Butch/Femme Chronicles* and discussing it at a university as "auto-ethnography."

He said, "Why do you feel you have to do that? You're making that script into social science when it doesn't need to be. It's just good writing. Let it be what it is."

Let it be what it is. This is the issue, right? "What it is" is socially constructed. "What it is," offers social analysis and an entreaty to action. The main reason I'm not interested in the word "memoir" to describe *The Daddies* is that it isn't meta-enough. It isn't about my life. It's about my experiences, which are something both less than and more than my life. Fiction and truth curve around like the horizon and meet somewhere we can't see. Magical realism even is the stuff of novels. I've been explaining my work as auto-ethnography for years in this way: Every story is about me, but I'm not the subject. The subject is culture, specific aspects of it that live and breathe through our personal lives. I'm a sociologist by training, I say in these explanations. Every writing teacher could have "show, don't tell" tattooed on an arm, we write it so much on student papers, and yet, I am not just a writing teacher, a writer. I'm a cultural creator and critic. I will not forsake "tell." I have something to tell.

In 1997 when I was first figuring out how to do my master's thesis, I recall talking to Linda Shaw, my favorite professor at the time, later colleague and friend. She tolerated my musings and misgivings in the way professors do with students they find unusual. I have always been one of these unusual students and as a professor now who is frugal with her time for students, I understand what a gift she gave me. I was carrying on about ways of knowing and the deeply personal experiences I was having at a community-based research and organizing job, how it was messy, but shouldn't that be the exact reason it's important to write about the personal stuff? I mean, from a social interactionist perspective, shouldn't we find that important? She handed me a copy of Carolyn Ellis' *Final Negotiations* one day with a stern admonishment. "This is one of the most important contributions to sociological literature I've read lately. But I swear to god, if you try to hand in a thesis proposal using this kind of writing, I'll kill you!" I read it that weekend while I was "supposed to be" reading other things. You can guess how I proposed (and wrote) that thesis.

I'm outlining the terms here because language is a proxy for meaning. That's part of why social fictions work. And by work, I mean, operate, effect, influence, describe, seduce, entertain, and labor. *The Daddies* may also disgust or arouse. Maybe both. I'd like for the text to prompt more discussion about why we don't discuss sex more often in the social sciences. Even solitary sex, in an image-driven culture, is a social act. After nearly a decade of performing artistic, auto-ethnographic scripts about gender, intra-gender gendering in particular (how gender is re-created within same sex and same gender groups) I realized I needed to discuss my sex life more than I'd been doing. One part of my head thought this was true. The other part said, *what the hell? You're not even an actor and now you want to be some kind of literary exhibitionist as well?*

When I first started writing about sexuality in my performance work, I was no exhibitionist. I had to rehearse the meaning out of the words in order to perform them. Even simple words like "cunt" and "fuck" were hard for me to say on stage when my first show toured. By the time I wrote my 2009 release, *Dykeotomy*, I had come to believe it was a cop out not to move further into how gender operates, is created and reinforced in intimate sexual relationships.

What do we think we're doing when we stop short of discussing the things people say and do in bed? I can answer that question because I've performed these shows on college campuses for many years now. Nearly every time I work with graduate students in Sociology and Performance Studies, colleagues implore me not to let students believe that they can write about sex primarily (whether auto-ethnographically or not) and expect to get a tenure-track job. What are we doing when we stop short in our analyses? We're not doing responsible social science on some of the themes that influence culture the most: power and eros. We're trying to keep jobs and bolster the credibility of our disciplines.

I'm taking the narrative route to tell you that this book is part novel, but also a biomythography – to use Audre Lorde's term – because I hope I'm not leaving anything important out. It became clear to me that I didn't want to make a life in the academy while writing that Master's thesis exactly because I wanted to write about things that the academy might not find important. I wanted to have an impact in the broader culture. (And as time went on, I learned more reasons why the academy was not the place for me – thank you bell hooks.) It was equally clear to me that I couldn't leave sociological ways of seeing and thinking and explaining behind. Arts-based research waxed significant after I'd been doing it for a while. My scholarly views and interests are interdisciplinary. I'm still worried that we're trying to get away with something every time we forge an explanation about our work. I make art for general audiences. That could be enough said too, but I believe we have the human responsibility to create a better, more fair and equitable world, so that's not enough either. I worry that we're trying to get away *from* something when we try to get away *with* something. I don't want my work to contribute to that deception or the inanity that accompanies it.

Here's the thing. If I want to creatively reveal the culture in meaningful ways that lead to positive change (and I do), things have to get personal. How do we manage to talk about sex and gender and sexuality without talking about how we have sex? And who is protected by that decision not to discuss our current cultural, erotic patterns? Patriarchy is protected, for starters. As more women are coming out as abuse survivors in the #metoo era, it's becoming clear to more people that our abuse is widespread. But what about the sex we choose and create? What about the ways in which "damage" begets creativity and then begets culture? We dare not ignore the erotic as a powerful font of creativity from which we form and respond to the world around us. And this brings me back to Audre Lorde, who understood this decades ago, and also struggled to find her way in the academy during her life, though her work is still revered by many, posthumously.

***

Biomythography was the genre given for Lorde's book, *Zami: A New Spelling of My Name*. Numerous reviews refer to the book as a novel, autobiography or memoir. Biomythography highlights her use of myth, history and biography in an epic narrative form. One of the things I respect most about Lorde's organization of her work was explicit naming. *The Daddies* uses personal narrative, news clips, "reviews" of other scholarly work and its relevance to the theme at hand: how we bring patriarchy into our private, emotional and erotic lives both to our detriment and as an expression of creativity, love and power. As Lorde has often been quoted, "The master's tool will never demolish/dismantle the master's house." In *The Daddies*, I hope to spark dialogue about how this is true, and also how our creative erotic responses to those tools and masters may indeed dismantle the master in each of us and thereby in the culture at large.

The Daddies is an indictment of patriarchy and also a love letter to masculinity. It's an intimate analysis of how gender hierarchy lives in our most personal interactions with our parents and lovers and patria. While focusing on what some might call a BDSM relationship, *The Daddies* shows how most people are complicit in re-creating gendered hierarchy, and how we might use a phenomenological understanding of gender to act and speak and create otherwise, in service of a fairer world.

The Daddies offers cultural analysis via critiques of pop-culture, television and news shows, etc. The references to articles and news shows here are real. I have used cultural analysis typical in qualitative methods and each is clearly referenced. For instance, the time-codes referenced in "The Purity Ball" section on Matt Launer's interview offer a real analysis of that show's manipulation of interviews and information. It's just that the chapter is written from the perspective of the book's "girl" character, rather than from the perspective of a scholar. This is similarly true with the "review" of Lakoff's book in the "The President and the Metaphors" section. Throughout, this book is influenced by my training as a cultural analyst and also by my twenty-plus years teaching and working with students from high school age through adult as a performer and speaker (as well as in the classroom as a college professor). These audiences have taught me how to tell stories about culture that "land" legibly and stimulate meaningful dialogue.

The question, "Who's your Daddy?" started showing up in mainstream cultural references during the 1990s. Those words can be spoken as a question, or a challenge, as a flirtation, a joke or a threat. It's all about inflection, intention and who's asking. Apparently, we have so much shared cultural meaning about "Daddy" the speakers and listeners can simply intuit meaning and proceed to laugh at the joke, or experience the shame, as appropriate.

But who is Daddy in American culture? *The Daddies* aims to find out more than who – but how the process of knowing Daddy can prompt readers to know themselves and their society. This allegory about patriarchy situates Daddy-ness in both men and women, indicting a system, and prompting individual responsibility for "growing up" and creating more conscious governments, communities and families.

The Daddies is a semi-fictional account of a disturbing truth – told through the first person "girl." She is called by my name, but her identity shifts to accommodate the girl as a stand-in for femininity. The primary Daddies with whom "the girl" interacts are her own father (an abused, but not abusive man), her stepfather (an incest perpetrator), her Daddy-lovers (female-bodied and masculine gendered), and her presidents (George W. Bush and Barack Obama).

At its core, the narrative arc is about erotic love and masculinity. There is currently very little scholarly analysis of these themes that dare to remain inside the topics, rather than creating academic distance from them. Through literary narrative the book addresses questions like: What is the appeal in "deviant" sexuality? How are we already playing out subtler versions of darker desires? Can we build satisfying relationships outside of strictly gendered paradigms? And also, how do our personal erotic choices influence the sort of nation, policies and religion we create and live in?

As *The Daddies* opens, the narrator has just had a terrible break-up with her partner. They were planning a life together when she's dumped for another woman – the three women had been friends and as the narrator's life unravels, she begins to understand the various ways in which patriarchy has influenced her life, decisions and relationships – even as a lesbian. She moves to a volcanic island and the presence of the "mythic girl" emerges – a fictional voice that speaks to "Daddy" (both the symbol of patriarchy and her masculine-lesbian lover), revealing the twists and turns of interpersonal kink relationships, along with their broader cultural influences.

The narrator is also a stepfather/daughter incest survivor and as the stories unfold, the narrator and "mythic girl" discuss this history. The first part, "Origins," establishes the foundation and ongoing influences of sexism from which we all grow. The second part, "Actions," progresses the reader's understanding of how patriarchal relationships are maintained, even within lesbian relationships and how our own fathers influence our lives as adult women. The third part, "Transformation," extends the metaphor of volcanic eruption – that which is destructive is at once generative. People of all genders may indeed be capable of remaking relationships outside the model of sexist gender norms.

The Daddies' loose narrative arc moves the reader through a series of stand-alone stories that illustrate the pact of gender conformity, how it's gone strangely, comically and horribly awry and then, how that might change. While the gestalt meta-analysis is of patriarchy, the story itself is scene-driven. *The Daddies* ends on a hopeful note – an invitation to remember that we are creating the world, even as it creates us.

***

The settings vary, as many of the scenes are based in memory. The narrator ends up living in Hawaii, on Hawaii Island where the volcano flows. She has previously lived in San Diego, Colorado Springs and some memories occur on vacations and in the narrator's childhood home of San Diego. The "mythic girl" resides in a fictional, dream-space where pop-culture collides with personal pathos. The pop-culture elements are taking place in the U.S. news media.

USES IN THE COLLEGE CLASSROOM

Audre Lorde's precedent-setting biomythography, *Zami*, showed that memoir, social analysis and fiction could co-exist to reveal cultural truths that emerge from the intersections of intimate relationships, stigmatized identities and cultural patterns. *The Daddies* does this as well, using memoir, social analysis, magical realism and contemporary journalism to explore the patterns many Americans have hidden about gendered living and life under patriarchy.

This book will be stylistically of interest to literature and writing departments and can be offered as a contemporary example of hybrid narrative, which includes social analysis. Thematically, it is of interest in sociology, women's studies, communication, anthropology, queer studies, rhetoric, and cultural studies. Not only is *The Daddies* "about" gender, it is a character and scene-driven account of how gendered interactions play out for a specific woman, and how those personal interactions are undergirded by and then re-create social circumstances as well.

Students studying gender roles, BDSM, patriarchy and the interstices of personal and political choice making will find new ways to link public and private communication. This text also challenges what can be discussed in college classrooms, ultimately allowing dialogue about how every part of human culture is the purview of the social sciences, though we rarely discuss the aspects of culture which shame us, or give us erotic pleasure.

Numerous questions emerge from the text regarding the themes covered in *The Daddies* along with the pedagogical implications of using holistic inquiry – in this case, stories that include violent or erotic content – to interrogate themes that each of us experiences quite personally.

ACKNOWLEDGMENTS

First, let me thank Patricia Leavy for doing her own work to show that "social fictions" have an important place in the social sciences. Then also for responding to *The Daddies* manuscript with "Wow. Oh wow." And meaning it in a good way. For all of those who reviewed this book in process and offered comments, Teresa Bergen, Carol McGrath and Lucy Aphramor in particular. Also, writing communities are super-important to me and to many others. I started writing *The Daddies* at CSU Summer Arts in 2008, continued at Vermont Studio Center in 2010 and finished at Djerassi in 2011. I was in residence at Dickinson House in 2017 when I received support to send out this previously rejected manuscript just a few more times. Thank you, thank you, thank you. This book was also significantly inspired by bell hooks' writing, in particular *The Will to Change*.

INTRODUCTION: *THE DADDIES*

I don't know why Pele called me home to Hawaii exactly at that moment, but here are my top three ideas:

1. When I first visited the Puna Coast, near Kilauea, I felt unsettled. My life and thoughts were moving more quickly than the island's energy and we weren't in sync. Five years later, life events had slowed me down and voila. We were in sync; I could hear the call.
2. Life events crippled me and in my disabled state I was unable to live anywhere else. The planet has a pulse, after all. Just like in the body, blood flows all beneath the surface. But you can't feel your pulse in your elbow. You can feel it in the tender places where the blood is close by. The planet is like that. Near an active volcano, the pulse is palpable. I'm developmentally disabled and had forgotten my connection to the earth. So she called me home; it was a benevolent act.
3. I have business near the volcano. And it's not my business to know it. I just have to show up. Bam. That's it.

She started speaking to me. That's what I know. Pele woke me from a sound sleep. It's not like she's speaking English but somehow my head translates the telepathic messages and I know what to do. Yes, I sound like some kind of woo-woo self-centered friend of the faeries to say a volcano took an interest in me, but people somehow believe "angels" take an interest in finding them a parking place that keeps them from walking and that's way weirder. You can buy figurines and plaques and stickers depicting parking angels. Maybe I'll make up some stickers that say "Listen to your volcano" and sell them online. People would buy them because as fruity as my story sounds, people wish it would happen to them.

You know those moments when you're so stressed out you're not in your right mind but you have a feeling that jittery, off-balance, emotional explosion feeling actually IS your right mind? Yes, I was in that state when Pele called me.

My relationship with my lover had dissolved. More accurately, she took up with someone she thought was hotter, simpler, funner and she no longer wanted to continue with me. What does one do with that? We had exchanged promise rings and were planning to spend our lives together. I still wanted to continue, but in the silence left by her absence, madness started to creep into my bed. It felt good, in an awful way. I had frequent past-life flashbacks in which she and I were playing out scripts of love and betrayal again and again. In one script, she was the Roman emperor who could not acknowledge a relationship with me, a common prostitute. In another, I was an angry, confused queen and she was the knight who loved me but found me somehow unapproachable, un-rescuable. I respect madness for its peculiar wisdom and though this felt like the worst breakup of my life (I would say that again and again "the worst breakup of my life") a deliciously painful change was occurring.

Look, it's not like I'd been longing for Hawaii. It's beautiful and the air caresses you giving you this tiny little skin-boner all the time. Sure, the water is alive with friendly mystery and sea turtles and dolphins are your neighbors and they really DO know more than humans. I had no particular relationship with Hawaii, nonetheless. I've never worn a little gold plumeria charm on a necklace to remind me of my time there. I didn't tack up pictures of palm trees pining to return. I had been there five years before the volcano called and, yes, whatever, stunning beauty. I felt … nervous. There was an eerie non-human presence that made me feel slightly unwelcome. Suddenly though, I was not just welcome; I received a direct order to come.

The breakup, and the capitulations prior to it, caused financial havoc in my life, so travel was not timely. And yet, so clear was the message, I got on the phone the following day to the retreat center where I had previously been in residence and then, for good measure, I called all of the female-owned bed and breakfasts I could find to explain that I was a writer and that I needed to come for a week or two. For free. Or, almost free. Inexplicably, within two days, I had three suitable offers. I purchased a plane ticket and departed that week.

Pele had not been specific about what I was to do there, so I figured I should just walk out onto the lava each evening and wait for the next message. Fields of pahoehoe lava stretched before me, as beautiful and awful and dangerous as my life had become. I was at a crossroads, and yet, there were no roads – just acres of ropy black, curly black, amazingly colorful, hard planet before me. The destructive, generative paradox – hard enough to walk on, but hot just beneath – comforted me. One night, I returned to my room in a daze. The next morning, I could barely move. Every part of my body was sore, though there was no bruising and no particular source of the pain. Fricking volcano! Pele had kicked the living shit out of me somehow. As I struggled to get out of bed, she said, *You are made to be torn down.* That was the only message.

Later that day, driving through Pahoa after a short walk onto the lava, I felt the car turning into a lot and parking. I got out of the car and read the sign on the building to see where I had parked. Pahoa Realty. The woman on the lanai said, "What can I help you with?"

And I replied, somewhat bewildered, "Apparently I need to buy real estate."

"Well come on in then." She said, as though this sort of thing happened every day.

I had no money with which to buy a house, but I looked at a few that day. I called my friend Pammie to say, "This feels nuts!"

Pammie had known me for years and she was no stranger to passionate moves. At that moment, she was living in Oregon because she needed to be closer to a river and ducks. Usually adults don't move state for ducks, so I guess I expected support for my madness. In a way, I got it.

"Well, it *is* nuts. And look, maybe the volcano is speaking to you, but here's what I know: never buy or sell property during a breakup. Give it three months and if the volcano is still speaking to you then, go ahead." This was the voice of reason. So, I waited three months and it was like a gong went off. I made an offer on a small two-bedroom cottage near the active volcano and less than a mile from the sea. I learned later that my new home was in an area sometimes called "Pele's lap."

When I called the mortgage broker recommended by my realtor, my tax return showed an income that wouldn't buy a pack of gum, let alone a house. With complete confidence, I said, "I've just put an offer on a house. I need a no-document loan at 100% financing. I have excellent credit, but no cash and no provable source of income." The man on the other end of the phone chuckled a bit and I heard his chair squeak as he leaned back, probably shaking his head.

"Just take a look and see what you have," I said.

"Okay," he said in that sing-songy Hawaiian English. He put me on hold for less than a minute and returned flabbergasted. "I think I have a loan you might be right for. This product just came in today and it can be no doc, if your credit's good.

"That's the one." I said confidently, already giving him my information.

"Unbelievable," he murmured as we hung up the phone.

***

What makes one break-up harder than another? Or for that matter, harder to accomplish? Why are some people harder to leave? I've never believed the story about finding "the one." During another breakup, my ex seemed merely absurd as she said unkind things to me. But this lover's words wounded me to the core. Why did I let her do that?

My mother remained married to my stepfather for eight years after she learned that he had been sexually abusing me from age twelve to fourteen. She chose him over me, and simply constructed a story about how she still had us both, even though I was more and more absent from her home. It became her home, not mine. She divorced him when I was 22. Or maybe he divorced her and I never got the full story. She's a story-spinner that way. A different story for every audience. She didn't see him as a pedophile or a rapist, that's for sure. I should've behaved differently. She should've forced me to behave. She was angry at something she perceived as competition from me, but what had I won? Her husband was just being himself. When you tell the story that way, how could he be to blame?

During my "worst breakup" I started realizing how difficult it can be to make choices that match one's values. She had become my partner, my beloved, and my Daddy – the one who would rescue me from all relationship difficulty. I couldn't easily give her permission to opt out of those promises.

"Do you think I was sexually abused as a child and just don't remember it?" She asked me at times. "I mean, I come up with some pretty specific scenarios when we're doin' it. Could those just come from nowhere?"

I considered it, sure. So many of us women have been messed with when we were children, by family members, by people who should be raising us. And if it's sexual abuse, it's usually men. Well, they are raising us into the world of adult expectations: women should prepare to take it; shut up and take it; look good and take it; take it and not want anything else.

I couldn't see sexual abuse on her. Sometimes I can see it on someone who's just walking down the street. I had to stop looking for it on strangers because that can really ruin the day, seeing one after another. But she and I were in it, so of course I looked for it. I couldn't find anything special, just the usual bullshit of being raised a girl. And maybe that's enough for re-enacting the particulars of patriarchy. We can pull the pattern for gender subjugation from so many small childhood experiences – the way dominance and submission lurk in so many corners of cultural and personal experience. Often, after asking questions like those, entertaining a few of my theories, she'd throw up her hands and say, "Whatever! I don't need to figure everything out. The sex we have is totally hot. That's what I know. So I'm a sick twist. You're right there with me and it's totally hot."

"Yes, but why is it hot?" I would ask. We had this conversation three or four times in the 18 months we were together.

She'd plant her feet in a dramatic stance and say. "I love the theatre of it. You are obviously strong and capable and don't need a Daddy. And I'm not your Daddy. I'm not even a man. I'm a dyke, playing a man, playing your Daddy."

And there it would end. Still, I wondered why she needed to get so far away from herself in order to feel hot. Or why the need for Daddy was so close that she was never playing. We see things on each other before we ever have the words in our mouths. Some mouths don't grow words the way mine does. She knew – strong and capable as I was – that part of me wanted a good daddy, more than I wanted a lot of things. I couldn't articulate it – or wouldn't – but I couldn't have let her hurt me like she did if I wasn't looking for some big reward.

***

Go ahead. Think the simple thing about me. But what about her? And what about all of the millions of men and women who can only get off on feeling their respective gender roles are being acknowledged and adored. Big and strong, small and fragile. Protect me while I take care of you, Daddy. Go ahead, keep thinking the simple thing about me. I'm damaged. You're so different.

***

My lover never seemed like my stepfather and that was the important part. I never felt like I was "reliving" my incest experience. Gross; who would want to do that? She was bold and assertive. She would come to me in the kitchen, after dinner, and tell me to go into the bedroom, take off my clothes and get in bed to wait for her. "Daddy needs you," she'd say. And she'd hug me and kiss me and I'd feel her hard cock, ready for me. My breath would quicken, my cunt slicken and I'd do as I was told. It was hot. Nothing like with my stepfather, who never spoke of need. He just had a creepy entitlement. For instance, as we'd sit on the sofa he'd grab my outstretched leg and place it under the blanket on his lap when my mother left the room. He always wore pajamas, maintained decorum as he took took took took. He'd use my foot to rub his penis and when he was done; he'd just shove me away and not look at me for the rest of the evening.

My lover looked at me. A deep soulful gaze, one hand on my chest – my heart – as she moved onto my body. I'd hold her around the waist with my legs and she'd fuck me deep and hard. "That's a good girl," she'd say. "You take it so good." And I was dizzy with the sensation of being seen, felt, her weight on me, the quiet joy of our breathing. I'd come and cry and cry and come again. Perfect connection; perfect catharsis.

Once I had purchased the house, and a car, the crazy deepened and I thought the crying wouldn't stop. I stayed in the Kurtisstown hostel until my house was out of escrow. That's where I read the news from my mother.

I often received email from her. Sometimes it was a check in. "How are you? Give me a call when you have time. I know you're busy." Usually, she forwarded me pictures of kittens sleeping with bulldogs, or the earth from outer space or cautions against smelling perfume samples in shopping mall parking lots. I wasn't expecting real news when I opened the email.

She told me that my stepfather had died. She read the obituary in the newspaper. Since their divorce, they had not kept in touch. He remarried and so did she. His children were angry with her for leaving him and had not invited her to the funeral. She wrote about her surprise and relief. She wasn't sure how she felt about not being told more personally that a man to whom she was married for twelve years was dead. She had decided not to go to the funeral, even though the date and time were listed in the paper.

My stepfather was a minister and author and had once been a well-respected orator and social activist. Her email was maybe a page long and in it, she tried to make sense of her love for him. She tried to make sense of her persistence in waiting for him to be a better person than he was. I wept as I read. I didn't feel anything particular about his passing, other than relief that he would not hurt others. Instead, I felt an overwhelming connection with my mother. It crept over me slowly as I read. My mother and I were cordial with one another but had not been close since my childhood. She made decisions in her life I felt I could never make – abandoning her child in favor of her spouse, chief among them.

As I read her words that evening, I began feeling that I was she – a different generation, different scenario and god willing, I'd never be faced with the choices she made. I read, with amazement, as she conveyed things I had said verbatim about my lover. She wrote: "He always had so much potential, so much passion and a desire to do great things. But he was never able to get past his own ego. He was never able to get past his ego and a feeling that other people were just there to comfort him, to serve him. I tried so hard to stay with him through the dark times, but I could never make a difference. I guess it was always up to him. And I needed to take care of myself."

I really had been sleeping with my stepfather all over again. Or, perhaps more accurately, I had been investing too much in the possibility of a better outcome with a Daddy – one that wouldn't leave me or hurt me or betray me. And that's just not real.

My life is all I can change – funny how a person needs to learn that over and over again. I live in a landscape that called me and I rumble with fire and newness. Pele is not a Daddy – she is the destroyer and the creator. She is not here to nurture. And thus I began the next chapter of my life – living on the lap of a goddess. No caretaker. Burn it down and build it up. This is a story about Daddy, in all the forms humans create. This is a love story, a hard and brutal love story. Once the burning is done, there's nothing left but love.

It is time for something new to be created, but something needs to be destroyed, first.

***

Dear Daddy,

I love you and I'm worried about you. You seem confused and saddened by my absence. When I spoke to you the other day, you said you loved me and you missed me and that you've been kept up nights wondering where you went wrong. You didn't go wrong, Daddy. I tried to tell you on the phone, but you just couldn't hear me. You couldn't hear me though you thanked me for my kind reassurances.

I admire your cordial concern for me. You are the best of the overseers, Daddy, always looking for my welfare. I have been at a loss to tell you how worried I am for you though. You are the one with whom I am intimate, yet formal. I must address you with certain respectful language, fold my hands just so and sit up straight and quiet at the dinner table. I must hold your queer silence under my tongue, like a sugar cube that fills my mouth with syrup, but I can't swallow. I can't speak and I do not swallow. I never swallow until you tell me to, Daddy. But this lack of speaking that has served us cannot carry us any farther now. I must speak frankly. I am an intimate, after all. We are more than intimate; we are related.

I am writing this letter because your state of mind worries me and compels me to intervene with comfort so that your pain and confusion do not turn toward harm. I dare not speak of what imperils you – your own hand, isolation, illness, or the brutal sanction of those who would have you be a different Daddy – hold me in line, chin to my chest, crying out your shame. Or worse than broken skin, through others' pity and loathing, you could come to loathe yourself. I am kept up nights sometimes too, wondering if harm is seeping under the doors of your house like fog, filling your lungs with a moist anger. External forces invade your cells, replicating rage. You contain a quiet rage. Breath in. Breath out.

I feel to blame, (though the feeling wanes) when you turn your pain inward, or outward. I know how easy it is for you to hurt yourself and this distresses me. I will not find you strung lifeless in your closet, hung by what you could not name. I am asking you to rally, Daddy. I know how easy it is for you to find another little girl to lick your wounds as she balances, kneeling, precariously on the foot stool next to the brass lamp with the green brocade shade, her wrists bound with pink ribbon, blood rushing to her head, flushing her cheeks as she licks, looking up at you with loving eyes. I know how you long for loving eyes looking up at you when you let a girl lick your wounds, Daddy. I know the difficulty with which you unbind those wounds. You have given me the gift of your gore; don't think I've forgotten. Even as I have taken the pestilence into my own body, holding my throat open and swallowing what comes, even as I have loved your bondage, your surrender, your release, even as I have left the room to heave out the poison you were made to carry, I have been blessed. And I had to leave you. But then, you knew that.

Every child, well parented, grows up and leaves home. Every one. Only the poorly parented stay behind to sleep in their parent's cupboards, nursing the wounds of the aging without first exercising the limbs of youth. My own mother was 32 when she left home. She loved to be needed after years of feeling tangled and unkempt in the corners of rooms she longed to inhabit. My mother's childhood home became her home. She began to live there rather than just rooting temporarily, until the pot broke, and then stretching forth toward deeper soil. She folded back on herself and bloomed within those walls. That is the way of children who stay children when their peers become adults. I love how you have needed me.

I didn't understand at first, and I'm not sure you did either, Daddy. I didn't understand what language we were speaking at the dimly lit corner table of the bar where you sat with me, so no one could view my age and ponder your impropriety. I didn't know why the barmaid cocked her head queerly when you and I spoke and laughed together. Each time she passed the table, she searched for meaning in my eyes. She seemed to think she knew me, seemed to understand what we were saying though her tongue spoke differently when it was time for the bill to be paid. I didn't understand why our language intrigued and horrified her. I didn't know why we seemed to be foreigners, even though we had always lived nearby, in the little cottage with the sloped roof, hollyhocks and pomegranates growing in the front yard of our tiny elegant house. We lived there our whole lives, you and I. We never left home and we never arrived from elsewhere. How could she treat us as though we came from afar and act as though our language was foreign?

But Daddy, I digress. I am writing to console you. I want you to know that I know what you have given me and I'm grateful beyond measure. I want you to know that my current distance is the proper way of things. You will come to see this too if only you do not harm yourself in my absence, if only you do not replace me with the girl down the block who doesn't have enough parents of her own and needs love, or the girl at the feed store where you buy oyster shell for the chickens. She thinks you are funny and kind, because you are, and though you tell me she isn't pretty enough for someone spoiled by my beauty, you could invite her over for gingersnaps and sweet lemon tea, Daddy. But I hope you reconsider. I hope you don't do that. I hope you don't do that.

Some part of you must surely feel abandoned, Daddy! And I want you to know that you are bright and capable too. Not just capable of being a good provider, of being in charge, of being a load of fun, *of sucking it up and being strong, of carrying all of my baggage up five flights of stairs when we go away from home for a few days and stay in a hotel whose elevator is always in need of repair. You are so much more than that Daddy. You are capable of so much more. You are worth so much more.*

Who would you be if you grew up too, Daddy? This letter is a gold-leafed invitation: Please find the tub of warm water for soaking in your own soul; light a candle for dinner with yourself. Every candle lit must not find its way to my skin. You can make sweet light for yourself; your fingerprints need not be sealed onto the envelopes of my body's messages in order for you to feel you've made your mark. I want you to come into your body and rearrange the furniture and throw away anything that has rusted or become musty or grown green with mold. Your inner barometer is screaming, Daddy! Why am I the one who dreams of drowning? Who would you be if you grew up too? Would you be able to rest and breathe and listen and relax? Would you be able to really relax, like when you hold me, like when we laugh together, like when you let the fluid part of yourself pour forth, rushing into every corner of my crayon box, touching all of my colors and howling with the delight of it? You have tinted the page on which I draw all of my life's pictures, Daddy. And you have shown me so much love. You have loved me and although I still hear you not-crying, not-begging, not-looking-longingly-at the back of my head, and my shoulders the curve of my derriere and my ankles, I have left you. It only makes sense. I have left you. And what I really want to know now, because I am not moving back to our home, is ...

How can I help you grow up too?

Metaphorically yours,
With Love

PART 1
ORIGINS

SHOOTING AND SPANKING AND WHO'S YOUR DADDY?

SHOOTING LESSONS

My grandfather was a police officer. He worked at the White House in Washington DC for years before he moved his family to San Diego. That was back when police worked at the White House in addition to secret service – now everyone guarding the White House Daddy is serving secret.

Even after retiring, my grandfather kept a loaded pistol under his pillow. He was a fan of firearms and their role in patriotism and family protection. Once, the house was under siege by burglars; he came home and interrupted the theft in progress. He didn't have his gun with him but he called out to the thieves, "You better get outa my house! I've got a gun!" He made his way to the phone that sat on the small phone table in the hallway (it was 1968 and phones sat on small tables in hallways) and he dialed the police. It was the right thing to do and he figured he'd slow down the thieves with threats until the police arrived. He picked up a heavy ashtray – the only weapon handy and kept yelling into the other room where the thieves were climbing out the window. "I'm coming after you with this gun!" And when he heard them run around to the front of the house to hop in their getaway car, he dashed out to the front porch where they shot at him with their non-imaginary guns. He dodged bullets, still moving toward them, and just in time, the police arrived and arrested the two burglars. He was a local hero. Their car full of loot was returned to rightful owners and they both went to prison for fifteen years each.

I was my grandparents' ninth grandchild, and the first girl. My grandfather called me "Grand-Daddy's little sweetheart."

"Where's Grand-Daddy's little sweetheart?" he'd call out, walking through the house with a bowl of vanilla ice-cream covered

© KONINKLIJKE BRILL NV, LEIDEN, 2019 | DOI:10.1163/9789004383562_001

in Hershey's chocolate syrup for me, one for himself. We'd sit on the back porch, gazing into the neatly manicured yard he kept. I loved the big fluffy pampas grass at the back fence, into which he had set three colorful reflecting balls. I was forbidden to run into the enticing pampas grass because, fluffy as it looked, it would cut me up with its sharp leaves. We'd finish our ice-cream and he'd take my bowl, then look straight ahead for a while longer, stoic. Then he'd say "Grand-Daddy's gonna getcha!" And I'd shriek and run. That was my 3-second warning to start the chase by running. Around and around the trees we'd go – there was a fig tree and a tangerine tree and a few of those trees with white bark that you could peel off with your fingers. Whenever my grandmother saw me playing with strips of the bark, she'd throw her voice a bit and moan, "Oh, ow, ouch, owwww!" Then she'd say in her regular voice, "Do you hear that? I believe that tree in the yard is hurt from someone pulling off its bark." I didn't pull much because I sort of believed her about the tree being hurt, but sometimes it was just too enticing, hanging in strips.

My grandfather would chase me until his shirt was untucked and my hairpins had started to fly out. My long hair was always pinned into a bun on top of my head.

"Now look! You've made her all a mess!" my mother would admonish when we came in from playing. She seemed a bit jealous that I was making her Daddy's eyes sparkle and getting his attention that way.

"Come with me now," my Grand-Daddy said one day. And I followed him obediently around the side of the house. It was a sunny afternoon and my grandmother was napping. No, she never napped. "I'm just resting my eyes," she'd say when someone disturbed her light snoring.

"Now, I'm going to show you something and you can't tell anyone about it, y'hear?" He looked quite serious and I nodded my head wondering what secrets could be relegated to such a private outdoor interaction. "I want you to see something – just so you'll be comfortable with it later," said my grandfather and he began to unwrap something in a cloth. It was his gun.

"A little girl like you can sometimes be unsafe in the world and, well, it's no secret is it? You've got a sassy mouth on you, little sweetheart!" He chucked my chin and his eyes sparkled when he said this. I was only six or seven years old at the time, so I couldn't quite sort it out – how being sassy could be a bad thing and a good thing. He sometimes threatened to hit me for being sassy and at other times seemed proud of me for it. Once, after dinner, when we were watching *Bowling for Dollars* on television, he told me to settle down and I didn't and he swung his leg to kick me, sitting on the floor in front of his recliner chair. My grandmother, still sitting in her chair in front of the television spoke sharply, "If you strike that child, I'll call the police!"

To which he yelled back, fury in his eyes toward her too, "Then you'd better start dialing because a girl with that much lip is gonna end up bloodied in this house or any other!" That surprised me and made me settle down a bit, my leg sore from the kick. My grandmother shook her head and took me in the other room to read a book and he finished watching the bowling show on his own.

In the backyard, unwrapping his gun, I felt I was being shown something special – and also something dangerous that I didn't wish to touch. "Put that in your hand now, girl." He said to me sternly and showed me how to hold the gun.

"Now, I'm not going to live a whole lot longer and you're still gonna get a whole lot prettier," his eyes sparkled then too. Again, a bad thing and a good thing all at once. I didn't understand. There was something dangerous happening to me that might prompt deadly interactions, and yet, it made his eyes shine with pride. "And I don't expect that professor-father of yours even owns a gun." I shook my head slowly. I had never heard talk of, or seen a gun at our house, not ever.

"Now, hold it in your hand like this. And never ever, get on this end of the gun – not yours, or anyone else's, y'hear?" He tapped the front end of the barrel and he looked very serious, so I nodded again. "Never turn it toward you," he emphasized.

Out beyond the pampas grass at the back of the yard was a thick wood. It was government property – nothing but trees and birds. I could hear the owls hooting at night when I slept over. My grandfather aimed the gun toward the woods and held my hand on the gun, underneath his. He showed me how to look just right to see where the bullet would shoot, then we pulled the trigger, and something big happened. I didn't really know what because I didn't see the bullet. Somehow I had expected to, like on the Superman show where he runs alongside the bullet during the opening monologue that says, "faster than a speeding bullet." On the show, the bullet is speeding, but I can see it. I didn't see anything when I pulled the trigger, but I felt a little sick, like I wanted to run away. I knew I dared not. My Grand-Daddy was showing me something special and I didn't want to seem scared.

Suddenly, my grandmother's voice was calling out the bedroom window, "What on earth are you shooting at out in that yard? The neighbors are going to think you've lost your mind!" And he quietly said to me, "That's enough for now." And quickly wrapped the gun back in the cloth. "Run on inside and play in your room for a while," he said, and slapped my bottom as he did sometimes when I was getting up to go somewhere.

"It's not a spank," he said once, when I looked offended by the pop, "just a little get-along." He gave me a final wink as I ran around the corner, knowing I wouldn't mention our secret to my grandmother when I ran into the house to play, like I was told.

SPANKING

Dear Daddy,

Do you remember how much I never wanted to be punished? And you said you never wanted to punish me either – but that a spanking was not actually a punishment. I still remember how you explained it to me.

"When you see a Daddy spank a girl with a bare hand, that's a girl he really loves. I'm talking about a real spanking, not just a little swat. That means he loves her enough to feel the pain with her – to take on more pain than she's feeling. He's right there with her and his hand is going to ache."

You slapped my ass with your bare hand. Skin to skin. First the left cheek and then the right. After every four or five contacts, you'd spank the middle, between thigh and ass, sending a quiver through my whole vulva. The blood flow to my bottom increased and my lower body began to feel more alive, but it didn't hurt. And then it did. An exquisite distance arose between your raised hand and my ass, the air tingling with heat between the two.

"For the Daddy, the hurt is all in one place." You described it as though the spanking was a weather front that would move through, affecting both Daddy and girl. Sometimes it would be light and frivolous, sometimes vicious, a potential for flooding, for damage. Of course there would be wetness, but the Daddy could choose to stay out in the rain too, or put on a raincoat against the torrent if he didn't really want to engage, if he didn't really love the girl in his care.

I started to understand spanking a little differently because of your careful patience with me, Daddy. I started to understand that it's complicated. It can be a punishment, or it can be loving, or it can be just a game you play.

So, if the Daddy was merely taking on a role, merely visiting – something like a social worker for that girl – he might want distance, isn't that it Daddy? Yes, distance would be best because he would not even be a social worker, really, rather the kind of worker being paid minimum wage and given no health benefits to shuttle the poor little creature from one appointment to another in the foster care of her miserable youth. If that girl were unloved, he would remain unaffected, a mere utility to her destination. Oh, she would be served, in the social service sense of the word. And he would be rewarded, though little, unless he's the sort that gets off on being needed, being wanted, doing good work. Of course he is that sort, at least at first.

But perhaps he loves her – like you love me Daddy. You said, "For the girl, the point of impact changes. For the Daddy, the hurt is all in one place."

I didn't let you spank me at first because I don't like pain, do you remember? Then I learned that barehanded spanking is something other than pain. I learned it's warm and connected. It's hot. As with a good massage, circulation improves and contact soothes. I also don't like the idea of punishment. My eyes glow with the gold of goodness, so my pleasure comes from activities other than punishment. The process of letting you pick my locks, come into the vault – inviting you,

7

shaking off the vines that cover my fortress and letting you come to get the gold, that is my pleasure. I know you are grateful. Why would I ever need punishment?

I let you spank me a little once and then I stopped you to ask. "But why do you want to spank me, Daddy?"

You had enjoyed giving many spankings in your years, if all those stories are true, Daddy. But surely you'd only spanked girls who don't guard and gift their goodness as I do. Surely they were the wards that key their workers' cars if left unattended in the parking lot of desire. Surely, they were the girls who goaded punishment so they could feel something, anything but loneliness or the fear of love. I'm not that kind. I feel fine. I feel fine. Surely there was pleasure in punishing those girls, but I was your own girl, Daddy. I feel the joy in ownership: 'belonging to' is one form of belonging. I am your own, and you love me, right Daddy?

"Why do I want to spank you?" you responded, and I nodded to affirm that you had understood my meaning. There was a pause in which you sat stoic until your mouth stretched wide in contentment.

"Because you like it and it gets you wet."

That answer made me smile, then laugh. It was the right answer. And from then on, you could pull out that answer as a tool for rolling me over and pulling down my pajama bottoms. That answer was a tool, but not a trick. Thank you for not tricking me, Daddy. I don't play and I don't have scenes. It's all real for me. We fool ourselves to believe that foster care is a type of parenting that moves a girl toward maturity. A really good Daddy who can't say 'I love you' and mean it is just a custodian. I want family, enduring connection. And now I know you do too, Daddy. You do too.

I always asked, just to be sure it was still about me. And you never used the paddle.

"Because you like it and it gets you wet."

Daddy, do your hands still ache for me?

Love,
Your Girl

THE ETYMOLOGY OF COLLOQUY

It can be a question, requiring response, or simply a statement of superiority, a demand, a boast, and an all around statement of dominance expressed in three little words:

"Who's your Daddy?"

Daddy is the name of the person in charge, cited in the Oxford English Dictionary back to the 19th Century. Daddy has been the title for the stage manager and then for the pimp in the early 1900s. Daddy has been the hardest man on a prison wing – one likely to use violence and rape, possibly murder with impunity. Daddy is sometimes synonymous with "Boss" in con vernacular, or simply meant to connote the masculine, dominant partner in a homosexual union. By the 1920's Daddy had come into usage in African American vernacular as any male lover. Variations such as "sugar-daddy" made their way into popular American usage.

"Who's your daddy?" is originally a sexual reference, regarding submission. The phrase arrived in mainstream American culture in the 1990s as a demand for respect. The comment's origins – either as a pseudo-Freudian outburst during sex, or as a reference to Sadomasochism/Bondage-Discipline sub-cultures – seemed to dissipate like fog. Few who sing along with Toby Keith's 2002 hit "Who's Your Daddy" would think that they are glorifying incest.

"Yes Daddy!" "O Papi!" These are sexual utterances denoting obedience. Perhaps the man knows subconsciously that the speaker loves and obeys her (or his) father. Especially outside of marriage, these utterances denote a surrender of self that usually only happens within the family unit. Daddy can enjoy submission without responsibility – without the long-term demands of relationship.

"Who's your Daddy?" as an interrogative, demands response. The respondent was perhaps not going to acknowledge submission, but now the point has been pushed. Daddy is naming himself and he is pushing the point. While "Daddy" as a nickname has become playful, almost synonymous with "Baby" within the realm of pet names or pillow talk, "Who's your Daddy?" means to evoke or force submission. As noted in an online blog discussing the term, "When someone says 'Who's your Daddy?' they are pretty much calling you their bitch. It's commonly used among testosterone-driven males when competing."

This behavior, being acceptable for men, has rendered the phrase "Who's your Daddy?" benign or even comical. When an unsavory term "ameliorates" (to use the language of lexicographers) it acquires a "better" or mainstream connotation. What was previously unspeakable in public, becomes common, unquestioned, de rigueur.

Nothing in the literature on origins or in the online discussions of these terms references the gendered nature of Daddy, as though it were not salient to meaning at all.

CHAPTER 2

THE FIRST TIME

My stepfather is driving the car as I sleep next to him, fully reclined. We are alone; my mother has driven the other car. We are on our way home from a party at the charm school that is our family business. He can see her on the freeway behind him for a while, but then he stops noticing whether she is there or not. He drives nearly an hour from the party to our home. He has been drinking, but he's not what he'd call impaired. He feels the fatigue of socializing more than the alcohol. He is relaxed, little traffic at ten p.m. to thwart him. He feels calm and in control as red lights drift slowly in the lanes ahead, white lights come toward, move past just to his left. His side of the car lights up briefly as they pass. He glances at his reflection in the rear-view, pats his thinning hair with thick, stubby fingers. He is on his way home, no one else will see him this evening; but practicing attractiveness is habitual. He is unseen as he looks at his own lap, sucks in his gut and shifts a little, admires the crease in his own slacks.

I am sleeping next to him. He glances at me and thinks I look peaceful at first, then comical, somehow vulgar the way my face is turned so far toward the left, head lolling, mouth open a bit. He drives and glances at me again, thinks I look sexual somehow, still comical, strangely vulgar. My mouth poised the way a woman's is when she wants it, or when she's drunk. There's no difference, really.

I am sleeping next to him and I am wearing make-up, for the party. It's that late-seventies kind of make-up where the black eyeliner goes all the way around the eye, drawn carefully into the lower lid, not outside the lashes. White frosty shadow on the lids matches the white frosted polish on the short nails of my summer-painted fingers.

'My God, she's an adult,' he thinks to himself, trusting only his eyes to tell him my age, though he knows that I am eleven, or perhaps I am twelve. Mine is a summer birthday and it is summer. He cannot remember whether we have celebrated my twelfth birthday yet or whether it's still to come. It's not his business to know my birthday. It's my mother's business. He'll think of something clever and warm to say about me to commemorate the day – or he has already done so. He doesn't know now which, and doesn't care.

'My God, she's an adult,' he thinks again, glancing at my sleeping body, lips parted in slumber. Brooke Shields is also twelve and she's on the magazine covers this year. She's twelve, on the women's magazines, an adult. He is smiling, with his wrist resting on the steering wheel of the car as he drives, gazing at the lights ahead, passing under the big green highway signs with ease. He is a lucky guy to be around so many pretty girls when he joins his wife at work. And they're all so young, which is a prerequisite for beauty. "You're a pretty girl." That's what he says to the women. Nothing more complimentary than that. That's what he says to me. He says it to my mother too. "You're a pretty girl." And then he kisses her cheek. He's a lucky guy.

He is watching my cleavage as I turn slightly to the side in slumber. I'm wearing a blue sundress with spaghetti straps and my breasts and hips have indeed become full within the last year. The short bolero length cotton print top is not meant to close in the front, only meant to cover the arms a bit, keep off the night chill. He has never considered the way a woman feels her own arms, what it might be like to be a woman with cold shoulders and a fashion sense. He has not considered this and does not consider it now. He thinks this lack of closure means something: access. The clothing means display and access. He loves how these are related.

I am wearing skin-tone pantyhose and a gold chain necklace with charms on it, hanging from a charm-holder. There is a gold K, for Kimberly, a little gold turtle, a gold kitten and tiny gold replica of a diamond ring.

"Those charms are expensive," my biological father would say around Christmas-time or my birthday, and his new wife would swat him and say, "She's a young woman now; the jewelry just gets more expensive by the year!" And he'd give her a knowing look and say, "Don't I know," and she'd wiggle her gold-ringed fingers smiling like a cartoon character. He seemed happy that the gift giving was easy though. The expense was worth the ease. He didn't struggle like when I was young and he really didn't know what I actually wanted. He still didn't see me very often. One gold charm for my birthday, one for Christmas. That's easy.

In the light of the oncoming traffic, my stepfather sees my high-heeled sandals tossed on the floor of the passenger seat. They hurt my feet by evening's end and besides, I wanted to curl up and sleep. They are the Candies with the thick plastic platform soles, thick spike heels. They have white cotton ankle straps and four thin cotton straps across the toes, knotted in the middle. At eleven, I stand five feet eight inches barefoot, six foot in those shoes. He sees the shoes and recalls me standing eye to eye with him at the party when he'd mischievously poured a shot of vodka into my punch glass from the bottle he found on the kitchen counter. He enjoyed my youthful exuberance, the way I always followed a beckoning finger into the other room to look for snacks hidden from other party-goers, to see some distant fireworks from a balcony or to sweeten the punch a little more with alcohol. He likes to take anything that isn't offered. Being in a host's home was enough permission, he figured. There is always something in the next room that should be explored, reasons his inner adolescent. My mother always crinkles her brow and shakes her head quickly – the whisper-version of gesture saying "No" when he tries to beckon her away from the group at a party. But I always follow, giggle, happy to be doing anything slightly naughty with adult approval.

He makes me happy. He knows that. He enjoys talking to me too. He recommends books for me to read and we discuss politics and current events. He knows that, given the choice, I would ride with him rather than my mother.

'She likes me better than she likes her own mother,' he thinks to himself.

He pulls into the driveway ahead of my mother. Her car is nowhere in sight. Perhaps she stopped for some milk on the way home. He hopes there is milk for cereal in the morning. He likes her to keep the kitchen stocked with staples. A person who grew up during the Depression shouldn't go without food or money ever again. He bagged groceries for ten cents an hour as a child and the family sometimes ate saltines and ketchup for dinner if there wasn't enough food to make a meal. He was the youngest of thirteen children. If he got dirty, his mother would say, "It'd be easier to have another than clean you up." Yes, she'd stopped for some milk and bread he told himself.

He glances at me again, car stopped in the driveway, my calf-length skirt wrapped loosely around my thighs in disheveled slumber. He remembers being happy that I was along at the party that evening, happy he could entertain me briefly in the kitchen with a shot of vodka before we rejoined the party guests. 'Such a pretty girl,' he thinks to himself. He reaches out his hand, pushing my skirt up with one motion and thrusts his fist down into the front of my pantyhose and panties. He enjoys the way my legs parted as my body shifted from the movement. He enjoys that a lot. He pushes his fingers past the soft hair, parting my labia, surprised almost at how hard it was to find flesh, my vulva closed and sleeping. But there it is, the dampness of concealed flesh. He knows what he is looking for and though he isn't sure he's found it, he begins to rub, and as my body relaxes after the initial intrusion, he truly feels that he has reached flesh. He rubs, watching the street out the driver's side window, dark and empty, no sign of my mother's headlights.

I wake and, noticing the intrusion, turn away from him, at which he pulls his hand loose of my clothes. My panties lie strangely against my vulva and my pantyhose are pulled down a bit or perhaps I would tell myself I have dreamed it. I don't know how to wake from a non-dream though, so I just keep right on sleeping, or at least acting like I am sleeping. And suddenly, he is tearing out of the driveway and making a quick left. He notices that I keep at the business of sleep, though my heart is pounding, not knowing where we are going.

He stops very soon, around the corner, in the secluded parking lot overlooking the sea. He looks at me, not knowing whether or not he has awakened me with his hand. He just wanted to touch it, that's all, didn't even give it any thought before it happened. But now he is thinking, damn it! He is thinking and I am still sleeping, or at least acting like I am and he is grateful for that. Perhaps if he could say what he needed to say, I would both hear him and obey, or I would really be sleeping and later would not have remembered anything. 'This is brilliant,' he thinks to himself.

"I don't know what came over me, Kimberly," he says. "I told myself I'd never do that sort of thing to anyone again, but I just wasn't thinking. You know I love you. You know that I would never do anything to hurt you. I've never done anything to hurt you. You know that. I haven't hurt you." He takes my murmuring and shifting in the seat as assent. He decides he needs a good night's sleep. It wasn't a very good party. He is tired and had a little too much to drink. No, it wasn't a very good party. It's not his fault when there's a woman in the car like that. When there's a woman who's been drinking in the car like that. He just needed a good night sleep. He arrives home in time to watch my mother putting milk into the refrigerator. He doesn't look at me as I carry my shoes into the house.

CHAPTER 3

THE PRESIDENT AND THE METAPHORS

PRESIDENTIAL DADDY

The television is on in the hotel lobby, the sound turned down to an audible warble. The men in suits are talking on the screen. We are watching their bodies from the desk up and they are nodding and blinking, leaning and speaking importantly. The man who will become America's president is talking now, for an extended time.

Absently, I glance around the room at the travelers taking breakfast. A man comes in from outside. It's chilly and he shakes himself for warmth, looks at the television for a moment and removes his jacket. He begins to pour coffee from the free continental breakfast buffet. He is the hotel shuttle driver. He drives back and forth to the airport, back and forth to the nearby university. In some part, many of us are in this hotel because of the shuttle it offers. The driver is important, in his own way.

The future President Obama leans back a bit and looks down and smiles, before opening his mouth to make a point. While he speaks, he leans forward, holds forth with great authority. This is clear from his demeanor, words inaudible.

"Oh hell yes," says the shuttle driver, rather loudly toward the television. "Who's your Daddy! Who's your Daddy!" He pokes the air a bit with one hand, steam rising off the coffee in the other hand. "That man is going to become president." He says, nodding his head vigorously.

All four of us – each sitting alone at our own tables on this Wednesday morning – are ready for work or travel, and we hear these comments. I glance around the room to see how the words have landed. A man in a suit has tightened his jaw and shakes his head a bit as he rustles his newspaper. A woman glances up and smiles. The other man doesn't seem to have noticed the words, intent on his cinnamon

© KONINKLIJKE BRILL NV, LEIDEN, 2019 | DOI:10.1163/9789004383562_003

roll and banana. I look at the shuttle driver. He watches the television attentively. He notices that I'm his only active audience and says to me, "And he's handsome too, right?"

I nod. "Yes, he's handsome," and after a pause I add – part joking, part coquettish, "you think he's gonna be *my* Daddy?"

The shuttle driver chuckles and shakes his head. "Ma'am, he's gonna be everybody's Daddy soon. That man is in charge. And got some folks doing things they didn't think they would." He smiles, repeats, "That man is in charge." He pulls on his jacket and says, a bit louder, to everyone in the room. "Airport. I'm going to the airport."

I first started to notice it on silent televisions – the way things would turn out. I don't have a television in my home, but I travel a lot and America's public spaces – airports, bars, hotels and restaurants – are replete with television sets. In the primaries, Hillary Clinton often looked disgruntled, while Barack Obama would look confidently irritated. This is a gendered interpretation of the same look. And even I make it. I wondered at this as I watched the silent screen, announcements of flights leaving for Tampa and Boston blaring around me. I watched the screens, Clinton's hand gestures, her hands dancing as she spoke. They looked slightly flustered and at one point, she gave Obama the hand, while he was talking. It was the "talk to the hand" hand. This contrasted to Obama's strong, punctuating hand gestures, his disdain expressed through keen, penetrating glances, brief chuckles.

But then I noticed the way others in the frame watched Hillary. And indeed, she seemed to have different reasons for being disgruntled by the discussions. She wasn't just debating Barack. She was countering everyone in the room with her position and presence. Where did their eyes fall? How did they show attention when she was speaking? These are the subtleties of gendered interaction. Gesture and glance carry the dismissal that words cannot in formal circumstances and no indictment can be leveled because, who knows if there was a slight? A glance can be misinterpreted, imagined. Only those who receive such slights often enough to make a clear analysis of the patterns really know. And whom can they tell without the perception of whining? This is the same with race, and indeed, given a black male candidate and a white male candidate, the nearly imperceptible favor given to the white man might have swayed a vote. But gender bias is also hidden, subliminal, and maybe more insidious because most of us live in mixed gender households. The word "bitch" is still everyday parlance, even in a presidential race. I started to wonder whether this had been strategy on someone's part – to run Barack against Hillary first – get the public accustomed to seeing his obvious superiority as practice for the deciding match.

In a restaurant bar, speaking above the movement of plates and glasses, the man next to me commented to his friend, "Did you see her face drop? He's nailing her." One of the debates was on. They could not hear the debate, but the two men watched the screen nonetheless. Then a little while later, he said, "She's got a li'l attitude now!"

The other replied, "Yeah, but she's still getting nailed!" Women's bodies and demeanors are the easy object of scrutiny, and what does it mean for a woman's face to drop when she's getting "nailed" vs. a man's face dropping? It's not a question I can answer, but I can see that it doesn't compare favorably.

She is not your Daddy. She's not going to be your Daddy. She may act powerful, but her power is as easy to dismiss as turning your head toward the papers in your lap, turning your head toward the wall, toward the other candidate. Her power is a mere entertainment. "She got him on that one, but just wait!" The man gestured with his beer, seeming to cheer her on for a moment, never expecting she'd win the joust.

She is not your Daddy. She is not my Daddy either, though sometimes women can be Daddies.

The Daddy gets into my bed, into my heart and knows what to do there, how to be strong, keen, penetrating with attention and caring.

My father, my stepfather, my patria – they are all men, but the intimate Daddies, in my case, were born women. Daddy is still maleness, but why would it matter what the dick is made of?

GETTING WHAT I WANT

I am running out of words. My vocabulary is getting smaller and smaller, but I am getting what I want, so perhaps I shouldn't worry about this triviality. I have started sucking my thumb. No, really.

Well, not really, but in my mind, I am sucking my thumb with an angry look on my face. Children wear this look when they don't get what they want. It's a form of self-soothing when the child feels cross and powerless. That's what the parenting magazine told me. I am very cross with Daddy. And I don't have enough words to express myself.

I told Daddy I wanted information and I wanted it fast. Daddy is not always good at giving fast information. Sometimes the story is slow to come and I put my hand on my hip and tap my pretty bejeweled toes. Daddy does not want me to get raucous with my dainty stompers so the story comes. Daddy said, "I'm only spending time with her to help her study for her tests. Would you have me be unkind?" And of course, I said no. Of course, I said that Daddy should be kind. Daddy is always kind to me and I am not selfish. Daddy knows I am not selfish; I am very giving. Daddy should know.

I am not unkind. I am generous because I have so much and I know why I should be mad at Osama bin Laden. I saw that on the news over and over and over and over and over. I hadn't heard about Saddam Hussein in a long time. Didn't we used to invite him over to dinner parties? Give him gifts? There was a picture on the mantle, wasn't there? Daddy put that picture away. Daddy is in charge of all photographs, all correspondences. Now we hate Saddam. "Don't you want to be supportive?" Daddy asked me when I expressed confusion. And of course I want to be supportive. I am very supportive. Daddy should know. Why did that girl need help with her tests? I asked Daddy to tell me why certain things are happening. I wanted to know so that I could be comforted. Daddy always comforts me.

The world started to confuse me and Daddy said I shouldn't worry my pretty head about everything. "Who can know everything?" Daddy said, "You just let me handle this." And that made sense. I like it when the stories make sense. I didn't want to have to know anything, let alone everything, about health care policies and the foreign affairs and the garbage. Where does the garbage go when the dirty, burly men take it away? Daddy just laughed and looked at me fondly when I asked this and I felt safe. As time went on, I wanted to know less and less but I still needed to feel comfortable, didn't I? Daddy is so helpful.

Daddy said he just wanted to take the new girl out for an ice cream. Daddy said, "I don't really want much from her. Don't be a silly princess. She was just wearing such a beautiful dress and it made me want to buy her an ice-cream." Daddy thought I would be comforted but this just made me cry and cry. I want to be the special one in the pretty dress, but Daddy didn't know this. If another pretty girl hadn't distracted Daddy, this should've been obvious. So I cried and cried. I didn't want to know about segregation in schools. It's worse than it was in 1954, but I don't know what to do about that, so Daddy took the word away. We just don't use that word any more: segregation. Now we say things like community schooling and cultural diversity. And so, I felt better.

I cried and cried, but it's okay because Daddy made another story: "We never went for ice cream. That was just a passing thought. I couldn't take her to your ice-cream parlor, ever, sweet girl." That's what Daddy calls me, "sweet girl." And usually, that makes me stop crying, but I am still cross. I miss ice cream. No one speaks of ice cream any more.

I asked for Daddy to comfort me and I have gotten what I asked for. Words keep disappearing from our vocabulary though and it makes the stories sound so strange. You should hear how long we have to talk nowadays to avoid words like racism and privilege and ice cream and pretty dress. We have to talk a long time and sometimes Daddy tears the pages out of certain magazines before I am allowed to read them. Daddy doesn't want me to be upset. Daddy loves me. That's the only explanation.

The stories don't always match up because sometimes, in order to make me feel better, Daddy tells me one thing, but then it doesn't quite work and so Daddy tells me something completely different. I'm starting to notice the disparities and it makes me mad at Daddy. If only Daddy had lied to me effectively in the first place, this wouldn't be happening!

Where does the garbage go? And why can't we swim in the bay anymore. Daddy says, "I'm tired, princess. I've been working hard." Daddy says, "I have a kink in my swimming shoulder; not today. Just give me a little rub right here." And so we don't go to swim in the bay, but I can read the danger signs. The ones written in plain English that say "Hazardous" and "Contamination," the ones right next to the immigrant, non-English speaking children swimming despite the peculiar smell. Daddy cannot take me swimming today but it has nothing to do with me, with the water, with the smell. There is a constant smell of something when Daddy talks. What is that smell and why did I never notice it at first? Daddy used to kiss me more often and I never noticed that smell. Where does the garbage go and who is that girl in the pink bathing suit looking at my Daddy as though something is familiar?

I am exhausted and cross with Daddy. Where is my pudding! Where are my new sparkly shoes? Daddy said we'd have more of everything and everything would be better than it ever was before and I believed it! I wanted to believe it because, after all, what could be wrong with more pudding and more sparkly shoes? Those things make me feel better. Well, I think they do – at least they distract me. Yes, and being distracted makes me feel better, better than – something. Where is my cake! The women in the Mariana Islands factories are sewing my party dress. The women in Bangladesh are assembling my fancy new coat. I said I wanted more shoes. More shoes! And this made Daddy chuckle with sparkly eyes. I love it when Daddy is happy. Daddy likes me to be an expensive girl, a demanding girl, a naughty, horny, little slutty girl just for Daddy. And I give everything I am to Daddy. And Daddy gives me everything too. Everything except what other girls get. Why am I home alone? Daddy said I'd never be alone again if only I didn't ask questions. Where is that smell coming from? I have gotten exactly what I asked for. But I miss swimming. I miss ice cream. I can't stop wanting things and Daddy does not seem amused any more. I have gotten everything I wanted, but the wanting doesn't seem to stop. Where does the garbage go? Why can't Daddy come up with a story that really works for me?

This is all Daddy's fault. I have started sucking my thumb and this feels foolish. I am a grown woman. This is all Daddy's fault.

REVIEWING THE LITERATURE

In *Moral Politics*, George Lakoff applies cognitive science to politics (Lakoff, 1996). Though he's published books on how we think in relationship to American politics since *Moral Politics* (*Don't Think of an Elephant* (2004), *Thinking Points* (2006) and *The Political Mind* (2008) to name a few), *Moral Politics* is worth discussion for the idea that people's political reasoning is determined to a large extent by unconscious metaphors. Our political views – on the republican and democrat ends of the spectrum derive from the metaphor of the nation as family. This is deep and unconscious, because that's how metaphors work. And Lakoff's no new-age spiritualist nor humanities-addled novelist. He's an MIT-trained linguist who went on to be a cognitive science bigwig at UC Berkeley and other esteemed institutions.

According to Lakoff, the political views of Americans, both liberal and conservative, derive from the metaphor of the nation as a family. But, the liberal and conservative worldviews are informed by two very different conceptual models of the ideal family. At the center of the conservative worldview is the "strict father" model, while liberals subscribe to an ideal of family life centered on the "nurturant parent."

"Strict father" is all about the morality of the traditional nuclear family in which Daddy supports the family financially and protects the family from harm. He also wields the authority and makes the rules. The children and the wife behave. His authority is super-legitimate – just the way it ought to be. In this worldview, self-discipline, self-reliance, and respect for legitimate authority are the crucial qualities that children must learn. Reward and punishment are important because people will be selfish otherwise. We will only be generous in order to gain rewards or avoid punishment.

The "nurturant parent" model, by contrast, stresses the importance of empathy, nurturance, fair distribution, and restitution. It's all about being cared for and cared about, getting and giving love, living as happily as possible; meaning comes from care. In this model, the obedience of children comes from their love and respect for their parents and their community, not out of the fear of punishment. Note that both men and women in this model can be nurturing parents – the doting daddy in the driver's seat is sometimes mama.

With the "nurturant parent" model, good communication is crucial because it is only when parents explain to their children why their decisions serve the cause of protection and nurturance that their authority is seen as legitimate. The strict father, however, need not explain himself clearly nor often. His power is unquestioned.

Lakoff says that both of these models "provide rich moral and political worldviews, rich enough to permit a wide range of variation." Nevertheless, the metaphors shape the political outlook and ideology of players. And since family-based morality is all-encompassing for most people, they tend to frame political questions in light of their family values. These are not just opinions about what makes for the best public policies, they are ethical views about what makes good people and a good nation. The family metaphor follows us outside of the home, outside of interpersonal interactions. It's everywhere.

Lakoff believes that conservatives are more aware of their metaphorical worldview than liberals. That's why they're sometimes better at exploiting the metaphor in the minds of those who take it for granted. Over the past few decades, they have defined their ideas and adopted the best language to express them. Liberals are less aware and take their views for granted, so they can't discuss them as easily.

Lakoff is clearly advocating for a liberal worldview, even as he is offering a scientific analysis of how these views become embedded and difficult to analyze. He is interested in how language and metaphor can make us do things we don't even realize we're doing – things that affect our personal lives and our national politics. With so many people nowadays wondering what the big difference is between the political parties – why they sound the same on so many issues, Lakoff would have us focus on what kind of metaphors they're invoking.

This reviewer can't help but wonder what other metaphor we might find for governance and how we can make the cognitive shifts that allow new metaphors to take hold. Still, it's worth considering – what kind of Daddy raised you politically? I prefer the love and respect model, rather than the fear-and-structure Daddy. And clearly, I prefer Daddy to be a woman, now that I've grown up. Still though, metaphorically speaking, Daddy remains in the driver's seat, and we're all just yelling for a pit stop, hoping Daddy brings us animal crackers when s/he comes back from the store.

CHAPTER 4

LOOKING FOR SAFETY AT DADDY'S HOUSE

WHAT IT MEANS TO KNOW EVERYTHING

I was exiled to my father's house while my mother learned the news that her husband had been molesting her fourteen year old daughter. For years. This wasn't my decision, though I was consoled by it; I shouldn't be there when she found out. I wondered aloud why this would be so – always questioning adult's decisions. My childish insouciance had been replaced at age twelve by the impression that adults were unreliable. By age fourteen, I questioned openly, though in this case, I thought I knew the answer. My absence would save me from the rage she'd feel toward me. Surely that was it. The adults outside of my family made this decision to shield me from further harm. And my mother, I thought – of course, my mother would soon be another source of harm.

It was like any visit to my father's condo – he never called it his house or even home. Often it was just "the condo." As in "Your dad'll meet you at the condo at three." My mother was busy and so I would spend the weekend with my father at the condo. That's all he needed to know. I quickly assumed he knew nothing; he treated me no differently than usual.

"Oh hi," he said as I walked in with my small backpack containing clothes for the following day. He rose from his spot on the thickly upholstered beige sofa, next to the sleek white Formica end table, where his Pall Mall Red cigarette perched on the edge of the ashtray. As he greeted me, it burned quietly down to its filterless end. Sometimes he'd forget them and light another elsewhere in the house. The condo with the late 70's furnishings was always tidy, except for the burn marks left by abandoned cigarettes on furniture, counter-tops, and kitchen linoleum.

He gave me a brief hug hello and I put my backpack in the condo's single bedroom where I slept on my visits. He slept on the sofa. He was sipping a glass of ice water – what time was it? Three p.m. Yes, it was still ice water though it would turn to vodka by five, the small lemon peel garnish marking the silent transition. I sat on the floor in my usual corner of the living room, watching television. I loved sitting in the corner of the living room next to the big floor to ceiling window that looked out on the driveway below. I faced the TV, but could still look out at the trees and cars to my left. My father's condo was just above the parking garage entrance. I watched the television absently, staring down at the tops of cars each time one would enter or exit. Nothing on the outside felt different than usual: the cool of the windowpane against my left hip and elbow, my boredom with the television, the view of car-tops passing beneath. I felt a chilly sweat on my neck and queasiness in my stomach, bile that would rise in my throat and then subside again before the urge to vomit really arrived. That internal change was the only difference.

My father didn't speak, as usual, until he asked the familiar question, "What do you want for dinner?" There were always three choices available to me on my something-like-monthly visits, but still he spoke them.

"I was thinking about going down to the deli for some roast beef sandwiches, if that sounds good to you," he said. "Or, I can get you some chicken taquitos at Picnic'n'Chicken if that sounds better." Then he'd pause. "I have some Salisbury steak in the freezer too, if you want that."

I felt grateful for his predictable monologue and the fact that it didn't actually cause me to think about food. If the choices had been different, or required me to consider the food, I might've been sick. I chose the roast beef sandwich. Everything was the same, as I stared out the window at the cars coming too infrequently to accommodate my need for diversion. The rumbling of the big metal gate comforted me. Each incoming tenant inserted a plastic card into the metal box that controled the gate. The coming and going was like the constancy of the earth turning.

The room too, was a comfort. When there were no cars, I chose to glance just to the right of the television. The fancy bottles of liqueur were arranged among small bric-a-brac on the glass shelves above the bar. These were comforting too: Frangelico in the tallest bottle, crème de menthe – the clear kind, not the garish green – Chambord in the small round bottle with the gold band around the middle. The vodka and gin and scotch were kept in the cabinet below; they did not warrant presentation.

When the phone rang, I was absorbed with gazing around the room, at the television, and out the window. I was sitting at my father's condo, as I had always done, nothing different except for the extra bile roiling in my belly. I was deliberately not thinking about my mother, about my stepfather, about the social workers and police officers, about the tutor who happened to be a psychologist-in-training who had become my confidant. "Just let me handle this and you'll never have to see him again," my confidant had told me. That seemed unlikely, but I was hopeful.

At the condo, everything was normal. And then, my father was handing me the phone, pulling the cord longer from behind the end table so that it would reach my corner perch. I had to scoot a bit further into the center of the room to accept the receiver.

I didn't fully register him saying, "It's Will; he wants to talk to you." The cigarette was dangling from my father's lips as he spoke, using both hands to free the phone cord. If the phone call seemed odd to him, he didn't let on, though my stepfather had never once telephoned me in this or any other location for any reason. But there he was, reaching into the sanctuary of the condo, forcing me to move to the center of the room before I could even consider the prudence of accepting the call. I was already taking the receiver and pressing it to my ear – a completely habitual movement.

Did everyone feel they had to accept a call from an outstretched hand? Would anyone have taken the call before even knowing who it is? I considered my obedience in that millisecond. The phone was already in my hand when I registered my father's voice saying, "It's Will." I felt like I would pee on myself. A horrible, heavy feeling in my bladder suddenly asserted and the prickly sweat climbed up my neck and into my hair. My whole scalp was sweating and I pressed my legs together to keep from peeing. My body suddenly wanted to wring itself dry, become dust. I wanted to blow away.

And too, I was aware of needing to sound nonchalant so that my father wouldn't question the phone call. I couldn't bear to explain this to him. I was in control and wanted nothing more than to watch the red and blue tops of cars driving into the garage and wonder what would make the paint job on the top of a car look so shabby when the rest of the car seemed new. I wanted nothing more than the endless drone of the television – the television my father turned off only when he was leaving the house, its familiar hum emanating from the living room while I slept, my father curled onto the sofa, snoring in the light of the picture.

"Kimberly?" My stepfather's voice was low and serious.

"Yes," I answered with no particular tone in my voice. I am pulling this off, I thought. I am not letting on.

"Your mother just called me and she's talking with some officers. You've really upset her, Kimberly."

He kept using my name in that way that we often did when my dog, Sammy, had peed on the floor because he was excited to see someone or had chewed something up that shouldn't have been in his mouth to begin with. You're a bad dog, Sammy. Sammy. Bad dog. One of us would say in a low voice.

"I see," I responded, as though listening to him giving me information about which bus I should take tomorrow to meet him at the ballpark to see a game.

"You've been telling some terrible lies, Kimberly," he said. "You're going to have to tell the truth. You're going to have to tell them I never touched you. Do you understand me, Kimberly?" He paused and I said nothing. "You've been telling some terrible lies." He said it again.

I didn't know what to say. I had not lied when I spoke to the tutor, then the social worker, and the officer. I had not lied. Many things in my life were a lie, or a mistruth, or a fabrication, or an exaggeration or an omission or a fib. But I still knew the difference. I couldn't speak for a moment. I knew that if I did as he asked – if I claimed he'd never touched me – I'd never know the difference between lies and truth again. I would lose the ability to discern. No, as much as my body wanted to evaporate and take to the winds, I wasn't budging. So I said, with careful nonchalance – my father still two feet away from me smoking his cigarette, sipping his drink, watching television – "Well, we were both there, so we both know the whole story."

Then there was silence on his end of the phone. I didn't let it rest for long. "Okay then." I said this almost cheerily, and then hung up the phone and passed it back to my father as though the call didn't even warrant explanation. And it didn't. I didn't owe him an explanation. With no expression on my face, I pondered my stepfather's audacity. The pee re-absorbed into my body and the urgency was gone. I pondered his audacity with a total poker face, poker-body, poker-aura. I acted as though I was not disturbed. And that was a lie. I still knew the difference between the truth and a lie.

I am the only one who knows everything, I thought. I know what he's done and I know what I said to the social worker and I know what my mother's being told and what my father's not being told. I am the only one who knows everything. I didn't yet know that so much was still to be revealed.

FORMALITY

Dear Daddy,

I am ready to go out with you, waiting on the divan in my party dress, wearing the earrings you gave me and a full mouth of lipstick, dark lines surrounding my big green eyes. You have given me your cufflinks to hold, shaking them first, like dice, and then dropping them into my hand with a wink. Here I sit, your attendant, until you present your sleeves, one at a time, for decoration and closure.

I am in love with you Daddy, decorated by your generosity and closed like a book until you open me and blow through my pages, smiling at the music of my giggles. You blow through me and choose the stories that you will read, leaf past the others. What is unknown to you begins not to matter, even to me.

You are my most intimate partner and yet I know more of your romance than of your soul. I will kneel before you later, untie your shoes and slip them scufflessly into their places, take down your braces and stow your tie. I know your fingers that caress my spine, fold my most pliable parchments. You fold me and fold me, make me joyful shapes. This I know for certain.

29

You are my own and I know the ways you hold me, close at night like a pillow and away at arm's length, pressing your palm into my forehead to avoid my mouth being able to reach any part of you. I just want to kiss you Daddy. You hold me away from your body when you wish. You are my first, Daddy. Whether you turn me away or not, I will long for your body, I am in love, the rest of my days.

You are my first, the first man that I love, that I try to love, that I want to love me. You don't come home from work until I'm in bed at night. You don't talk to me about my day. You drink too much. You stay busy. You read the paper. You watch the games. You bruise my face. You break my bones. I break away. I return. You don't come home at all. You don't come – you are my first. And I long to curl against your body like a kitten, pressing long for the most contact, sleeping with my tongue out, belly up, against your heartbeat.

We have a relationship whether you are in it or not. You are the one, Daddy. I dress properly for your friends, wear my hair to please you. We are formal, and yet, you are my most intimate partner. I just want to kiss you Daddy. I will not bite. You are my first. You are my second gestation, my first man, the man I long to know most.

Love,
Your Girl

MON CŒUR EST À PAPA

"He was so nice to me and I didn't deserve it. When I came back from a day off set," Marilyn said of her time working on *The Misfits* with Clark Gable, "he patted my ass and told me if I didn't behave myself he'd give me a good spanking. I looked him in the eye and said, 'Don't tempt me.' He burst out laughing so hard he was tearing." Ms. Monroe added, "I wanted him to be my father. I wouldn't care if he spanked me as long as he made up for it by hugging me and telling me I was daddy's little girl and he loved me." She said, "Of course, that's a fantasy" (Schneider, 2012).

Girls can need Daddy, but that's not for boys. After age 8, age 5, age 3, boys are in charge. They are the ones who ask, "Who's your Daddy? Who's your Daddy!" And when the girl says, "You are," they drawl, "That's right babe." And they smile like Burt Reynolds with Dolly Parton in *Best Little Whorehouse in Texas*, like Sean Connery with Ursula Andress in *Dr. No*, like Brad Pitt with Angelina Jolie in *Mr. and Mrs. Smith* or one of those People magazine articles, or one of those news stories or one of those family photographs.

Who's Your Daddy? A girl is always waiting with an answer. She is Marilyn. She is Dolly. She is Angelina, part powerful, part pliant, part frail, part pretty, part pouty, part primal urge to be plundered and cared for. She is a trophy, a charm, and a muse. Lara Croft loved her Daddy. "I will do it for you Daddy." Cool and dangerous, she'll lick her lips and look up when asked, "Who's your Daddy?" She'll say, "You are baby," and we know that what she gives, what he takes, what she chooses to let him take – which is, of course, different from giving. Daddy is a big job, Brad. Are you up for it?

She is on the screen wearing lip-gloss. She is on the screen with her hair falling over her eyes. She is on the stage surrounded by men, wearing nothing but a blue sweater, singing, "My heart belongs to Daddy." We are not worried about her. She is not a hero, but an idol – a shape used for worship. We are not worried about what she gives away, leaves out, makes less of, we are not worried about her strength though we see her reckless and starving and selling her looks, her form. She is the shape of things to love. Oh little girl, how grown up you seem. How sophisticated you are. How calculated; how capable; how wrecked. A lot is expected of you. Pretty. Jolie. Pretty.

CHAPTER 5

COMING INTO MY ROOM AT NIGHT

My biological parents were married until I was eight years old. They divorced during the remodel of the second house I called home. Remodelling is stressful on a marriage – that's what the adults always said during that time.

Before we moved out of the house on the cul-de-sac, in the valley surrounded by ice plant and dirt that felt like suede, my father would come into my room at night. My crib had been in that room and then I got a big bed, with drawers beneath and a small lip around the outside of it to remind me to stay in. My two favorite dolls, Nancy and Peachpit, sat on a shelf where I could see them from my bed at night. The butterflies, under glass, on pins that let their wings cast iridescent shadows on the background paper, hung on the wall. I practiced sounding out the names beneath their bodies when I started school and began reading and writing. I began by sounding out my own name, in kindergarten. It seemed so long and unruly. My name has lots of soft edges and hard angles and lines and a swoop at the end.

Before we moved out of the house, where snails roamed the ice plant on the slope in the back yard and the dirt was so perfect, my father stayed up late at night in his den at the end of the hallway. It was his den, though we all watched television there on the hound's-tooth sofa in the corner. My mother would make popcorn and set it on the end table next to the big black and white ceramic ashtray with an archaic looking Sagittarius symbol in the bottom of it – my father's sign. I sounded out that word too, when it wasn't covered over in ashes. I don't know why the dirt felt like suede in one particular corner of the canyon. My friend and I discovered it and immediately we took off our shoes and socks, put our feet in to feel it between our toes. It was the color of a camel and I went back later with a brown paper lunch bag to fill, handful by handful. I kept the bag of dirt in my closet, on the floor in the back. I wanted to see Nancy and Peachpit each night before I fell

© KONINKLIJKE BRILL NV, LEIDEN, 2019 | DOI:10.1163/9789004383562_005

asleep, but it was enough to know that my dirt was there. I didn't need to see it, but I thought about it each night before I fell asleep. Beautiful dirt that made my body shiver with delight when I touched it.

Sometimes, when I couldn't sleep, I'd pad softly down the hall in my long pajamas and sit next to my father on the hound's-tooth sofa. A thick smoke hung in the air, making swirling patterns across the top of the dimly lit room. I walked beneath the smoke in my yellow pajamas that reached down to my feet and ended in bumpy white plastic footies that I tore out so I could see my toes.

"Can't sleep?" My father would say as I'd climb up next to him on the sofa and sit, about a foot away, both of us staring in the direction of the stereo turntable, playing show tunes. My father propped up the album cover for *The Fantasticks* where we could see the picture, and the title of what was playing.

"Soon it's gonna rain. I can feel it. Soon it's gonna rain, rain pell-mell." The man's voice and the melody soothed me. I recognized that word from the red package of cigarettes from which my father smoked, only it didn't sound out exactly right.

My father got up and went to the kitchen and then I heard him rustling in the bar cabinet. He handed me a small glass that looked like milk and I said, "What's this?" suspicious.

"It's a bedtime drink," he said, and sat back down next to the end table and ashtray to watch my face as I tried it. I knew I should try it and though I was finicky with food, I sipped the milk. It tasted sweet, and a little chocolaty, but not like chocolate milk. It was wonderful if I sipped a little at a time. If I took too big a drink, it bit my tongue. So I drank slowly, quizzically as he watched me.

"Is that good?" he asked. I nodded and we sipped our drinks together until the end of the album and then he took me back to bed.

Sometimes I had a bad dream where aliens came to earth to collect little children and take them away forever in their spaceships. The aliens did something to hypnotize all of the parents so that even if the children were hiding, the parents would betray them and stand by while the aliens took them away. In the dream, I was being chased by the aliens, who looked like regular men in suits. And I ran to the kitchen, where my mother was washing dishes at the sink. I pushed past her and crawled into the cupboard under the sink, smelling the bleach and cleaning solutions that my parents had showed me and told me never to drink because I could get sick and die. I sat with my legs hugged up to my chest, smelling the chemicals as I heard the aliens approach. They said to my mother, "Where is she?" And my mother replied in a cheery tone, "Why, she's right here under the sink." Then I'd start to wake, thrashing in my bed, not wanting to see where the aliens were going to take me. I'd wake as I was knocking over the bleach, kicking and screaming and watching my mother's smiling face, not even saying goodbye to me as they dragged me away. Perhaps I imagined that last part, because I was already waking, whimpering, thrashing in my bed.

On those nights, my father would come into my room, having heard me from down the hall. He'd tell me to roll over and rub my back a little bit and then he'd try to ease away gently.

"Don't go." I'd say softly and he'd sit on the floor next to my bed. The red glowing tip of his cigarette comforted me, the only light in the room, moving toward and then away from his face again and again. Still there. He was still there. I watched the darkness around the little red glow through the hair that fell across my face as I lay on my belly, head turned toward him.

Once he told me that when he was a little boy he had nightmares about a purple man who would come to get him with a gun. And I could see the purple man in my mind, though he was still wearing the alien's suit. My father told me he stopped having those nightmares when he used his thoughts to put a bouquet of flowers into the purple man's hand, instead of a gun. Then the dream became funny. I didn't see how that would work, but I always imagined the purple man in the suit with a bouquet of flowers nonetheless. It was easy to see it that way because it wasn't my nightmare. And I fell asleep watching the movements of the little red glow in the darkness, the side of my father's face coming in and out of view.

CHAPTER 6

DADDIES, DAUGHTERS AND STRIPPERS

DADDIES, DAUGHTERS AND STRIPPERS

We drove past the big pink building nearly every day. It was just off the freeway, on the way back to our home in Point Loma – a middle class suburb where the property values were rising every day in the early 1970s. It was great to live so near the sea, and so near the bay. The naval bases reminded us of freedom and the tuna fishermen were prosperous – out to sea for long stretches, then back again with money for presents for their Portuguese-speaking mothers, their good Catholic daughters. Point Loma was a good place to live and it's where I was raised – at the very end of Interstate 8. We took the Rosecrans exit and just off the ramp – there it was.

The building was big, like a warehouse, but it was bright pink and it looked like fun! Big pink and yellow bubbles floated up the side of the building and each of the windows was pinked-over so you couldn't see in. The windows were painted with little white lace curtains and bows too. Outside, was a lavender-colored bus. It looked like a school bus except for the color and the fact that the windows were painted and curtained with pink fringe. The words "Party Bus" were painted across the side of the bus too. It made me think of the way the Partridge Family painted up their bus all fancy to ride around in while they played music. I loved watching that show on TV.

The sign on the building was a big rolling script that said *Les Girls* and it lit up with big white bulbs against the pink building. That place looked so enticing! And it was something for girls – though I never saw any children around the building, going in or out. I sometimes saw sailors, or men my father's age and older – never any girls at all, nor women.

Sometimes, as we drove past, I would say to my father, "I want to go to Les Girls!" I pronounced the "s" in Les and he never corrected me. He just said, "No you don't." Or, "That place isn't for you." Or,

© KONINKLIJKE BRILL NV, LEIDEN, 2019 | DOI:10.1163/9789004383562_006

"Why don't we stop for a hamburger on the way home." If he said that place wasn't for me, I'd sing out, "Yes, it is! It says girls! I want to go on the party bus!"

"Let's get a hamburger." Or, "Let's stop for an ice-cream," was always a better response to my questions about Les Girls. Next door to Les Girls was a much smaller brown building with an orange and beige painted sign. It said, "The Body Shop" in big letters up the side of the building and it had a huge sign up above it that said, "Bottomless too." I couldn't figure out what that meant, but somehow, I sensed a competition between that business and my favorite one: Les Girls. It made me giggle to think about what a person might look like with no bottom.

One time, when we drove past Les Girls, and I came to attention and pointed, smiling, mouth agape, my father said, "That's a place where girls work, not play. It's for women to earn money." And my mother, who was also in the car, added, "But not girls like you." I was baffled. It looked like fun – and if it was fun, why shouldn't someone like me work there, or play there for that matter. Who were the ones playing, if not the girls? That place was the same color scheme as my Barbie townhouse and her pink plastic convertible. Someone was not being honest with me, and I couldn't figure out why or who.

And what was the proper way for girls like me to get money, when I was all grown up? It was the early 70's and although feminism hadn't really visited my idyllic white suburban neighborhood, it was affecting the bigger world around me. I was being told that women could go anywhere, do anything. My third grade class put on a performance of *Free to Be You and Me*. And yet, I was also being told that some places weren't for me – even if they had the word "girls" in the name. Those girls were different, and I shouldn't be different. The party bus also had smaller printing on it, "Be king for a day!" and there was a little crown hanging off of the word "king." I wanted to be king for a day – somehow the gender switch between girls and kings didn't register problematic. I could be a king if I wanted to. I could.

Why didn't my father tell me the truth? That my body is a commodity and that it's possible to sell it for sex, or for voyeurism or for the sake of product sales? Why didn't he tell me? How should I get money in order to make my way in the world, and from whom? Should I get money from women, or from men? Should I act more excited to get a gift from a man than from a woman like my mother and her friends? Should I save money by hiding it from a man – not letting him know what I bought at the mall or that I took a friend to lunch? In addition to working for a living, should I use my sexuality to get things from a Daddy? What does it mean to be a "good" girl?

The images of women on the windows of Les Girls were all slithery silhouettes with their long hair curving up in the back. Sometimes at home, I stood with my body in an S like this and it's true, if you lean your head back and curve your body just enough, someone could cut a silhouette into black paper that would make you look just like that. Well, almost. More like a cartoon version of a woman with her body slithered into an S and her long hair sticking out like in a photo-still moment. I practiced at home in the mirror, for when I could go to Les Girls. Les Girls. It looked like so much fun.

After I finished high school, my friend Jenny went to work at The Body Shop. By then, I knew why children weren't allowed and why my father never spoke of the place. How could he? What would he say? By then, I didn't want to discuss such things with my parents either. It's in men's best interest to keep those jobs hidden, along with the women who do them – it's in men's best interest to keep it all on the down low, away from their wives. Keep it in the realm of sailor's stops on shore.

"Nothing to see here, move along!" That's all anyone knew how to say. Both men and women in polite conversation just turned their heads as they drove past the big pink building, the giant Body Shop signage that still read – now in neon – "bottomless too." I too had learned the rules – I wouldn't have mentioned that place to my parents because it would be uncomfortable. Those buildings were huge.

Jenny worked there and even she didn't speak much about her work to those of us who weren't in the business. It was as though she made a pact not to discuss the other world. She had entered an occupation where her non-stripper friends were not welcome, though perhaps she'd come to know our boyfriends, fathers and husbands in a different way than we knew them. Our other friend Kathy worked at a store in the mall and she felt jealous of Jenny somehow – like maybe Jenny was prettier, had a more desirable body. Kathy was concerned about the attentions of men too, and the gifts they could give her in order to help prove her worth.

So, what is the "proper" way for women to get money, status, wealth, without it always seeming like someone's giving them something? Even after high school, that was a question I couldn't answer. And I started to wonder, every time I drove past Les Girls: how is it legal to advertise "nude girls." A girl is a female child, by definition. And it's not legal to sell children for sexual purposes. If there really were girls in Les Girls, they'd be closed down, right? I mean, wouldn't they?

WHEN SEX IS ABSENT

Dear Daddy,

I know you thought about having sex with me a long time before you thought you should. Isn't that true, Daddy? Come on. Be honest. Here. Let me tell the story for you ...

Daddy thought about having sex with me long before we did it. She'd think about it and wrap her hand around her cock and squeeze, just squeeze – driving a sensation into the body and the mind that was part pain, part pleasure. She thought about it at length, often not the act, but the preparation for the act, the angling for a sweet surrender. An orgasm is fast, lasts for a few seconds at best. The angling for surrender can last for days, weeks, years. The moment of surrender where Daddy feels power with all her senses, the whimper, scent, soft skin, warm breath, the mad give of flesh when pressed, the weight of a body that when pushed off-balance, returns to push back – that moment of doing it can last forever. That memory can prompt many orgasms. Daddy thought about it for a long time and squeezed, sometimes hard. She just squeezed.

Daddy kept those thoughts to herself for a long time. At first, when she knew me, she thought more often about the last girl to receive her Daddy-love. She became obsessed with how sweet that girl was, how sweet, how distantly sweet. She was gone, who knew where. No card on Father's Day. No flirting over email. Gone. And yet, Daddy's jaw still ached with the sweetness of her. At first Daddy thought it was that girl she missed. But it was me. She missed me and we hadn't even done the things she missed. When she realized it was me, her thinking shifted to very private thoughts and Daddy turned marmoreal around me, cold and beautiful, my glances slid right off of her. If I touched her shoulder and leaned in to whisper something, at a movie perhaps, Daddy's lips would purse, almost imperceptibly, then release. That was the only sign that my action had moved her, like a firm squeeze, a combination of pleasure and pain.

Daddy contented herself with the idea that the right moment might never come with me. She might never have the chance to brush my hair or kiss my pretty toes or make my knees sore, fistful of my ponytail saying, "Just a little bit more. Be a good girl. Just a little bit more."

But then the right moment came. There were a series of right moments and Daddy knew just what to say to make my ears burn, my head turn and my heart race. And then there I was, standing on Daddy's porch with an empty cup in my hand, asking for some sugar. "Give me some sugar, Daddy." That's how I asked it. "I don't know how much I can take." I said to Daddy, "But I think I need some sugar."

We were nothing but a toothache until dawn, until well into the next week. For a few months, we were nothing but a bright-eyed sugar-rotted grin. Daddy was careful, but firm. She was overflowing joy, now that those urges could be acted upon. The right moment came.

"But really," Daddy said later, "I was content to just love you and have those thoughts about you, all to myself."

See, Daddy. I know the score. Whether a man has sex with his daughter or not, there is still a sexual relationship to be navigated. How could there not be? Female youth is sexualized. Even someone as old as Hugh Hefner still has sex with women far younger than his daughter, than his grandchildren. It's not just the Daddies, the abusers, and the pedophiles. All girl children must navigate sexual relationships. Even when a man makes the sane and compassionate choice not to have sex with his daughter, with a girl, the rules of propriety still focus on sex. There are proscribed guidelines for how to avoid doing it, how to eschew references to it, when it's okay to talk about it. And of course, every man must learn how to keep getting a hard-on for youth and innocence and girlish bodies while keeping the girls sorted so that he doesn't do something he shouldn't.

You don't think I understand you, Daddy, but I do. You never asked me for my stories – how I know the ways of men like you. But I will tell you anyway. I will break the rules and tell you what I know, unfold my histories like maps, fill the table where you sip your morning coffee. Before you are fully awake, too busy, before you are too clever and put my stories aside, I will tell you. I will point to the map and explain. I know you. I have always known you, even before I understood my knowing.

My stepfather went to church when he wanted the support to abstain from having sex outside his marriage. He went to the country club when he wanted support for philandering. Sex with a minor, his wife's own daughter, was a particular indulgence for which it was more difficult to find support. Difficult, but not impossible. Some of the men with whom he played golf found it humorous that he could always get a young girl. He was a trickster, so they didn't really know whether he was doing it, or just joking about doing it. Never admit to doing it. That's rule number one. Always take credit for doing it. That's privilege number one.

As I exited the car on the passenger side, we drew the stares of two older women because we were quarrelling loudly about something – likely something I wanted to do. Perhaps I wanted to stop at the bookstore or go somewhere specific for lunch and he had provided his standard answer, "Well, there's just no way I'm going to do that." And so I quarreled. He stopped the argument by saying, loudly enough for the nosy passers-by to hear, "This is the last time I'm marrying a woman as young as you! You're nothing but trouble." They looked aghast and then we nearly fell down laughing.

If anyone from the church came by while we were out to dinner, my stepfather would shift his glass of scotch and the ashtray over in front of my plate, and hand me his cigarette. After chatting and passing by, he'd retrieve his illicit objects and wink conspiratorially at me. My mother once admonished him, "Don't do that." And he acted like she was a tight-ass, a real downer.

Once when we dined together alone, at the country club, one of his friends came by the table and my stepfather referenced me and said to the man, "She's a pretty girl, right?" And the man nodded appreciatively, appraising my beauty. "It's not easy to find a date like her," he added. "She's twelve." The man looked more closely at my made-up face, my woman's body. Then they both laughed as though it was a really good joke. Alone in the elevator with this man later that evening, he smirked at me and casually reached out and gave my twelve-year-old breast a squeeze.

All women are for sex, and all men must want sex. Men just have to choose when to do it and with whom. Girls and women wait to be chosen – unless they offer – and woe be to the one who offers and is turned down. Men are in a position to choose and when women become Daddies, they too can choose.

When our sexual relationship began, you struggled, didn't you Daddy, with how to relate to the last girl who called you that – the last girl who was your very own. It's not exactly the same negotiation as when one has an ex-lover. At first you tried on the term Uncle, but I protested, remember? Uncles can have sex with their nieces too, and share special things, and go out for ice cream and make secrets and take time away from ... me. I protested, though I could understand the need to establish some relationship that honored the more-than-lover pact – the familial relationship. But then slowly I realized that brothers too could have sex with their sisters, so can cousins and grandfathers and so can neighbors and godfathers and ministers and friends of the family. Daddy can do what he pleases.

Even when sex is absent, it's still there. Daddy, you can't put anything past me.

Love,
Your Girl

PART 2

ACTIONS

CHAPTER 7

THE FIRST TIME II

I am interested in finding out what she means. She is articulate and open with a confident stance. She is tall, not particularly attractive, grey-blue eyes and ruddy white skin. Her hair is fluffy, not quite curly, as though it carries its own small wind. Still, she seems strong; she speaks with curiosity and good grammar. She has good posture. These things attract me. I react. I am a spasming muscle; she is the stimulant. We flirt – in that ambiguous way that can never convict us.

I meet her at a university where I am giving a talk. I am the expert on gender for this evening. She is in attendance. It could be any city, any university – but it isn't. I used to live in this city – Colorado Springs. I have a history here, finished my undergraduate work at this very campus. I have connections here – and here she is, connecting to me.

After my talk on gender roles, she lingers to question, to hold my gaze, to touch my elbow in conversation as we walk together to the parking lot after the event. I want to know what she means when she says, "There are complexities to this butch/femme thing that I wonder how much you know about. Some things I don't know who to talk to about. The sexual identities …" She pauses, and then continues. "I don't know how much you know about the leather community …"

She pauses again. It wasn't really a question; she intended to continue all along.

"In the leather community, I am a Daddy. But because I pass for femme, I don't get much recognition, much respect. And I think, I could change my appearance, but I don't want to. I like to be soft too."

She seems to read my attentive silence, renegotiates her admissions and adds, "But you know, I also used to be a bottom, and I looked a little more butch then."

This admission is unique – her timing, bold. I am nodding, pondering the creation of balance between appearance and behavior. I could say, "You're so big and strong, so forward and in control of this

© KONINKLIJKE BRILL NV, LEIDEN, 2019 | DOI:10.1163/9789004383562_007

conversation. I think you have the credibility of a Daddy, despite the long hair, the eyeliner."

I don't say this. I think it. Fascinating. And so it begins, an academic discourse. She is a seeker. I am a teacher. She is a Daddy. I enjoy a considered submission. And so it begins. She watches me, listens, responds, leans in. She uses the same tools of communication I use: disclosure, analysis, physical openness, negotiation, and re-negotiation.

Later, about 5 a.m., I ponder how she presented herself to me. I agreed to have coffee with her, so I will interview us both further on this theme. To what, in me, was she responding, in order to create this response in me? She is remarkably skillful, or perhaps, I don't know that I am an easy mark for this sort of intellectual and erotic tension. I am an easy mark for curiosity about what "leather daddy" means to her, and how she does that role – what "femme" and "passing" mean to her – what "bottom" means to her.

A few years later, we are lovers – more than lovers – we are something like family. She asks me, "How did the Daddy thing start with us? Did you ask me for it?"

I stare, incredulous. "You brought it up the first time we met."

"Right, but we were just *talking* about it. How did we get around to doing it? I mean, we were lovers for a few months before that came up." She wobbles her hand around the word *that*, assigning it indescribable meaning.

I am fascinated that she really doesn't remember, that she really doesn't know what she chose in me, the first time she laid eyes on me. We have had time to think about this. I have thought about this, but apparently she hasn't. I don't recall my exact words – how I gave her permission to do what she did for the first time, but I know I gave permission – the soft, steady reassurance that a violation would be allowed, appreciated.

She stood on the balcony smoking her pipe, watching the light retreat over the city skyline. She was wearing her black bathrobe over her white boxer-briefs – the snug kind that keep the soft-pack in place, hug the thighs, the gluteal muscles. ("I'm developing an ass like a Clydesdale fucking you as much as we do," she chuckled once, admiring her rear in the mirror.) She stood alone, smoking against the pink sky. We'd been lovers for a few months, but tonight, something was different. Before she walked out, she held me for a kiss, made sure I felt her cock, soft but assertive, against my pelvis.

She was quiet, and felt somehow unapproachable, enjoying her pipe in the warm night air. She was quiet and yet, entirely legible to me and I knew not to say much. I knew to wait patiently. I already loved her and had already begun making sacrifices. I tingled with anticipation that her inflexible ways would soon reward me.

I became small and quiet, a transformation prompted by her rigidity, prompted by my permission, prompted by her assertion, and prompted by my invitation. We fell like dominos, a brutal, beautiful cascade. With a different entitlement in her hands, she felt my breasts, held me around the waist and pulled me in. She kissed me differently, her tongue so deep down my throat, I couldn't breathe for a moment and I liked it – knew not to speak of it, but I liked it. "Go get in bed, sweet girl. Take off your clothes and wait for me." She patted my ass and I turned from her, obedient.

I saw moments of her, through the bedroom door, emptying her pipe, methodically stowing it away, washing her hands, and brushing her teeth. My skin tingled beneath the sheet. I saw her change the soft dick for the hard one, long and black, protruding beneath the bathrobe. This part was nothing new, but something was new – and I knew not to speak of it. She joined me in bed. I was on my back, her body next to me. She was propped on one elbow, gentle but assertive, touching my breasts, my belly with tender fingers, pulling me in occasionally for a hard penetrating kiss. The mutuality of our passion suspended, I became shy and waited, thrilled and a bit frightened – could I do it? Was she going to do it? We'd been talking more and more about Daddy. Still abstract, still talking. I could feel it coming. Could I? Stay present and genuine, really do it?

Deep breath. Let the body decide. Breathe. The body is deciding.

Her soft hand still on my breast, she leaned toward my ear and asked, "Are you going to give your Daddy what he wants?"

As she spoke, my throbbing thickened, slipped. The body is deciding. "Uh-huh." I managed, and my willing embarrassment, face flushing, fueled her. She was on top of me in an instant, her hand holding my wrists above my head and pushing down, hard. I had neither the strength nor will to move and a fear of both truths fluttered gently in my stomach, the sensation drowned out by my slickening need. Her tongue down my throat, my wrists aching beneath her significant strength, she straddled me, pressed her hard cock against my belly. Her body held my legs shut.

"Daddy's cock is going to be too big for you. Is that going to be okay?" She was speaking into my ear, between kisses. I managed a whimper and she said with a small chuckle, "That's right, it's going to be just fine. And afterward, when Daddy's all done. When I've taken all I want, I'll kiss you better." She gently kissed my forehead. "I'll clean you up with my tongue, where I hurt you. I'll take care of you because every part of you is perfect. Every part of you is mine." She kissed my cheek and released my wrists with a stern look and said, "Don't move now."

Indeed, my wrists were still bound.

My eyes wide, no words, the mind reeled briefly with astonishment. Could she not have started a little slower with the Daddy-thing? But I could feel the answer in her touch. It was too big. She was going all-in. And I would take it just as she gave it. The body was deciding.

She gently knelt between my legs and spread them. "That's my good girl," she said, gazing at my glisten. "Legs up," she said. I obeyed and as she nestled down onto my body, she put one arm around my back and held me, tighter than she'd ever held me, more lovingly than I'd ever felt her. The other hand found her cock, so she could move into me slowly, her forehead against my sternum, she was feeling every moment of her entry. Her first, in a way. She said, "I'm going to go slow at first, but because you're so good, I won't be able to hold back once I get started." And in she went, little by little, "Are you my good girl?" And I was nodding against her head. "That's so good. You *are* my good girl."

And my mind was lost, belly fluttering. Already all in. My body was choosing this. My body was saying yes in every language it knew and she was listening so attentively. It was bringing her so much pleasure; I couldn't conceive how exponentially mine was multiplied. How could I not have known this joy before? Her pleasure was amplifying and the mind went deaf in the soaring sound of it. Her fierceness and release became one and I felt the holiness of it. How could I not have known?

As soon as she pulled back and pushed all the way in, her restraint was spent. She was talking, as she started moving faster, not an apology, but an explanation. Not a request for permission, but a surety, a deservingness that was so beautiful, so beautiful, my mind was blinded by it. "Oh yes, good girl, that's it. Remember, I'll kiss it better after." She said as she fucked me harder, "That's it. I know it's big, but you're doing so good. It's so good."

I had to have something to hold onto. And though afraid of breaking the invisible restraints her hands had put upon my wrists, my arms sailed down and I wrapped around Daddy's thick back and she moved to accommodate. Her one hand around my left breast, squeezing hard for leverage, the other arm still holding me close and solid, she affirmed me. She did not admonish my move to hold her. She affirmed it.

"That's a good girl. Hold onto your Daddy while I fuck you." Accommodating my need, she said, "You hold on." And a warm, tingling light spread through my body, emanating from my pussy, emanating from her piercing. The point of her pounding ready to supernova, she was within herself and still with me. She was within her own pleasure, yet spurred by mine.

"Daddy needs to fuck you hard now, princess," she said and how could it be any harder? I didn't know, and everything felt right. I wanted to please my Daddy more than anything, more than anything and my body was choosing. My pelvis was tipping forward to give her all I could and then I had to hold on. The impact was so great, I had to hold on. I had never been fucked so hard before and she was commanding, "You take all of your Daddy."

And I was screaming, "Yes!" And filling up. "Yes!" I had never felt so full of love before. "Yes!" Her anguish overflowed into joy, and I contained it all. I didn't spill a drop of Daddy.

And by the time she was done closing my wound with her tongue, licking up her come and mine too, so no one would see, I was exhausted and wordless. I would've made my fortune on the business of sleep, if she hadn't awakened my drifting, her eyes blinking at the ceiling, chewing her lip with worry.

"What is it, baby?" I said when I sensed the shift. I expected the post-Daddy-sex trauma to be mine. She had done this before with a lover. I had not. I was frightened by her urgency, looking for the right answers when she asked, "What do you think about what we just did."

"It was good." I offered, dumbstruck by the experience itself, this question, too much.

"Because you know, that's not just sex for me." She sat up, cross-legged on the bed, searching my face. I felt suddenly exposed, any move might be wrong and I knew no matter what we called it, I could not lose her. Right then I knew: I would do way too much not to lose her.

"I know." I said, and I sat up too.

"No, I don't know if you know." She was shaking her head. "We have to talk about this, have a talk. Because we've been having good sex for the last few months, but that's not just about sex for me." She said *that* with bulging eyes and an emphatic glance toward where my body had lain. She continued, "I mean, I don't know how that was for you. But for me, right now is the time to decide. We can still say 'okay, we tried that out and we're never doing it again.'"

My mind reeled. I had no words yet to discuss what we had just done – no words at all – and now something had to be decided? I chose words carefully and each felt like a failure in my mouth. "If you don't want to do that anymore with me, it's okay."

Perhaps she saw the confusion in my eyes, "But you wanted it?" she asked.

"Yes, I was there with you." I said, holding her gaze.

"I know you were," she said simply. "But you have to be sure, because if I go there, it's all the time. It's not just sex for me. It's all the time. It's in our lives." She was nodding while she was speaking. "It's big. For both of us."

I didn't know what to say, so I crawled across the big bed toward her seated form. I crawled into her lap as best I could and I felt her worry soften.

"Yes." I said.

She held me, and rocked me a little bit, soothing herself as much as me, I think. She kissed my forehead and we were silent for a time. Before she loosened her hold on me, she said, "Okay?"

I reiterated, "yes."

The gentle teacher, she added, "And you say, 'Yes Daddy.'"

My whole body tingled. And I whispered it into her ear.

"Yes, Daddy."

CHAPTER 8

UNIVERSITY DADDY

I wanted so badly to be respected among the people who 'count' in my field – most of whom are men – that I labored long and hard to express my thoughts about such things as myths and movies in arduously constructed arguments I thought my detractors could not penetrate. My essays were girdled by pages of heavily cited theoretical substructure before I even got to the film I was interpreting ... I continued to thicken my veil of language and thought until even I was hard pressed to penetrate it when re-reading my own articles years later. The desire to gain respectability by meeting the standards of patriarchal language and custom is also very strong among women with whom I talked. In one sense, we can say that women don the veil voluntarily in order to hide their too-feminine aspects. But the standards we try to meet are so synonymous with academia that we seldom identify them as masculine – they are just 'the way things are' in academia if we want to succeed. It would be misleading to say that hiding behind the veil is completely willed; sometimes we are not really aware that is what we are doing. (Rushing, 2010, p. 139)

I don't have three letters after my name, just two. I am a Master, not a Doctor, and though I've made my way with one letter fewer than many of my colleagues, I sometimes fantasize the third – the simplicity of a title that doesn't reference gender at all, the simplicity of a title that precedes the name, rather than trailing behind it. But the university is Daddy's system – not mine, and I fear its excesses.

© KONINKLIJKE BRILL NV, LEIDEN, 2019 | DOI:10.1163/9789004383562_008

It's hard to find a good Daddy at the university. Stern, mean Daddies abound. They become what the system demands, sell scholarship for status, trade outlook for overwork. The pleasure comes in release from the bondage of effort – a glass of wine and sleep after too many hours at the computer. Nary a doting Daddy to be found. Not my type at all.

Everyone becomes a naughty boy seeking Daddy-love at the university. Some thrive on the waiting and the worry, the promise of eventual Daddy-love that few receive. Many are left ABD: Absent Blessings of Daddy.

Everyone takes on the boy role at the university, sending endless emails that will not be acknowledged, enduring stern glances from professors across conference tables. I have no time for you. You are dismissed. Did you look up the articles I told you about? Do it again. Do it differently. Do it right. Do it again.

Boys bond at the university. What else is there? The graduate elite lean together, huddle around the campfire in the cold night telling tales of Daddy. Ghost stories of the bloodied specters sweeping through corridors, zombies exuding entrails, still walking toward the next class. Both men and women can be Daddy's boys at the university, and you would think that, as in my bed, the women can be Daddies at the university too. It's rarely true. They are Daddy-paper-cut-outs; they are placeholders. There are tales of the occasional non-boy-non-Daddy – vampiric women with high round breasts pressing forth from tight-fitting bodices, nipples issuing bile, skin like ice. They cackle like witches in fairy tales and their cock-sucking can suck the life right out of a boy.

The boys know their place. They are in Daddy training and they sing songs to praise their leaders, their institutions. Both dominated by Daddy and dominating undergraduates, their time for glory is nigh.

The university is a gay leather Daddy scene. Posture and privilege are important. It's not about the muscles; it's about the steely stare, how long they make you wait. I'm not a boot-licker. I like a pillow under my pretty knees when I suck my Daddy's cock, not gravel, not glass. I won't rim a dirty asshole to prove my love. I don't like filth on my pretty face, won't be consoled by the adoration of those with lesser status than mine. I don't tremble with anticipation when I wait too long. I want real love. I didn't choose to get the PhD.

I still fantasize about it. I stroke my soft throat thinking of the speaker's slight shift in posture when putting Dr. before a name. I dream of eyes brightening with respect before I've done anything to command it.

I once met a university Daddy I really liked – thought I could respect and make a home with him. John was a special Daddy. Soft and praiseful, stern and loving. I spotted him immediately across the crowded courtyard. I spotted him immediately, though I was only visiting that campus. "What department are you from, Daddy?" I didn't say it out loud of course. I know the drill. I started asking around.

Soon, we were out to dinner, John and I. Daddy had my full attention.

John talked about his relationship with his children, and I listened very considerately. He spoke mainly of his daughter; he spoke with pride and fondness. I enjoyed his happiness when he told of her schooling, her new job. He also told of a son and while I felt let down by his parenting imperfections, I also felt thrilled. He expressed a combination of remorse and dismissal with this boy child. There, there Daddy. You've done the best you can and I love you for it. Surely that boy was no good anyway. I licked my lips and listened. His relationship with his daughter propeled my fondness forward. I enjoyed his mouth moving as he told details about a relationship I had only previously read about in his writing.

"He's the father of the program – a strong gentle patriarch," relayed Charlotte, my friend, his former student. "It's not just that he's fatherly with the students – stern at times, strict, but very kind. He's also the patriarch of the department. He seems to be a calming force – one that guides the work of the department through the channels of the university that might otherwise be difficult to navigate. He helps to unify the department too." She spoke easily, as a child well parented and comfortable in the world will do. Her chair was comfortable. She knew her place was meant for her.

"Yes, they really do seem to work together well," I said of the department, "in a respectful, familial way." I looked for that dynamic and I found it. The good family draws in good neighbors, good friends. They think, "What a great guy." And, "How does he do it?" And, "They're all so great!" I looked at it and saw the beauty. Everyone wants to do good work when they feel supported. When they feel loved.

"Who knows what will happen when he retires," my friend concluded. I nodded and feared the day. It may already be too late – I may have missed him and when would I find another?

This is not even what I want! And what if the moment of bootlicking arrived? What if he tired of open-handed skin-on-skin and brought out the paddle one Friday dusk? It could happen and where would my fantasy of gentle deliverance be then? How would I submit – too close to the prize to turn back? How would I flee, penniless, no respect, knowing none of the boys would look back from the songs and the bonfire to find me in the dark wood.

I look for this Daddy on campus after campus, create him from the remnants of interactions I've witnessed and imagined. I stitch them together into the pattern for which I long. Satisfied with the look of the garment from a distance, it is so flawed up close. I pick at seams, gather and tuck to conceal the shabbiness of the fabric when I don it. Daddy, you are always incomplete, and yet, I long for you next to my skin.

I am fantasizing about matriculation. John is waiting for the likes of me, surely. I know it's not just him – it's the whole department. The whole family will welcome me. And then I refocus on the life I've made outside the Daddy-Scholar Factory. I am my own sort of scholar and I make my way well. Would I do something so impractical as matriculate for a good Daddy? Move house and re-form my life around a good Daddy? A graduate program re-builds the scholar in its own image. The leather Daddy models discipline so the boy can learn about structure, benevolence and protocol. Academics learn how to dominate by first learning how to yield. I have remained outside their systems, but I know their ways.

Could this department be different? No adversary among the professors, between professor and students? The students seem – dare I say it – supported. They seem encouraged and mentored. It looks like a happy family and I am fantasizing.

Tolstoy wrote, "All happy families resemble one another, each unhappy family is unhappy in its own way." I have seen the unhappy families in which funding is inadequate for the children, or in which the girls must submit unduly to their Daddies, as their mouths and asses toughen, just like the boys – their softer regions close completely. I have seen the incest departments, where sex and domination are the norm as the work gets done and then of course, there are the departments, more and more of them, where the parents work too hard and cannot buy their release in order to sit still and breathe with their charges, in order to form the relationships that will lead to maturity. Time passing, people aging – this is not the same as maturity.

I nearly cried during dinner with John. It shocked me and I don't know why I started talking about the topic of dysfunctional departments anyway. What came over me? We don't speak of such things, ever. I don't know why I chose to share that I felt a longing for more education – a longing to which I don't often allow myself to admit. But there it was, and there was a concern, an intimacy in the way he listened and looked at me that nearly brought me to tears. At some point, I made a comment about my father being a professor, then a dean. When John asked what his degree area was, I was surprised to hear myself form the word: Communication. Same as John. I had not let myself know this before the word was in the air.

Charlotte encouraged me to reframe my perception of spending five years under the care of John and his crew. She had been a student and received the rewards. "Think of it as a retreat. It's funded and it's in the middle of nowhere. You'll get to hang out with great people, read and write a lot, smoke pot and drink wine with your retreat-mates in the evenings and just create for a few years."

Charlotte looked wistful, remembering her experience. "It's not a bad deal." I hesitated, pondering this. "I know what worries you," she added, perhaps seeing something on my face. "He was kind of a father figure to me too. But a good one," she said knowingly. "He really is a loving patriarch."

After dinner with John, I made a list of reasons why I had never pursued a PhD. These are the top ten.

1. I'm afraid of doing a lot of work, mainly for approval. The desire for approval could flourish within me, nourished by the academy.
2. I'm afraid I will be changed in negative ways – as well as positive ones – that I will lose touch with other ways of seeing in favor of Daddy's way.
3. If I learn to connect my thoughts, in constant dialogue with everyone who's ever considered my topic of study, what's to keep me from being lost among the voices? What if I lose my way?
4. I am good at one thing at a time. I create in silence and leisure. Will my own rhythm of knowing, feeling and learning survive?
5. The fragile parts of wonder and enthusiasm might be shamed into hiding.
6. I don't want to anticipate all arguments. Be Right. I like to be surprised.
7. My father became white and middle class when he went to university. And then he forgot he was ever anything else. What will I forget?
8. My stepfather had two doctoral degrees, and he wasn't a nice person. He was a good thinker, a good conversationalist. He knew how to make people feel small, unworthy with the nuance of communication. He was especially good at this with women. Will I wake with a headache and the tattoo of oppressor in my skin, coloring my choices?
9. I don't want to become adversaries with people I admire in order to prove I am worthy of their intellectual company.
10. I don't want Daddy to dominate me with excessive work and call it the secret handshake, the decoder ring. I don't want to find I've been fooled by childish rewards. I see them sit in their little cells so long the back deforms, the mind brittles.

Daddy, I still fear you. And I still long for you.

John is aging. And I have not yet applied myself to sit by his side.

CHAPTER 9

DADDY GOD

DADDY GOD

Back in the 1970s, the college campus near my house built the little chapel for quiet prayer and contemplation. It didn't have lighting at first; a group of graduating seniors paid to have that added in the 1980s – small lights just beneath each pew showed where to kneel. You could rock back on your heels a bit and use the light to see the pages of your bible or your book of reflection.

The chapel is carpeted throughout, just enough space for seven kneelers – strange, swooping angles – a modern meditation hall with dark chunks of stained glass showing a disciple receiving illumination from above as he gazes skyward, supplicant. It isn't meant for gathering, just somewhere to stop on your way to class, or after some heavy discussion in the dorm room when you need to clear your head in peace. Upon entering, a small pathway leads to the front alter. Or you could veer off into one of four prayer areas on either side of that pathway. Solo prayer to the left, a duo and a trio on the right.

When I was nine, my friend Kathy and I would veer into the prayer chapel for a brief run through the prayer cubicles. Really, a run. It was one of the mischief-stops on our afternoon bike ride through the college after school. We'd enter quietly, in case someone was kneeling in prayer. Sometimes someone was and whoever entered first would poke the other to turn around and leave. Our breath sounded suddenly loud in the small dark space with another person crouched and still. Outside, our voices thundered again, laughter swinging our legs over our bike seats. We'd ride on.

When no one was in the chapel, we'd kneel side by side in one of the larger prayer-cubicles for a moment, quiet. Did Kathy feel it too? – A sense of peace and awe. It made me pinch my legs together, afraid pee would come out. A kid can't feel that for too long without an authority around – at least we couldn't – so one of us would start laughing. We'd make sounds and holler, testing our voices in the echo chamber. Alone in this architectural oddity, we'd start to climb over the kneeling stations and through the carpeted cut-outs that allowed each person kneeling to see the stained glass altar. Around and through. Echo, moan and shrill. Around and through – we'd pick up speed. Two or three times through the obstacle course, gasping for air, we'd dash back out into the sunny day. Sometimes someone would come in and we'd immediately bolt, yelling, "Sorry!" behind us. We knew we were bad. Pleasure outweighed guilt.

After years of childhood visits, I didn't go again for a long time. I was surprised to see – when I entered the chapel in 2007 – that the manner in which prayer was conducted had shifted. Pile after pile of written notes and prayers littered the pews – probably three dozen in all. Most looked like elementary school love notes with hearts and flowers drawn on them; most bore feminine handwriting. Some were full letters, asking for forgiveness or seeking guidance. Many of the shorter ones appeared to be scribbled in haste requesting a good grade on a test, guidance about a boyfriend, or a request for direction in the scribbler's life.

The chapel is now a place to leave love notes for God. And I wondered if anyone still paused in quiet contemplation, seeking internal guidance or fortitude, as they once had, kneeling quietly? I'd tried it too as a child, without Kathy around to see me. I went alone and tested the idea of quiet meditation, waiting in the still dark silence for something to happen. I was never sure what happened, but I often felt calmer, when I strolled back out into the bright day.

Do these girls ever get impatient with Daddy-God? Do their hearts fill with emotion when they feel their surrender? Do they get turned on talking to Daddy-God? Intimately, sweetly, they make flowery trellises of the yellow-ruled margins. They dash in for a quick benediction. One particularly girlish looking note, written on the torn edge of notebook paper, requested blessings in her life and signed off with, "Please and thank you Daddy God!"

All you have to do is ask. Is that you, Daddy-God? Daddy? God? A few notes said, "I love you sooooo much."

OUT OF THE WOODS

In my dream, my father and I became lovers. We were both adults, neither one of us a child. In a dream, anything can happen – we can both be children. He can be a child and I, a crone. I can be my father's child in a dream – yes, even that could happen. But in this dream, it was different. We were both adults. We were lovers – nothing really weird – some intercourse; he went down on me. Then, once we were intimate through sex, he told me this story.

In my dream, my father told me a story about his childhood, about what it meant to survive and have people hate you for it. He told me a story about the day religion came to town and strung him up, murdered the children – the boys he was playing with. It happened like this.

In 1943 a small group of boys are playing in the forest by the river – the place where the Bosque and the Brazos rivers meet and swirl together, sheltered by tall trees and ferns. There's a fresh spring pump that the boys drink from when they're thirsty. They run around and slide down living hillsides, rubber soles gliding over rocks, pants greening, canvas sneakers damp from rich banks. Small hands grasp the silver pump handle, one by one, an elbow to the sky, muscles working the pump as their mouths lower to the spigot. One by one, they drink and breathe hard and look at the blue through the canopy of trees. When their breath comes easier again, one runs, and the others follow. On that particular day, a lot of them had gathered in the woods near town – ten, maybe eleven boys. Sometimes there were only three or four boys, released from household chores, sent to play in pairs, sometimes solo. On that day they were a small crowd of piercing voices, laughing enthusiasm. They were young boys, still seven, eight years old, some just six, or nine. Single-digit river-revelers, released with a nickel for a Dr. Pepper or maybe just a mind for the trail, the river, the green.

Did anyone know where the men came from? My father didn't know, even as the adult storyteller, lying in the tangled sheets, telling me the tale. He certainly didn't know, as the boy in the woods, rattling the blue bonnets on their stems as he ran by. They must've come from somewhere – men like that don't just appear from nowhere, I thought to myself as I heard the story. Still, they came. They walked through town, talking crazy – talking aloud to no one, and to anyone who'd listen.

"Prepare to bury your children," said one.

"I'm here to help you die," said another. Each seemed to be speaking from within his own experience, as though he were alone, but somehow the messages converged, just as the men had, to tell one tale. They validated each other. Together, they made a pack of what might've been individual hard times, individual stories that the mind can tell to make the mouth bleed. One man's mouth was bleeding. He said nothing, just held the mouth open, with blood trickling out. It looked like he'd been hit with something, hard, but didn't raise a hand to wipe away the blow.

They walked through the town and no one stopped them to ask if they needed any help. When a person is angry, it's hard to see they need help – or hard to ask, in any case. When a group is angry, who can help? How can anyone help an angry group? My grandmother, usually ready to meet anger with anger, even stood stone still on the sidewalk, next to her sister, staring down the paper barrel of her straw into her Sun Tang Red crème soda as they passed.

"God died a bloody death," said one man as they marched. Another continued his sentence, "as a human man, while others watched." A third man added eerily, "And it was all about YOU." Maniacal laughter punctuated his comment.

So, they walked through town, a spectacle, a moving threat; they harmed no one, but threatened all. "Prepare to bury your children!" one yelled again, as they disappeared into the woods. There were knives and ropes. That's what my father recalls. Surely, someone would've come forward to stop them if they'd seen such weapons moving through the town. My father said there were knives and ropes and he should know. The children smelled a wrong moving toward them and stopped their running and laughter for a moment, standing all along a wooded trail. Little boys stood, staring at the men, or looking away, mouths open, breathing hard and frightened. Two boys hid, but not well, in the viny brush. My father looked down; concentrating on the leaf between his fingers, ear to shoulder. I can see him there, his black hair covering one brown eye.

When the men lunged, the chase was brief. Each man grabbed a boy, some men took two, their small bodies wriggling like fish pulled from current, urgent against the airless press into which they were compelled. And then the blood flew, swift and stunning. Such purpose in these men! My father seemed shocked still, as he told the story, in a quiet tone, a whisper. All these years he kept the secret to shield others. One boy's ribs were run through with a knife again and again, until his body looked perforated, tenderized for broiling. Another boy was filleted like the fish for frying. One boy's spine was broken as the man took his clothes, pushed his face down in the muck and raped him, hand mid-back for leverage, then snap. One man strung a noose, a fast, practiced meditation, looped it, looped it, tied, my father all the while pinned beneath his heavy thigh – being sat-upon really, as he watched the rope sail through the air and then swing where it caught the tree. My father was strong enough for nothing. Nearby, another boy's throat was being cut, ear-to-ear. The man shook the body and my father watched the heavy skull flop back, so deep the wound.

"Do you see God yet!" one of the men bellowed. Not so much a question, my father wondered what he should see but freedom, his own dinner-table after a run in the woods, the long black hair slicked back into a large high knot on his mother's head. His chin came to rest on the rope knot and then his feet were off the ground. He told me how the earth looked like Christmas, so much blood on leaves, on little boy's white t-shirts. He told of the iron smell in his nose as he ascended, jerk by jerk. The men's work was finished now and they all watched the last, more intricate effort of the hanging.

"Rise to heaven!" one man called. The rope was tied against the tree; my father's eyes closed. He heard the branches cracking with footfall, voices retreating. His eyes were closed, the scent of child death and green life in his nose, the river still running beneath him.

The people in town began to wonder where those men had gone. They began to talk about where they had come from and what might make them speak that way. "A man's got a right to talk any way he pleases," one reasoned. And as the sky moved to dusk and no children emerged from the forest, the mothers sensed it first. Each asked herself, "Is my child in danger?" And then they began to ask their families "What about the children?" And soon a group of townspeople took the path into the woods.

"I thought I heard my mother's voice," my father said in awe. He seemed childlike again, remembering the experience. "She had such a big voice – you remember," he looked over at me, invoking my memory of my grandmother's presence – an imposing, somehow handsome figure with a volume to match. I nodded.

"But I was dead, how could I hear anything?" He lit another cigarette as he relayed what happened next.

The parents wailed and cursed and mothers held their dead babies, rocking them as parents of dead children have done through time. They rocked the little bodies hoping for peace. At first they didn't see my father. Their flashlights trained on the ground as the light was nearly spent. My grandmother searched the ground. Wailing, she searched. My father was trying to think as loudly as he could, "Look up. Look up!" And then they did and quickly unstrung him. For my poor grandmother's sake, watching, they did so gently, and good thing! There was still life in him. The rope was so large against his tiny head and neck; there was a notch against which his chin had held up his lightness. The back of his neck was as sore as the front from holding his chin that way through the time it took the town to wonder, then arrive. But sure enough, he gasped air as soon as his body found the earth. He gasped air and my grandmother knelt in the ferns and rocked and rocked him.

My father stayed in bed two weeks after the murders. No need, the doctor said, but my grandmother said different. She was keeping an eye on him, packing a soothing poultice on his neck twice daily and feeding him tepid beef broth for strength. "Drink this now, mama's baby," she'd say. "You've been spared for me and we're going to forget this ever happened. You're going to forget this ever happened."

"That rasp in his voice will go away with a little time, but those rope burns might last," said the doctor. And they did. They were the first and the last thing anyone saw when my father finally rose from the bed, returned to school. The townspeople watched those rope burns as the throat moved with drinking, swallowing a sandwich, looking up at the sky. My father began to look down to escape the gaze.

And of course, he didn't forget losing his friends. He didn't forget the forest, which he was never allowed to enter again. He still went there though, slipping off the sidewalk onto the path when no one was looking. More and more, no one was looking. They either stared, or didn't look at my father in that town from that point on. It was too hard to remember, too hard to forget something like that. He could feel them wondering, "Why him? Why wasn't my boy spared?" They never spoke about it in his home either, because he WAS spared. That was that, according to my grandmother. Best to forget a nasty business; don't let it move in on your living.

In my dream, my father cried when he finished the telling, and I held him. In my dream, my father and I were lovers and we were nude, in bed, when he told me the story of the red crease that is visible only when he tilts his head back, only if you're looking for it. The thick beard of manhood, the way the skin chafes with frequent shaving, a move to a new town ceased the staring. And no one ever thought to ask again – razor burn, ingrown hairs, nothing more. The price of a strong manhood, thick beard, frequent shaving. In my dream, I ran my hand across his face, down his neck, with tenderness while he cried.

When I awaken, it all seems so real. I am picking up the phone to call my father. I want to ask him if he'll tell me the story of what happened in his childhood, tell me what will happen next in his life.

Then I realize that I can write his fiction just as well as he can (Dark, 2016).

CHAPTER 10

DADDY'S TERRITORY

TWO POINTS ON A MAP

We are always traversing the landscape between two places.

That's right, Daddy and I do not live together full-time. We have separate lives in some ways. My life is naturally transient because of my work. I am a professor, a consultant, a performer, and a public speaker. I am always in and out of one hotel or another, on the stage, on the road. Daddy is a firefighter, a rescuer, and as a sideline, she repairs motorcycles. In particular, she encourages other women to ride and learn about their Harley Davidson motorcycles. She enjoys a long ride through a beautiful countryside. Daddy is one of the few women to become a certified Harley-Davidson mechanic. She has broken many boundaries related to gender – only 3% of American firefighters are women, after all. She crunches on the hearty flakes of gender norms for breakfast – holds the milk high as it pours into the bowl. She laughs and crunches with a mighty smile on her face.

Daddy stays put. Other than the trips she takes with me, and the occasional solo jaunt to see the countryside on her motorcycle, Daddy stays put. I flutter like a kite across various skies. Daddy holds the string as she rests on our picnic blanket, eating a sandwich and drinking lemonade. We talk on the phone every day – sometimes two or three times. Sometimes I think Daddy is needy. Sometimes I think I am needy. Sometimes I can't tell. When I see that it's her call coming in on the cell phone, I always pick up.

The physical terrain we traverse stretches between San Diego California and Colorado Springs Colorado. Sometimes we fly over this landscape, taking in the landscape of our region from above – the Navajo nation, the Grand Canyon, the Rocky Mountains. Sometimes we drive through the lands that were once home to native people – the lands that were once Mexico, that were once sovereign tribal

© KONINKLIJKE BRILL NV, LEIDEN, 2019 | DOI:10.1163/9789004383562_010

territories. Ownerships shift. People move. People stay put. We are always traversing the landscape between two homes.

And we are at home in both of our dwellings, both of our landscapes. We each have roots in both places too, so neither of us feels disconnected from friends and family when we move between the two points on the map. I attended university in Colorado – Daddy grew up in Southern California and she still has family there. My son was born in Colorado and hers was born in California. We both have sons. We are both rooted in two places and so this endless migration between the two seems natural to me.

Daddy hates the endless migration. She says, "You should be at home with me." She pouts about my extended absences. She pouts about my short absences too – if she wants me handy, any time away is too long, too far.

And Daddy also makes the best of it. She relishes her job as navigator when I am away. I get lost on the road and I call Daddy on my cell phone. She sits at the computer using GPS to help me get back on track. I could pull over and do it myself, but Daddy likes to put me back on track. Although she doesn't like it when I'm away, she loves the fact that others – total strangers – adore me and think I'm smart. She sometimes meets me when I travel for work too. We have weekend getaways before or after my engagements. She jokes with me about needing to come to my presentations as a body guard, about needing to play the role of security when I am on stage. She puffs up her chest and puts on a smirk as she stands in the back of the room, her eyes welling with tears of pride as she watches me. She says, "You shouldn't travel without a body guard, baby. Don't you worry. Tonight, I'll be in the back of the room with my sock full of pennies in case anyone gets out of line."

Daddy is good fun on a long road trip. When we travel with our boys, we stop for donuts; we stop for a go-kart ride; we stop for a nice meal overlooking a beautiful vista. We show our sons the good life. Daddy does most of the driving. Daddy pumps the gas and checks the tire pressure. Daddy packs the cooler with sandwiches and cake that I've made. Daddy puts in extra blankets and pillows in case any of us get sleepy. When Daddy is driving, I am the navigator, but I am also one of the kids in the car. She brings me a box of animal crackers from the gas station mini-mart as a treat when she's in paying for the gas. I don't ask for the cookies, but she hands them to me with a private wink. I am both mother and girl.

When Daddy and I travel alone, we take a different map. We stop at hot springs, sit in hot water together and enjoy cocktails overlooking the countryside. Hot water is one of our simple pleasures – we were so delighted to learn that we shared a penchant for "taking the waters." Daddy is competitive though – sometimes she rankles at the idea of me sharing her interests. She thinks it's great when I arrange a trip to an exotic spring that she wouldn't visit on her own – when we sat in hot water in Iceland, she was all praise and glory to my ability to expand her horizons. And sometimes, Daddy is just plain bitter and moody about my worldliness. What kind of girl knows more about the world than Daddy? What kind of girl is better-traveled, sits in foreign waters. It's just not seemly for a girl to get around so much.

Daddy is good fun when we travel alone. I have never been so at ease. Daddy helps me relax after a hard day of work. Daddy comes to an event and feels pride that I am her own. She rubs my feet back in the hotel after my workday and then we do naughty things. Daddy sets the stage and tells the stories that give me permission to do naughty things. Daddy says, "You look so scandalized!" And then she chuckles and forges on with the naughtiness. "Don't worry," she adds with a lascivious grin, "I'll take responsibility for wanting to do what we do – you just keep being innocent and letting your Daddy corrupt you."

The landscape we travel is at once ordinary and extraordinary. We are rolling along in our 4x4 vehicle, taking the big freeways and the small, unpaved roads with ease. We are taking in unbelievable beauty between the Southern California coastline and the Rocky Mountains. We are so lucky – oh yes, we know it – lucky to have each other and be in such beauty. Daddy doesn't like the cold in the winter, but she loves the skiing, the snow-mobiling, the hot springs surrounded by snow. Daddy doesn't like the cold in the winter – and yet she's afraid to leave home. We're always planning on it, planning on it. Colorado Springs is a place with a certain set of values, a certain population with conservative, patriarchal Christian values. We don't hold those values, those beliefs

71

– at least we don't hold them in our mouths – we speak against them with ease. And yet, this is Daddy's home. Year after year, this is where she lives. She says, "This might be my last year of scraping ice off the windshield." She says, "This place is so provincial." And then she stays. There are things to love too – the landscape. And we have the ability to travel. We are so lucky. She says she wants to live somewhere else – Southern California, Hawaii. She just wants a little more money, a little more security. I don't say so of course, but I know she's afraid.

"If you want to move, do it. We'll figure out the details," I say. I don't say this too often because I know that if she leaves, I'll be the one to plan it, make the move comfortable and we can't talk openly about the ways in which I take charge. Daddy is fragile about things like that. And what if things between us didn't work out? Daddy is fragile about things like that.

So, for now, we enjoy traversing the landscape between two places.

DADDY'S DINNER

Vegetable Quiche

6 eggs
½ cup shredded cheese
¼ cup secondary vegetable,
1 ready-made pie shell

½ cup milk
½ cup primary vegetable,
large chunks
½ tablespoon crushed garlic
small chunks

Beat it all furiously; eggs and milk first, and then put it in the pie shell. Cook at 350 degrees, 45 minutes. Once the chopping and crushing is done, take a whisk and beat it like there's no tomorrow. Quiche is a simple way to impress. The effort isn't in the kitchen; it's in the ingredients. Pay close attention to the following instructions on choosing ingredients. Your ingredients are everything.

She didn't like for me to stray too far away from her in the supermarket. Lagging behind warranted a stern look. Moving to another aisle was cause for a lecture. I like to peruse the cheeses, confident that my partner is retrieving the easy items, like milk and eggs. Some years ago, eggs were sold in different sizes and colors. Now the grocers know we want nothing but large and white. Choosing the eggs is easy. They're going to be large and white. Free range, please. But if not, buy them anyway. Dinner must go on.

"Stop wandering off," she'd say with a grand sweep of her hand. "I'm going to round the corner to find some mustachioed character trying to buy you candy. If you wander off, someone will snatch you up!" This was too theatrical to seem truly possessive. She enjoyed the idea of me as a recalcitrant five-year old in the supermarket. I want to report that really, I just wanted to be choosing between the Gouda and the Havarti. But I should suspect I'm lying. Why would I have strolled with her behind the cart if I didn't enjoy being the little girl on whom she doted?

If you have a Daddy-type tapping her foot nearby, sharp cheddar is always a good choice. The cheese has to have a strong voice. A Havarti along with Bleu is good. A Gouda can hold its own. Consider the flavors along with the vegetables you choose. Your palette is sovereign. Remember that.

Choose the vegetables that look the best on your shopping day. We're led to believe that all vegetables are created equal in this era of worldwide produce transport that renders seasons but a travel-brochure frivolity. I'd be buying only organic vegetables if Daddy didn't require us to use the big well-lit supermarket instead of the small cozy health food store to which I am accustomed. Indeed, I chose the customs of the doting shopping-guard over my own customs.

Seemingly, all vegetables look good in the big well-lit supermarket but look closely. Some hum more loudly than others: more chi. Choose a primary and a secondary vegetable. Asparagus and red pepper, for example, Broccoli and leek. Artichoke heart and shallot. The secondary vegetable should be chopped into smaller pieces. It is an invited guest whereas the primary vegetable is hosting the dinner party.

You'll never regret fresh garlic, though in a rush, the pre-crushed and bottled variety is suitable.

The nightly dinner party for two: I had a Donna Reed apron; a Martha Stewart smile. My Daddy loved Martha Stewart. "She just wants the world to be more beautiful. Is that so bad?" she would say, in defense of her mornings with coffee and Martha on the television. She watched Martha when she was at work too, in the firehouse, hoping that the alarm would remain silent until the petit fours had been frosted. I smile and make the food. I let her choose the menus and mealtimes. If I really were Martha Stewart, I would've made piecrust. The frozen, deep-dish variety, made with vegetable shortening, was good enough for us, however. I decided this and she didn't quibble.

"I don't mind cleaning up and taking out the trash," said Daddy, "as long as you keep me well fed!" She'd say this with the plate in hand, steaming slice of quiche next to a simple field greens salad spritzed with vinaigrette. She'd flourish her hand over the top of the plate as though I were the food and add, "Baby, you're the best!"

THE PURITY BALL

IGNORING THE NEWS

Daddy and I are climbing into bed in our Colorado Springs apartment. I have recently been thinking about how a relationship like ours – one that acknowledges a power exchange – is somehow more "honest" than "normal" male/female relationships. Sure, we use storytelling in bed, but so do a lot of people; they just don't tell themselves they're doing it. If they did, they'd have to confront their cultural biases about attractiveness, thinness, needing to like someone's stories before an attraction can occur. What I do is more honest than shaving my body, striving to look youthful, putting on girlish prettiness, watching my lover's turn-on and calling it normal. Most people are deceiving themselves. Nothing funny here – the masses opine – this is just the way adults behave in a relationship of equals.

We're all just fetishists, I thought to myself. At least Daddy and I are erudite and clever as we sort out our cultural propensities. At least Daddy and I are intellectuals – we often fuck and then marvel at how great we are in bed – what it must be like for those having pedestrian sex down in the valleys of maladroit love-making. They have no idea how great it is to be us.

I have been thinking about this – and I know my Daddy shares some of my views. We talk about things. For a working class butch-dyke Daddy, she's very smart; she reads; she thinks. But when it comes to who we are in bed, I'm never sure my Daddy and I are making the same meaning of what we choose to do. How could a person ever be sure? The stories we tell shift based on the response we want, after all. They shift based on our current thinking in the day, based on the images and stories we see outside of our homes. What's happening between Daddy and I is never just between us in private. There is a permeable field between public and personal always.

© KONINKLIJKE BRILL NV, LEIDEN, 2019 | DOI:10.1163/9789004383562_011

Daddy often initiates the stories – and sometimes they surprise me. Not the themes, per se. The themes are very common – ownership, virginity, beauty, innocence, purity, ownership. Even the stories follow typical archetypal patriarchal lines. Daddy is not at all creative – she just embellishes the stories we were handed, personalizes them with my name and attributes. Daddy is a hack, really. Nothing original in our themes.

No, the stories don't surprise me, but my reactions do. I'm surprised by the fact that she is so sincere in telling those stories – as though she made them up and they've only ever happened between us. Her full attention focuses on me; she watches my surprise and pleasure. She watches me bask in the stardom of her stories. When I think about the stories later, I'm often surprised by her sincerity. The way she can call up my turn-on with her sincerity – her total pleasure – about things that we would both rationally denounce. Daddy's stories are my stories are my culture's stories. We are not inventing anything. And sometimes, it even feels like we are tapping into the great cosmic dance of masculine and feminine. (And perhaps we are, but is this the only way to do it – or just the way we know best?)

It feels so good. And when we're all singing the same tune – me, Daddy, the media – there's something so beautiful in the harmony. My body just responds. I am surprised, horrified at times even. I love being the receptacle for my Daddy's pleasure, and the body responds.

Tonight, Daddy settles onto my body, her giant boner poised to own me and as she kisses my neck and squeezes my breast she tells the story about my wedding night. Of course I will eventually get older and marry, but even when another man comes into my life, she says, I will still belong to Daddy. Daddy will always own me, even when I someday wear another's ring.

She slips her cock in, calls me, "good girl" and, "sweet princess," and I can feel her pleasure, her release and dominion are wound together like her pleasure is wound with mine. She is fucking me and I hold onto her back with my legs, with my arms. I am prone and she is fucking me and telling me how Daddy will be right next door on my wedding night. Daddy will have the room right next door at the fancy hotel on my honeymoon and she asks me – as though there could be any other response under these circumstances – as though I could say anything against Daddy under the circumstances where I feel fully adored and fully needed and fully successful at fulfilling my beloved – she asks me, "Are you still going to be longing for your Daddy, even on your wedding night?" And I nod, skin tingling. My commitment to Daddy will forever supersede any commitment I make to others. We cannot be parted. Daddy is Daddy forever. "Are you going to slip right next door as soon as your new husband steps out and spread your legs for your Daddy like a good girl?"

And I feel that slight nausea that sometimes comes when I understand the story with some conscious part of my mind, but the body takes over again and my cunt slickens and I whimper, "Yes Daddy." She is on my body, after all, covering me, protecting me. She is giving me pleasure and she is in charge in so many beautiful ways at this very moment. I am in surrender and it feels more than good – it feels beautiful and right and like the promise of every fairy tale. No matter what could ever go wrong out in the big world, my Daddy will always be there to love me and take care of me – to fold me back into loving arms. I cannot conceive of anything better than Daddy. Daddy will always be there.

This is just a story of course. And it's just between us. No one ever needs to know what happens just between us, within our private places. It's just between us in our cozy, stylish downtown apartment. Daddy goes to her job as a firefighter. She puts out the fires. She makes the rescues. She gets in the big truck when the alarm rings and Daddy makes everything all right. I am the smart, pretty girl – Daddy likes a clever girl – and I plan the parties and I bake a delicious cake and I put a good meal on the table. We have a good life. It's just between us in our little home in Colorado Springs in 1998.

I was so focused on our story; I didn't see the ads in the paper that very week. It was that very week when Daddy wrapped me into her arms and told me the story that prepared me for my wedding night. I didn't know that the big party was starting, across town, as my Daddy whispered these things in my ear and fucked and fucked me until her considerable strength was spent and my body ached with pleasure. I didn't know that across town, at the Broadmoor Hotel – the most fancy hotel in our whole city – Lauren Wilson was wearing her fluffy white formal dress. She was proud and sparkling in her tiara, taking Randy Wilson's hand for the waltz. At age 13, Lauren Wilson was afraid of dating – she just didn't want the turmoil of it all, so she took the purity pledge and her Daddy loved her so much, he made this huge party, just for her. Other girls could join her, with their Daddies. What they pledged didn't need to be private. They were having a big party.

I hadn't seen the news. I was so absorbed in my own life. I couldn't even imagine Lauren, receiving the single white rose and feeling so adored, so loved. Her Daddy pledged to protect her and to love her. Her Daddy pledged to hold up the best of himself for her, and she in return, promised her virginity, her purity.

I didn't know that was happening at the Broadmoor Hotel, just as she didn't know what was happening in my home. I know how she felt though. Just across town, I was having the same feelings. I am beautiful. I am loved. My Daddy will always protect me.

The New York Times
May 19, 2008
Dancing the Night Away, With a Higher Purpose
By Neela Banerjee

***

COLORADO SPRINGS – In their floor-length gowns, up-dos and tiaras, the 70 or so young women swept past two harpists and into a gilt-and-brocade dining room at the lavish Broadmoor Hotel, on the arms of their much older male companions.

***

The girls, ages early grade school to college, had come with their fathers, stepfathers and future fathers-in-law last Friday night to the ninth annual Father-Daughter Purity Ball. The first two hours of the gala passed like any somewhat awkward night out with parents, the men doing nearly all the talking and the girls struggling to cut their chicken.

***

But after dessert, the 63 men stood and read aloud a covenant, "Before God to cover my daughter as her authority and protection in the area of purity."

***

The gesture signaled that the fathers would guard their daughters from what evangelicals consider a profoundly corrosive "hook-up culture." The evening, which alternated between homemade Christian rituals and giddy dancing, was a joyous public affirmation of the girls' sexual abstinence until they wed.

***

Yet the graying men in the shadow of their glittering daughters were the true focus of the night. To ensure their daughters' purity, they were asked to set an example and to hew to evangelical ideals in a society they say tempts them as much as it does their daughters.

***

"It's also good for me," said Terry Lee, 54, who attended the ball for a second year, this time with his youngest daughter, Rachel, 16. "It inspires me to be spiritual and moral in turn. If I'm holding them to such high standards, you can be sure I won't be cheating on their mother."

***

Relying on word-of-mouth that brought families mostly from the thriving evangelical community in Colorado Springs and from as far as Virginia and California, Randy and Lisa Wilson built their Purity Ball into an annual gala that costs about $10,000, financed by ticket sales. This year, about 150 people attended the dinner, purity ceremony and dance.

***

The purity pledges for the fathers to sign stood in the middle of the dinner tables. Unlike other purity balls, the daughters here do not make a pledge, said Amanda Robb, a New York-based writer researching a book about the abstinence movement who was at the Broadmoor event.

***

"Fathers, our daughters are waiting for us," Mr. Wilson, 49, told the men. "They are desperately waiting for us in a culture that lures them into the murky waters of exploitation. They need to be rescued by you, their dad."

***

The Wilsons organized what was considered the country's first father-daughter purity ball 10 years ago, as their oldest girls entered adolescence. Randy Wilson is the national field director of church ministries for the Family Research Council, a conservative advocacy group, and Lisa Wilson is a stay-at-home mom.

***

"The culture says you're free to sleep with as many people as you want to," said Khrystian Wilson, 20, one of the Wilson's' seven children, including five girls. "What does that get you but complete chaos?"

***

For the Wilsons and the growing number of people who have come to their balls, premarital sex is seen as inevitably destructive, especially to girls, who they say suffer more because they are more emotional than boys. Fathers, they say, play a crucial role in helping them stay pure.

***

"Something I need from dad is affirmation, being told I'm beautiful," said Jordyn Wilson, 19, another daughter of Randy and Lisa. "If we don't get it from home, we will go out to the culture and get it from them."

***

Recent studies have suggested that close relationships between fathers and daughters can reduce the risk of early sexual activity among girls and teenage pregnancy. But studies have also shown that most teenagers who say they will remain abstinent, like those at the ball, end up having sex before marriage, and they are far less likely to use condoms than their peers.

***

No one knows for certain how many purity balls are held nationwide, because they are grass-roots efforts. The Abstinence Clearinghouse, an advocacy group, says it sells hundreds of purity ball kits annually to interested groups all over the country and abroad.

***

Abstinence is never mentioned at the Colorado Springs Purity Ball, but a litany of fathers' duties is – mainly, making time to get involved in their daughters' lives and setting an example.

***

In a ballroom after dinner, bare but for a seven-foot wooden cross at one end, the fathers and daughters gathered along the walls. Kevin Moore, there with his three girls, told the men they were taking a stand for their families and their nation. Then he and Mr. Wilson walked to the cross with two large swords, which they held up before it to make an arch.

***

Each father and his daughter walked under the arch and knelt before the cross. Synthesized hymns played. The fathers sometimes held their daughters and whispered a short prayer, and then the girls each placed a white rose, representing purity, at the foot of the cross. Mr. Lee and Rachel walked away holding hands.

***

The girls, many wearing purity rings, made silent vows. "I promise to God and myself and my family that I will stay pure in my thoughts and actions until I marry," said Katie Swindler, 16.

***

Her father, Jim, said he brought her to show her how much he cherished her after almost losing her in a car accident two years ago.

***

Loss tinged many at the ball. Stephen Clark, 64, came to the ball for the first time with Ashley Avery, 17, who is "promised" to his son, Zane, 16. Mr. Clark brought Ashley, in her white satin gown, to show her that he loved her like a daughter, he said, something he felt he needed to underscore after Ashley's father left her family a year ago.

***

Mrs. Wilson, the organizer, said that her father abandoned her family when she was 2, and that Mr. Wilson's father was distant. One father said he had terminal cancer and came with his two daughters. Others were trying to do better in their second marriages.

***

"I've heard from fathers that this challenged them, to guard their own eyes, for example," Mr. Wilson said. "It is a call to covenant which basically says, 'I as my daughter's father will be a man of integrity and purity.'"

***

If most teenage girls would not be caught dead dancing with their dads, the girls at the ball twirled for hours with their game but stiff fathers. Every half-hour, Mr. Wilson stopped the dancing so that fathers could bless their daughters before everyone.

***

The dancing continued past the ball's official end at midnight. Mr. Wilson had to tell people to go home. The fathers took their flushed and sometimes sleepy girls toward the exit. But one father took his two young daughters for a walk around the hotel's dark, glassy lake.

DADDY VS. GIRL PURITY SHOWDOWN

It's a showdown! Right here on the TV screen – pop up the popcorn, pull up a seat! It's a showdown the likes of which you'll rarely see on national television. Daddy vs. girl! That's right – she's showing the pluck to take him on. She's cagey. She's tiny, but thinks she's mighty. Everybody get ready to watch – it's a showdown!

Shelby Knox took a purity pledge when she was 15. She comes from Lubbock TX, a city with one of the nation's highest incidence of teen pregnancy and where the schools teach an "abstinence only" curriculum on reproductive health. Shelby took a stand. She spoke out in favor of complete education, including information on contraception. She spoke out on reproductive rights. And eventually, though a self-proclaimed conservative Southern Baptist, she also spoke out on gay, lesbian and transgender rights. She was the subject of a 2005 documentary – The Education of Shelby Knox *– and that's what put her on the Today show, opposite Purity Ball founder Randy Wilson. As though they were two sides of a morality debate, two sides of a power-struggle, two sides of a Christian coin tossed into the air as though there was some question about how it would land.*

It's a showdown! And the talk shows are set up to showcase the story, the battle, and the fight. The media is there to give us a good story, an exciting competition – a story with some tension. It's not about fairness; it's not about investigation. It's definitely not about context. Those don't make for pleasing entertainment. Shelby's in for a fight with the Daddy whose daughters are, one by one, becoming crusaders for purity. The eldest three, close to Shelby's age, have written a book (for sale on the family website) called Purity Woman. *Khrystian – the second of Randy's four daughters writes regularly for various Christian blogs as well.*

Shelby is up against Randy on the talk shows, on the news shows, and even on nationwide morning television – Ding! The bell rings for Round One on the Today Show.

Matt Lauer will offer the story about the Purity Ball. The focus is on the Purity Ball and while he describes the event, a video clip plays showing happy girls dancing with doting dads. He introduces the interviews by saying, "It sounds simple enough, but some people think these dances are controversial." He draws out the word controversial, as though there's something not quite bright about saying such a thing. Ding!

Round Two. Randy is seated next to Matt Lauer on the guest sofa. Matt Lauer introduces him first, as the founder of The Father Daughter Purity Ball movement. Then he introduces Shelby by saying that she took a purity pledge at fifteen and that her story was chronicled in a documentary film The Education of Shelby Knox. *Shelby is further away on the sofa – Matt leans awkwardly forward to address her. Randy is invited to speak first. Ding!*

Round Three. Matt begins by confirming to Randy, "You've got five daughters, right?" And Randy proudly affirms this fact. Randy is given time to speak in a comfortable, authoritative speaking voice and Matt listens intently, his gaze steady and respectful. He questions – the need for the virginity pledge – and as Randy answers, the scene shows a room full of thin, graceful white girls dressed in white dresses swooping and twirling to a beautiful instrumental score. They are like Swan Lake ballerinas en masse, their dresses swirling around the fancy ballroom. The caption under the dance, while Randy talks, reads, "2 in 10 teens report having a sexual experience by age 15." Ding!

Round Four. Without yet allowing Shelby to speak, Matt Lauer states her rebuttal for her. He says, "But to Shelby this sounds like 'until I'm married, my father controls my life and then once I'm married, my husband controls my life.'" And then, Shelby still waiting, leaning in, ready to talk, waits while Randy is given the time to rebut her sentiments (as delivered via Matt). Ding!

Round Five. "That's not what we're saying ..." he begins simply. As he speaks about allowing his daughters to succeed, the caption at the bottom of the screen reads, "33% decrease in the teen birthrate between 1991 and 2003," as though there is some correlation between this statistic and the work he describes. Then, as he continues speaking, the statistic changes, "In 2003, 47% of high schoolers reported having sex, down from 54% in 1991." Ding!

Round Six. Matt Lauer leans toward Shelby and says, "Hey! His take is a different one. He says these girls aren't making these vows to their fathers; they're making these vows to themselves. And what's wrong with that?" He says this as though she weren't sitting right there and somehow she, and the audience need to hear the point again. He says it as though she needs to speak directly to Randy's point rather than having a point of her own to make. Ding!

Round Seven. As Shelby begins to speak, for the first time in a segment that is now more than halfway finished, the caption beneath her name reads, "Made purity pledge at age 15." And who among us is not wondering when she failed her pledge, broke her pledge, unpledged her pledge due to someone else's influence. Sure she looks thoughtful and self-possessed, but there was a pledge involved and a person who can't pledge a pledge and take it seriously is somehow suspect. She is prepared to answer Matt's challenge however, but she's right to speak quickly – she knows the score – as she describes girls not knowing what they're pledging to when they are so young and so much pressure is upon them. They can't possibly be pledging to themselves, she asserts. She is articulate, but her point comes off strident. She is not given much time to make any point at all. Ding!

Round Eight. As Shelby talks, Randy looks at her politely. Is it a smirk of condescension? Hard to tell. When she affirms part of Randy's point, "I think father-daughter time is great –" Matt Lauer then interrupts her with the question, "Well, what did you know at 15?" He is leaning forward in his chair, almost aggressively, his voice still cordial, probing. His pen in hand and outstretched palm challenge her to respond. Ding!

Round Nine. Shelby is resilient in her response – she says she knew nothing. She says her pledge just meant that she wanted to please her parents, her church. This was something they wanted soooo badly. She states clearly that she was pressured and threatened with ostracism if she didn't give the correct response. The caption beneath *her image as she speaks reads, "Pledging Purity. A father-daughter dance." She says, "So many girls take these pledges because their adoring fathers are watching them. And that's what he wants." Ding!*

Round Ten. Matt Lauer interrupts her again. This time he references the statistics. He directs his comment to both of them as he speaks about the Purity Ball, "Purely, this is not a cure-all because if you look at the statistics – and we had them in the piece – 88% of girls who take this vow end up having sex before marriage." Randy is shifting in his seat as though he knows this part is coming. He is murmuring "right" and "yes." He is letting us know that he has not been surprised and that he's got this one covered. Matt then asks Randy directly, "Why do you believe that is happening." Ding!

Round Eleven. "This is all about fatherhood." He speaks and seems to hear his words as he goes on and he self-corrects as he goes to leave no chance for intervening views. "Again, this is not about a father controlling his daughter. It's about a father knowing the heart of his daughter and being there to work through life issues, relationship issues that she has ..." At this point, a picture of Randy's family – his wife and seven kids – comes on the screen. They are posed in matching shirts in front of the beautiful Colorado Park called Garden of the Gods. He has been asked a specific question about the high numbers of girls who don't follow through with the purity pledge and he is using his time to set up an unrelated point – about father-daughter relationships. Ding!

Round Twelve. Shelby tries to speak. She gets out "ah" and then Matt speaks the viewpoint that he believes would've been hers, had she been allowed to enter the conversation. He says, "Some people think those daughters fail because they're abstaining from sex, but they're also abstaining from talking about sex." Ding!

Round Thirteen. Shelby leans in and takes the floor! She says, "Well, I do have to take issue with the word 'fail.' First of all, a young woman making a responsible sexual choice whenever she wants to, whether that's in marriage or whenever she decides to – that can't be considered a failure because that's her decision. And if it's an educated one, then it's one that everyone should respect. I do think that a lot of young women feel a lot of pressure to stay technical virgins though they break these pledges in other ways by engaging in other risky behaviors to do everything but sex, which is very scary, not using safer sex techniques because they don't really have good sex education." *She has made the point she came to make, despite the focus of the segment being on her rebuttal of the Purity Balls. Ding!*

Round Fourteen. Matt Lauer steps in immediately to say, "Well, we should just mention, that though this started in religious community, this is very much a mainstream activity." He goes on talking about the Purity Ball without addressing Shelby's comments at all. "It's interesting to me to get some education on this," Matt says to Randy directly. Ding!

Round Fifteen. Randy speaks again – gives his final remarks about his relationship with his daughters. Matt Lauer thanks Randy first, then Shelby, for being on the show.

And – Game Over. Go Shelby for speaking a full 69 seconds during a five minute segment on the Today show – it clearly would've been less without your calm, clear, assertiveness (The Today Show, 2007).

Shelby Knox and Khrystian Wilson are close in age and similar in upbringing. On Shelby's blog, The Ms. Education of Shelby Knox, *her writing presents her as smart, humble and self-assured. She's aware of her privileges, her fallibility and grateful for her various connections to a feminist community that helps her unravel the intersections of gender, race, class, sexual orientation and other social indicators as she continues to work to make the world a better place* (Knox, 2008). *Khrystian also works to make the world a better place, by waging war against premarital sex. She describes the hell – with endless toil and flames and a futile longing for peace – that besieges American women today if they let themselves choose sex out of wedlock. For Khrystian, purity is the answer and she is grateful to God, and to her mother for being a shining beacon of good Christian motherhood, to her father for protecting her virtue and to her husband for modeling integrity and holiness.*

I am still wondering: What was Lauren Wilson afraid of? She said she didn't want the flirting, the taunting, and the breaking up that was going on around her in school. And this makes sense – but why connect any of that to the sex act itself? She first kissed her husband on their wedding day. What did she fear? Not conforming to the virginity fetish? Not pleasing her Daddy? Not being seen as fully pure and righteous – beyond reproach in a reproachful community?

Maybe she feared the way all boys are portrayed as lustful animals who will manipulate a girl for sex, who will take sex and give no reward, maybe of the way all men are portrayed as idiots on television commercials for washing machines and power tools. Once they marry, they can't figure out how to work anything electronic except the television remote control, how they objectify women and then look at one another, palms upturned shoulders shrugged and go, "What?" "Wha – ?" "It's just the way we are!"

Maybe she fears becoming the maid – the scullery maid, the milk-maid, the French maid. Maybe she fears becoming the whore. She fears the way her father could lose respect for her if her behavior slips outside the realm of "pure." She fears the way her father looks at women – any women, different women, his wife, and his daughters. Lauren is not stupid – she is paying attention to every glance and she knows that any wrong move might remove her from the light of her father's smile. Maybe she fears losing love – the love she has. She fears finding love, then losing it. She fears being the one who is loved for her purity, for her goodness, for her workhorse flank and her thin, trim, hand-on-hip sensible detergent commercial mom demeanor. She fears being the one who's loved for her beauty, but not her sexiness. She fears being loved for being sexy because if she's not sexy, she won't be loved. That's just the way men are. She was thirteen and stepping onto the tightrope of adult expectations about femininity and her parents had given her no net of reason to help her navigate these fears. She was stepping onto the tightrope of adult expectations about femininity and she was a smart girl. Suddenly the crowd below sounded like they were hooting and hollering watching a stripper on a pole. Suddenly they sounded like a church choir. Suddenly they sounded like they were waiting for blood, lions just let loose in the coliseum, women being stoned for infidelity, executed for killing abusive husbands. What was the crowd shouting? Lauren couldn't tell. She was afraid. She just didn't want the "turmoil" of dating. She turned on the platform, above the crowd, and saw Daddy holding out his hand. Daddy's voice was closest to her ear so she heard him clearest. He said, it's okay princess. Better if you just stay home with me. I will pledge my protection if you pledge your chastity. It's that simple. Daddy loves you. Just stay here with me.

I know how Lauren felt.

This is no debutant ball or quinceñera party or cotillion, the girls are not being presented to young men for display, preparing to be passed off into their own generation of coupledom, into the next generation of Daddy-dominion where they have some chance of reforming and revising the rules by which they will live. No. The custom has folded in on itself. These girls are pledging to their fathers, to stay true to the Daddies who raised them, to take on the customs of that generation. They are pledging not to move forward. And the origins of this custom make perfect sense. A regular guy – Randy Wilson – just came up with it all – assisted by the fears and concerns of his regular daughter. Lauren.

I want to love Randy for his attention on his daughters. I want to love his pledge of integrity, the idea that he needs to be a good role model. I want to love the intention and the time he's taking to know her, how this might transform him. I believe that this intention to uphold his best self could transform him.

But it's hard to trust the best intentions of men who can't first denounce patriarchy, who can't first say, no, I will not take my place in the hierarchy that will always place me above my daughter, below my God, above my wife, below the men who hold a higher position, above everyone in my household. It's true: I can't easily shake the assumption that the environment of patriarchy will poison any good intention that individual men have in some way. Randy Wilson is explicitly answering to a bigger Daddy, the Daddy-God whose words were written by men and passed down through an institution that has burned women's bodies, tortured women's bodies, keeps anyone woman-bodied from being in contact with her God and able to translate the divine for her culture.

Really, I want Randy Wilson's best intentions to succeed – along with the best intentions of the tens of thousands of men who've held their daughter's hands at Purity Balls around the nation and now the world – the increasing numbers of men who take their daughters to these balls each year since Randy and his wife Lisa organized the first event.

I see the Daddy holding out his hand to his daughter with pride on his face, in his stance. I want to believe that he's not leering at his daughters, that none of the men at the Purity Ball are sporting boners or ducking into the bathroom to jerk off, or fondling their daughters in the car, or planning on showing them how it is, for their own good, in preparation for their wedding nights, because their virginity is now a specific, signed and delivered possession and they can. They can.

They still can.

I want to believe they won't.

How can you measure the value of your eleven year old looking up into your eyes (as you clumsily learn the fox-trot together) with innocent, uncontainable joy, saying, "Daddy, I'm so excited!" wrote Wesley Tullis in a letter describing his grateful participation. "I have been involved with the Father-Daughter Ball for two years with my daughters, Sarah and Anna. It is impossible to convey what I have seen in their sweet spirits, their delicate, forming souls, as their daddy takes them out for their first, big dance. Their whole being absorbs my loving attention, resulting in a radiant sense of self-worth and identity. Think of it from their perspective: My daddy thinks I'm beautiful in my own unique way. My daddy is treating me with respect and honor. My daddy has taken time to be silly, and even made a fool of himself, learning how to dance. My daddy really loves me!" (Wilson, 2001, pp. 140–141)

CONFUSION HURTS

FUNNY BUSINESS IN THE BROADMOOR

We met in college. Taffy and I were among the few students not fresh out of high school – and we had a similar fashion sense – a little tarty, despite being a little chubby. We flaunted our sexuality and I found her refreshing, so we started hanging out. I was busy working – I tutored students for a living – made my own business of it. At first, I tutored foreign language because there was a need, owing to the three-semester requirement for a BA degree. I was already multi-lingual, so it was just a handy way to make money. Then I realized I could tutor almost anything – most students didn't know how to listen and assimilate texts and pay attention to requirements and make connections the way I did. The truth is, I was indeed the same age as my fresh-out-of-high school peers. But after finding the gumption to leave home at fourteen after the telling-on-my-stepfather-about-the-incest experience went awry, I found the gumption to travel and make a life. I wasn't fresh-out-of-anything at that point.

Taffy was actually middle-aged. She had two kids and a husband who was never home, though he paid all the bills and gave her an adequate allowance to feed the family and go to school. He was a trucker, she explained. "You'll meet him eventually," she waved off my curiosity about her "other half."

Taffy's two children were a boy, Mark – just finishing high school and intending to go into the Navy – and a girl, Tabitha, still in high school. She was fifteen when we first met. It was important to Taffy that they live in a good neighborhood, so Tabitha could go to a good school. Though they rented their home, it was in the most expensive suburb of Colorado Springs – the Broadmoor area. Dan – the absentee husband – didn't like the idea of buying property, Taffy explained, so it was better for them to rent. I was impressed that a

© KONINKLIJKE BRILL NV, LEIDEN, 2019 | DOI:10.1163/9789004383562_012

trucker's salary could afford their lifestyle – especially with Taffy as a full-time student, but who knows what people have going on. It's not polite to meddle.

We spent the first few months of our friendship getting together for lunch and studying – well-intentioned meetings that would devolve into conversations about who Taffy would try to fuck for a better grade, or what kind of houses and lives we thought our professors had. Taffy was not the best student. She was ditzy and thought I dressed cool and that's why she originally liked me. She worked to keep her C average, and well, I was good at school, so I could afford the goof-off time with her.

Once, when we were sitting at a downtown café having lunch, Taffy's husband Dan showed up to say hello and to meet me. Taffy introduced us and Dan nodded a hello, but didn't sit to join us. He said something to Taffy about picking Tabitha up at school. He said he was taking her out to a movie that night. Taffy said, "Oh that's great," and then when Dan left, she said to me, "Isn't he ugly? I mean, really Kim, I find him disgusting."

I chuckled at this and considered his appearance. He was tall and white, thin, but barrel-chested. He wore jeans and a t-shirt and his curly hair fell almost to shoulder length. His thick mustache almost obscured his mouth. He looked like a middle-aged biker, trucker, yeah, whatever. I reported that I didn't find him particularly ugly.

"Well, I just want you to know I haven't fucked him at all in the past three years – haven't kissed him for more than five. I think his teeth are all rotted out anyway! Who'd know under that moustache? Makes me sick to think about it!"

We laughed at the level of her disgust like naughty schoolgirls smoking in the bathroom considering what a first kiss – or a first fuck – would actually be like. "Why do you stay with him?" I asked simply.

"Oh my God, Kim, how would I live without him?" She said, wide-eyed, as though I hadn't seen the obvious. "I'm not smart, like you. And now I'm old and fat. I'm not even pretty enough to find someone else to take care of us. He's gone most of the time anyway. And he sends us money." Taffy ate another bite of her sandwich, then added, "Oh, and Tabitha just adores him! I couldn't take her Daddy away from her like that!"

I nodded, because I understood every word she said.

"He does that pretty often when he's in town – pick Tabitha up from school. On school breaks, sometimes she even goes out on the road with him. He says he gets nicer hotel rooms when she's with him – like Holiday Inns or something. I don't like the idea of her staying in those truck stop motels. He really dotes on her, Kim. That's the best thing about our relationship really – the money, and how much he loves his little girl."

I took this in with as little judgment as I could muster, given my own past. Still, I was thinking about the man I'd just met and the sweet, simple Tabitha I'd only met once or twice.

One Christmas, Taffy invited me over to their house for a small party. She had told me ahead of time how Dan never liked her to have anyone over, but this time she put her foot down.

"I'm having people over for spiced wine this Christmas, Dan. Punch me if you want to, but I'm doin' it!" I asked her if he ever really punched her. She waved me off. "He doesn't have to. I mostly do what I'm told."

Apparently he approved the party reluctantly because it'd make them seem more normal to the neighbors. Taffy said some thought he looked too rough for the neighborhood, given that most of them were lawyers and bankers. Taffy and the kids looked like a good upper-middle class family though. I was the only friend of Taffy's whom Dan approved for the party. The other guests included two sets of neighbors – one couple were parents to Tabitha's friend from school. Mark's girlfriend was also in attendance.

Taffy decorated the house in beautiful reds and golds, candles and evergreens. She made hors d'oeuvres and cookies and served spiced wine. Dan sat stoic the whole evening. He drank beer instead of wine and the only time I saw him talk all evening was to Tabitha. She'd go sit next to him, on the edge of his recliner chair, leaning onto him affectionately.

"Daddy, will you get me some new boots at the mall tomorrow. I don't like the ones Mommy got me for Christmas." I heard her say at one point. Taffy overheard too and said, "Just listen. He'll give her anything she wants and he barely speaks to me if I ask for something."

"Seems like you're doing okay," I said and she smirked and giggled.

That's when I noticed something about Tabitha. She put on a different, little girl voice when she spoke to Dan. And her demeanor became something more than childlike – she became airy – diffuse. A childlike air is innocent, sure, but exuberant – interested in things. Tabitha wasn't childlike with Dan; she acted like she was in a trance – almost catatonic, acting out the demure daughter role. This is a look I've seen on women before – in private settings, and public ones. Marilyn Monroe was famous for it. I think of the way the model, Anna Nicole Smith, looked in the videos just before her death. I watched her diffuse airhead ways with interest. Some celebrities learn to hide it better, be on cue with their gazes, words and glances. Everyone thought Anna Nicole was just stoned, but no. I watched her on television and thought, no. She's not stoned. She's just retreated so far into herself that she can't snap back to attention when someone speaks. I've noticed that women do this particularly around their abusers. You learn to retreat so far into yourself that you're just observing the way the body moves, the way the face tilts, you're just observing the reflection of what you're doing on the face of the Daddy. And if he's pleased by a staring, pleading, wanting kind of innocence, that's just what the face and body learn to do.

Oh sure, I'm a damaged goods kind of observer. And this is a subtlety. Oh sure. I could've been imagining things. That's part of what we're taught too. Don't trust what you know. Don't trust the body; the body is all an act. Fuck that. The body doesn't lie. Observing and connecting seemingly disparate moments is how I survived – and learned to thrive. I have a certain mastery of the world that precludes being blind to human dynamics, cultural forces. Holy shit, I thought. He really is having sex with his daughter.

Well, this is a touchy thing to try to share with a friend. I asked her, shortly after the Christmas party, if she thought Dan would ever be violent with – or molest – the kids.

"Oh no!" she replied. "He's an asshole, and it wouldn't surprise me to know that he hires and beats up whores when he's out on the road, but he looooves Tabitha. Nothing gives him more pleasure than doting on her and spending time with her." She was pensive. "He's smacked Mark around once or twice, but sometimes that kid deserves it."

I listened to this answer, wholly unconvinced. Taffy and I spoke easily about sex and how men could be assholes in particular ways and she knew that I had endured some incest – as had she. This line of questioning didn't offend her, and though she blew me off at first, it made her think.

"Kim, did you see something between Dan and Tabitha when you were over at the house?" Taffy asked me a few weeks later. She added, "I swear that's why he doesn't let anyone come over. They'll see how he is! And I'm so dumb; I just take him for granted. Someone else might see something I can't!"

"Nothing specific," I said to Taffy, "but I wonder, when he's home, does he ever spend time with Tabitha alone – like in her room?"

"Oh Kim, sure! Ever since she was a little girl, he's doted on her. He just lives to protect her. He sometimes sleeps in her bed even now! He'll lie down to rub her back and just fall asleep there. I asked Tabitha once if she minded him in there – said I'd kick him out if she did – and she said no, she just slept like a rock. She didn't even notice he was there." Taffy reported.

"Taffy, that's funny business." I stated directly.

"No! I can't imagine! Do you think?" Taffy stammered.

"I think lots of things," I said, and the conversation took its turns from there.

Just after I finished my BA, my son was born and I moved out of Colorado Springs with my new family. I didn't see Taffy again for a few years. When I started to spend more time in Colorado Springs again because of the charming Daddy I'd just met – my firefighter, my lover – we got in touch again through a previous professor. Taffy was still in school, somehow a perpetual student. I told Taffy a bit about life with my sexy new Daddy and she said, "That's hot Kim." She looked at me, impressed and said, "Fuck, you're so cool. I can't believe you found a woman to do that shit with! You're a genius!"

"But hey," she said, changing the subject, "there's something else I want to talk to you about. Something happened to Tabitha a few months ago and it was just awful. She's doing better now, but Kim, somebody raped her. Maybe more than one guy." Taffy seemed beset with grief at the thought and all of my memories fearing her sexual abuse returned.

"I'm so sorry, Taffy." I said, holding her hands. "I'm glad she's doing better. What happened?" I asked.

She told me a story with no entrances and no exits – no details, no real information. It went like this: Dan took Tabitha out to a party with some of her friends. They went out to the lake to drink beer and listen to music. Dan left and came back to pick her up and he found her there, in a parking lot alone. She was bloodied and her clothes were torn. He took her home and told Taffy to clean her up.

"We have to go to the hospital, I told him!" Taffy reported. He said no, Tabitha wouldn't want to talk about this. Whatever happened to her, she wouldn't want to talk about it.

And indeed, she didn't want to talk about it.

"Kim, she's nineteen now and she didn't want me helping to clean her up too much – you know, she didn't want me to see her coochie. She said it was fine and I asked her what happened – Kim, she couldn't even walk for days. And I thought, my God, what should I do? But Dan said she'd be fine. He spent so much time with her, Kim. He brought her favorite food home every night and he brought her presents. Her room was just full of flowers and stuffed animals. But she wouldn't tell me what happened!"

"I'm so sorry, Taffy." It was all I could think to say to her, as I shook my head listening.

"But then we did have to go to the doctor because after she could walk again, she had a sore on her eye that wasn't healing, and she had a sore throat and it was like she had some kind of flu. And Dan let me take her to the doctor for that, because it didn't seem to be related to the rape. But do you know what they said after doing some tests?"

Actually, I did know, but I let her say it first.

"It was the worst case of gonorrhea they'd ever seen in someone's throat and eyes! And she had syphilis too.

"Kim, I didn't know what to do. I just sat there crying and when the doctor asked her about her sexual history, Tabitha just said, 'I guess my boyfriend's dirty.' And I just sat there. She didn't say anything about the rape. I didn't even know anything about the rape to tell! I just sat there."

I held my friend's hands as she told this news – now a few months old – news she hadn't shared with anyone, other than to discuss it with Dan.

"You thought something was wrong with Tabitha when she was younger, Kim. And you're so much smarter than me. What do you think is happening with my baby?"

"Of course, I couldn't possibly know," I began. And then I couldn't help but share my thoughts. She was asking, after all. I couldn't help but share my thoughts and wondered what I – an outsider to their family, not even a close friend any longer – what could I do? They're all adults, I thought. And she's asking my opinion. So I just said what I was thinking.

"Taffy, from the information you've shared, and from what I've seen in the relationship between Dan and Tabitha, I'd say that he's been molesting her for a long time. I also think it's unlikely that he's able to afford your lifestyle by delivering oranges to Iowa – I think he's likely involved in either drug trafficking or human trafficking. It's possible he's been pimping Tabitha for years – that's why she goes on trips with him. And, it sounds possible that something got out of hand this last time – or perhaps Dan orchestrated the gang rape – because that's what I think it was, probably oral, and anal too – because she threatened to leave him. Either way, Dan did not try to exact revenge, or report the crime against his darling daughter for some reason. I'm guessing it was a good one." I paused and her mouth hung open, but I can't say she looked surprised.

"I'm so sorry, Taffy." I said it again.

And then I went back to my life. It's a little hard to believe, in hindsight. I went back to my own dramas with Daddy. That whole discussion feels like a dream.

A few years later, I was still living between San Diego and Colorado Springs, I heard from Taffy again. It was a bad cell phone connection. Taffy said she was calling from Montana – that Dan had moved them to a new house about a year ago. The call was breaking up. "This isn't my phone," Taffy said, and she started to speed up her speech to get to what she had to tell me quickly, "so don't call me back here. Kim, I have to tell you that you were right about so many things. I had no idea what he was capable – o – an – need your help – can ou – an"

"Taffy, I can't hear you!" I was trying to give her my full attention as I was walking out the door on my way to work. The call came at a bad time. The call was breaking up. I thought she'd call back. I tried to call her back but the number she was calling from didn't come up on my cell phone – and she'd told me not to call anyway. I kept hoping she'd call back.

Even after a year, two, I still try to find her on the Internet. I search and I can't find a trace of her. I still hope she'll call back. I hope I'll know what to do.

CONFUSION HURTS

Dear Daddy,

Everything about you is starting to confuse me. And it hurts to be this confused. It hurts in my belly and in my breasts and in my uterus. I'm sure you are not lying to me, because how could that be? And still, I wonder why I am even thinking about the word "lying?" Why am I telling myself so often how impossible it would be for you to lie to me?

When I wake up in the morning, you still make me waffles – the ones that come out of the waffle iron looking like four hearts with the tips touching. You still smile at me, though you don't chat nearly as often. The presidential-Daddy said there were weapons of mass destruction and that I should be scared, really scared. And yet, he said I shouldn't worry, just act normal. I am acting normal as I pour the syrup. I think something is growing in my right ovary.

Daddy, you said I was the only and the best and the sweetest girl. You said "in love" and "best lover" and "sweetest girl." I can't find the news clips anymore. I can't find the web links. I can't find the tools to know anything on my own. I think Daddy threw them away. Someone told me that was called data cleansing.

I wonder about the data that has been cleansed from the long phone calls to the other girls I can see on the phone bills. I wonder what you say to other girls and when I wonder aloud you admonish me. "Well, obviously I love you. I'm still here, aren't I?" And I cannot argue with that. You are still with me. I think you are still with me. Suddenly, you are not with me as often, and not in very meaningful ways. The presidential Daddy is not on the television anymore – just gone, just gone. Approval ratings have dropped and it is best to stay out of sight. I try not to take this personally. Surely, it has nothing to do with me. Daddy, you keep telling me, "This has nothing to do with you. I could never stop loving you." And of course I believe you. All of this is starting to confuse me.

I found a letter you wrote to another girl. It spoke of your hubris when looking at photographs of this girl. It spoke of a love that would never end. And the photographs were not for me to see. All of the praise, the conversations, the meetings, the coercion, the satisfaction – it all takes place elsewhere, in a foreign land. It wouldn't make sense for it to happen here. So you make sure it happens elsewhere, Daddy. This keeps me safe. I am safe. Daddy says so. Daddy is extraordinary. You invoke extraordinary rendition to take praise to other girls. The torture happens right here in my cells. I think there is a growth in my uterus.

Daddy, you said the letter didn't matter because it was never sent. The girl didn't receive it and so it didn't matter at all. I wondered how this could be if you really felt those things – enough to write them – then surely they matter. You tried to calm me – you said I am the best, the best ever. And then went on talking to the other girl in hushed tones, on the telephone, on the computer, giving the other girl all of the laughter that used to be for me. You don't laugh with me now, more often you sigh, look put out. If the sore on my nipple doesn't heal soon, maybe you won't love me. Where are my fancy pajamas? I am acting normal. I am afraid, but I am acting normal.

The phones are tapped. The records have been shredded. I am under surveillance, but I can't see through the two way-mirror. I'm not the one who can see everything, know everything. That's Daddy's job and it's necessary to keep me safe. My phone is tapped, but I can barely hear my own conversations, let alone anyone else's. My stomach hurts and you said I should be afraid, but that you would protect me. Be very afraid. Why is my nipple so sore?

Daddy, you are starting to confuse me, but I don't worry. It is just confusion. The pain is starting to get to me though. And the fear. I am carrying it around, code red. I am carrying it around, orange alert. I used to love the brightest colors of the rainbow, but now I don't know what they mean. I think they mean something and there are alarms on all the doors. I can't leave home without my identification. I can be taken in for questioning. It has not happened; surely it wouldn't happen to me, and the others surely deserve questioning. Daddy, will you always protect me?

I no longer look like the photograph on my identification. You keep all of the photographs in a file somewhere and I cannot see them. You don't come home every night now, sometimes don't call. I am turning the channels, turning the channels. I am being sold something. I am trying to act normal. Where are you, Daddy? Where are you Daddy and why do I have to have so much fear? You are starting to confuse me, but just when I get really scared, you kiss my forehead and smile at me. You still smile at me – at least in my mind. Where are you Daddy? It hurts to be this confused. I try to forget that I can't go to the doctor. I'm sure you are not lying to me. That's just not possible. Why is lying always on my mind?

Love,
Your Girl

CHAPTER 13

ABROAD WITH DADDY

DADDY GETS A PASSPORT

She never had a passport until she got involved with me. Most Americans don't have a passport, I was surprised to learn. In fact, before we needed a passport to travel to Canada and Mexico, fewer than 10% of Americans had been issued a passport.

Americans don't get out much.

I told Daddy I wanted to travel with her. Daddy is fun on a trip; why would we not go abroad? I took Daddy to Mexico first – just for a few days. Daddy hates poverty, and she's a little racist too. "I just want everything to be attractive." Daddy said. "Is that too much to ask?" During the time we were together, I came to understand that "attractive" usually meant wealthy, white, European – only certain types of beauty are legible to Daddy.

Daddy hated Mexico, but she agreed that we could take a trip to Europe. I made all of the arrangements, of course. Daddy said she never wanted to travel to countries where women are second-class citizens, where women are devalued. I laughed and said, "That's all countries on our current socio-political globe, Daddy!"

She scoffed at this and pointed out that we couldn't have a relationship like ours just anywhere in the world. We couldn't be two women in love just anywhere in the world. We certainly couldn't be all gender-twisted-kinky everywhere in the world either.

Daddy had a point. That point is so easy to see, it obscures everything else. I didn't argue this with Daddy any further – I also would've been afraid to travel to the middle-east or parts of Africa, parts of Asia with Daddy, as a couple, for example. I didn't argue the point – happily, I started looking up well-located Parisian hotels and Amsterdam museums. And the baths! I found a Turkish bath in Paris that we would visit for sure. Daddy and I were not wealthy, so the trip required a little

© KONINKLIJKE BRILL NV, LEIDEN, 2019 | DOI:10.1163/9789004383562_013

planning. This pleased me – making us comfortable within our means. If it were up to Daddy, I think she wouldn't have left U.S. soil without being certain of four-star comfort and the safety of wealth-privilege.

Planning a trip with Daddy got me thinking though – about the different ways that the U.S. Daddy-patria has affected the world landscape. The U.S. Daddy is a big bully, everyone knows that, but U.S. also exports a culture where women are devalued – and that mixes with other forms of female devaluation in some strange and dangerous ways. Of course we are devalued in the U.S. Earning less money than men for the same work is the very definition of de-valued. Our work has less value; our bodies have less value. If there's a frat party or a super-bowl party, our bodies are part of the fun, the entertainment. We have less value on all levels.

Daddy doesn't see it because she has used her race privilege, literacy privilege, her big strong body and winsome ways to chew up gender norms that might stop her. She feels triumphant. The American myth of meritocracy shines like a sun in Daddy's belly.

Sometimes, the U.S. patria exports this way of seeing things to countries that have gentler forms of sexism and things get worse for women. And when capitalism is added to existing gender hierarchy, women suffer even more. Sometimes, the U.S. Daddy exports American democracy – our particular brand of corporate-rule democracy – to countries where other political regimes have been repressive and this seems like progress. People's lives will improve when they can speak more freely, make art more freely, organize themselves more freely.

But when my Daddy spoke so vehemently about only wanting to travel to certain parts of the globe because in some places, women are devalued, I started thinking more carefully about women's value. Perhaps one message of American democracy is that it's possible to change your political structure without changing your social structure. Don't worry guys – women's bodies will still be at your disposal. Under U.S. Daddy democracy, you can just make more money on them.

DADDY ON HOLIDAY

Daddy thinks he already knows her. He thinks he couldn't possibly know more. He thinks by buying her an ice cream he has the ticket.

He purchased the privilege. He has collected a butterfly that can be pinned to a board and when he places the tiny black letters beneath her suspended body with care, he will feel a sense of participation, a sense of effort. He thinks he has participated, but he did not even spell her name right. He can't even say her name right. Daddy is standing on the deck of his cruise ship afraid to do more than smell her spices. He may have come to shore, smug man, but he deceives himself! He can visit, and visit and visit, every day for a year, but until he learns her language, tends her fields, cries with her father and eats cake on the lawn of her church, he is still a cruiser. He could stay a lifetime, and still be cruising by.

Stop calling her exotic. Stop calling her different. Daddy, with his dollars and his curiosities and his big fat hard-on for her and her ways. He has spent nothing of value to him, invested none of his private currencies in knowing her. Daddy makes children of everyone now that he loves her, fucks her, buys her gifts, all the girls are wearing pigtails and the store has sold out of the fabric she uses to make her dresses. All of the girls think they want a Daddy too. She tells them it was fun at first. She tells them the games were easy, his requests amusing, but then he looked away from the depth of her like a dullard. She wondered if Daddy was brain-damaged, but then she saw it: he only likes one story. He only likes his own story.

"Run sisters!" she said. This casting call is for his movie, his view of the world. He did not learn her name or her songs or go fishing with her brothers. Something smells of rot when he speaks of love.

She is different from other girls and he can't even tell! She is not an exotic destination, an outing, a pin on a map. She is not a clever handle, a cute moniker, a tiny square picture next to a description of what she will and won't do.

Daddy was a bomb going off in her village. They're not stupid, but he flashed and devastated so quickly, who could plan? He flashed and fascinated so quickly, who could foresee? He wanted her and her curious, winsome ways and she got some pretty trinkets. Now all the girls are wearing her smile on the beach, hoping to catch his eye. She tries to warn them because she has seen the future. But no one listens; they must find out for themselves. He will leave a genocidal fall-out where the girl-children litter the streets, their bodies torn apart by bigger dicks and bigger dicks – each man in her town will have a missile strapped to his pelvis because they covet Daddy's ways. She didn't know he was a murderer. She didn't know he ate the faces of children for dinner. He seemed so jovial, so funny, and so stupid. How could he be so dangerous and speak of love? How could he raise his hand to her after all that talk of love, call her different, brown, savage – who is this Daddy? Too late to walk away.

Suddenly, he became what girls want. A promise of payment for the pain, a promise of protection for the pain. They do not know how small his prizes truly are – Daddy, striding from his ship with his shock of red hair unkempt, his red-tuft merkin tied atop his puny prize. He is just visiting and he has set their fields on fire.

Daddy does not know her, but he'll want to and then it will be too late. We will all be wise or dead. Daddy will want to know her, not because she's cute, or clever, or submissive, or looks at him like a newborn doe, but because she is herself, precious and unique in the world. He will cry and yearn to know someone who does not remake herself according to his next whim. Daddy has something to learn here, and he will feel it, the moment he's made the lessons unlivable. She heard him say it, "She's so authentic." Ha! She is authentic. She is different. Her sons have started wearing Daddy's mustache. Her beauty has turned to gore and her home doesn't look like the pictures on Daddy's travel brochure anymore.

The New York Times,
April 29, 2011
CBS Report Recounts a 'Merciless' Assault
By Brian Stelter

Lara Logan thought she was going to die in Tahrir Square when she was sexually assaulted by a mob on the night that Hosni Mubarak's government fell in Cairo.

***

Ms. Logan, a CBS News correspondent, was in the square preparing a report for "60 Minutes" on Feb. 11 when the celebratory mood suddenly turned threatening. She was ripped away from her producer and bodyguard by a group of men who tore at her clothes and groped and beat her body. "For an extended period of time, they raped me with their hands," Ms. Logan said in an interview with The New York Times. She estimated that the attack involved 200 to 300 men.

***

Ms. Logan, who returned to work this month, is expected to speak at length about the assault on the CBS News program "60 Minutes" on Sunday night.

***

Her experience in Cairo underscored the fact that female journalists often face a different kind of violence. While other forms of physical violence affecting journalists are widely covered – the traumatic brain injury 'suffered by the ABC News anchor Bob Woodruff in Iraq in 2006 was a front-page story at that time – sexual threats against women are rarely talked about within journalistic circles or in the news media.

***

With sexual violence, "You only have your word," Ms. Logan said in the interview. "The physical wounds heal. You don't carry around the evidence the way you would if you had lost your leg or your arm in Afghanistan."

***

Little research has been conducted about the prevalence of sexual violence affecting journalists in conflict zones. But in the weeks following Ms. Logan's assault, other women recounted being harassed and assaulted while working overseas, and groups like the Committee to Protect Journalists said they would revise their handbooks to better address sexual assault.

***

Jeff Fager, the chairman of CBS News and the executive producer of "60 Minutes," said that the segment about the assault on Ms. Logan would raise awareness of the issue. "There's a code of silence about it that I think is in Lara's interest and in our interest to break," he said.

***

Until now the only public comment about the assault came four days after it took place, when Ms. Logan was still in the hospital. She and Mr. Fager drafted a short statement that she had "suffered a brutal and sustained sexual assault and beating."

***

That statement, Ms. Logan said, "Didn't leave me to carry the burden alone, like my dirty little secret, something that I had to be ashamed of."

***

The assault happened the day that Ms. Logan returned to Cairo, having left a week earlier after being detained and interrogated by Egyptian forces. "The city was on fire with celebration" over Mr. Mubarak's exit, she said, comparing it to a Super Bowl party. She and a camera crew traversed Tahrir Square, the epicenter of the celebrations, interviewing Egyptians and posing for photographs with people who wanted to be seen with an American journalist.

***

"There was a moment that everything went wrong," she recalled.

***

As the cameraman, Richard Butler, was swapping out a battery, Egyptian colleagues who were accompanying the camera crew heard men nearby talking about wanting to take Ms. Logan's pants off. She said: "Our local people with us said, 'We've gotta get out of here.' That was literally the moment the mob set on me."

***

Mr. Butler, Ms. Logan's producer, Max McClellan, and two locally hired drivers were "helpless," Mr. Fager said, "because the mob was just so powerful." A bodyguard who had been hired to accompany the team was able to stay with Ms. Logan for a brief period of time. "For Max to see the bodyguard come out of the pile without her, that was one of the worst parts," Mr. Fager said. He said Ms. Logan "described how her hand was sore for days after – and that she realized it was from holding on so tight" to the bodyguard's hand.

They estimated that they were separated from her for about 25 minutes.

***

"My clothes were torn to pieces," Ms. Logan said.

***

She declined to go into more detail about the assault but said: "What really struck me was how merciless they were. They really enjoyed my pain and suffering. It incited them to more violence."

***

After being rescued by a group of civilians and Egyptian soldiers, she was swiftly flown back to the United States. "She was quite traumatized, as you can imagine, for a period of time," Mr. Fager said. Ms. Logan said she decided almost immediately that she would speak out about sexual violence both on behalf of other journalists and on behalf of "millions of voiceless women who are subjected to attacks like this and worse."

***

More than a dozen journalists have been detained in Libya in the past two months, including four who were working for The Times. One of the Times journalists, Lynsey Addario, said she was repeatedly groped and harassed by her Libyan captors.

***

For Ms. Logan, learning about Ms. Addario's experience was a "setback" in her recovery. While Ms. Logan, CBS's chief foreign affairs correspondent, said she would definitely return to Afghanistan and other conflict zones, she said she had decided – for the moment – not to report from the Middle Eastern countries where protests were widespread. "The very nature of what we do – communicating information – is what's undoing these regimes," she said. "It makes us the enemy, whether we like it or not."

***

Before the assault, Ms. Logan said, she did not know about the levels of harassment and abuse that women in Egypt and other countries regularly experienced. "I would have paid more attention to it if I had had any sense of it," she said. "When women are harassed and subjected to this in society, they're denied an equal place in that society. Public spaces don't belong to them. Men control it. It reaffirms the oppressive role of men in the society."

***

After the "60 Minutes" segment is broadcast, though, she does not intend to give other interviews on the subject. "I don't want this to define me," she said.

***

She said that the kindness and support shown by Mr. Fager and others at CBS and by strangers – like the high school class in Texas and the group of women at ABC News who wrote letters to her – was a "very big part of picking myself up and restoring my dignity and my self-worth."

***

Among the letters she received, she said, was one from a woman who lives in Canada who was raped in the back of a taxi in Cairo in early February, amid the protests there. "That poor woman had to go into the airport begging people to help her," Ms. Logan recalled. When she returned home, "her family told her not to talk about it."

***

Ms. Logan said that as she read the letter, she started to sob. "It was a reminder to me of how fortunate I was," she said.

CHAPTER 14

PLAYBOY, PANTIES, PAPI

DADDY LIKES PLAYBOY MAGAZINE

I found the first Playboy magazine in my father's bottom dresser drawer when I was 12 years old. I wasn't snooping – I always felt like someone was watching me when I visited the condo, so I didn't really snoop. I was looking for something – who knows what – my bathing suit perhaps, or something of mine that had been misplaced. The second drawer in that dresser was designated to my use when I was visiting my father. Every once in a while he did a bit of my laundry and then folded those items and put them into the second drawer. I'm sure I was just looking for something, and there she was.

The woman on the magazine cover and then in the centerfold was a slender Asian woman – I couldn't tell much else. She looked childlike because she didn't have giant breasts to go with her slender hips. She was also almost hairless – though as I look back now, her sparse hair seemed natural – her pubic area hadn't been shaved.

When he was about eighteen, my son was doing some construction work at his granddad's house. He reported that my father had a big box of Playboy magazines in the closet and that sometimes, the new issue of the magazine was left lying on the coffee table. He found this slightly creepy and wondered aloud why an old man would want to look at pictures of naked women that were his age, 18ish. I commented to my son that Playboy was an obsession of my father's generation – the first socially sanctioned medium for men to objectify women and seem sophisticated, intellectual even – if they also read the articles. The male urge to look at naked women, posed and beauty-conforming was presented as natural. And besides, those were "girl next door" beauties – innocents. They weren't porn stars and prostitutes. They were fantasy girls who just really loved their bodies and liked sex. That's what the magazine presented. I also commented that my father

© KONINKLIJKE BRILL NV, LEIDEN, 2019 | DOI:10.1163/9789004383562_014

had never left those magazines where I could see them – not even as I entered adulthood. It must be some sort of male bonding thing that he leaves them around for you to see, I commented to my son.

"Gross," he replied.

When my father died, I found no box of Playboy magazines in the closet or anywhere else. In preparation for his death – and knowing that I'd be the one to clean out the house – he got rid of them. Once again, he protected me from something I shouldn't see – but what? What shouldn't I see? Of course, he's dead, so I can't ask him directly. Would he have been able to say?

There were four copies of Playboy in various piles of magazines and paperwork, however, as I cleaned up after his life. He kept cooking magazines and furniture catalogs – the few Playboys were stashed among those, probably forgotten in the tidy-up, or perhaps even saved for a certain article, or a specific photo display he wanted to look at again later. One was a particularly thick anniversary issue from 1986 – the rest seemed like average monthlies. 1986 was the year after I finished high school and then another was from 1992, then 2004 and 2011 – one of the most recent.

As I looked through those magazines at the centerfolds, considering a grown man – no, an elderly man – looking at pictures of women who were never older than 23 in that particular sample, I thought about my son. Would these girls date him? Would they date someone like my father, who died before he reached Hugh Hefner's age? Hefner's wives are young and blonde and busty and always comment publicly about how much Hugh satisfies them in bed.

In the progression of photos from 1986 through 2011 the striking change is the presentation of the woman's vulva. Some of the photos were all about the boobs and the pretty panties the woman is wearing. In the later issues, the panties were gone. In the earlier two issues, the woman's pubic hair looked silky, nicely trimmed away from her panty line, but lush coming into a triangle where her legs met. Many of the women were posed with a jut of the hip, an hourglass curve lying on their sides. They had youthful faces, but curvy women's bodies. In the 2004 issue, the women each had but a Hitler-mustache of pubic hair, childlike vulva just visible beneath. And in 2011, all of the women were clean shaven and more often posed standing or sitting front-on to the camera. Their hips were so slender and their legs are spread, tiny little lips of their sex pursed together, few curves and big innocent eyes staring at the camera. In the later issues, some of the women even lacked the jutting breasts – ubiquitous on all the women in earlier issues.

One woman was pictured standing on a beach. Except for the large breasts, except for the lack of childlike exuberance, except for the lack of actual movement or activity, I thought that woman looked just like a naked three-year old spending one last summer clothing-free at the beach before being told forever more she had to dress proper or be thought a whore. She looked just like that. I could even see the small goose bumps on her tiny labia, as though there had just been a breeze when she came out of the water looking for her mommy or her Daddy to wrap her in the beach towel.

She stood staring, waiting.

She looked just like that.

PANTIES

I left the black lace panties in her bed, as a memento, after we first had sex. Who knew she'd keep them, cherish them? I meant them as a souvenir, rather than a gift really, though I wasn't attached to their return. A souvenir – a memory – a connection to those private moments of darkness – to be found while she was making the bed in daylight.

She stuffed the red panties into her pants pocket after a kiss goodnight – a good kiss. They are cotton with a small broken heart next to the cupid and the words "heart breaker" on the right hip. It was a good kiss, but a departing kiss nonetheless, as we stood on my front porch, lights out, invisible to all, including each other. She whispered to me, "Take off your panties." I squirmed in hesitation at first, knowing that my desire to sleep would collide with carnal wishes if she touched me again. I tried to evade, but then followed her straightforward, somewhat stern instruction. She put them in her pocket, my vulva aching with anticipation. She gave me another peck on the cheek and moved down the stairs, got in her car and drove away.

I put the panties with the cherries on them in her suitcase like a secret love note after our weekend in San Francisco. I still considered them mine, again a memento. When I said I wanted to wear them again, a few weeks later, she scoffed. "No." she said. "Those are mine." I pouted. I liked the cherry panties. She gave them to me to wear, but two months later, I left them under her pillow the morning after I ejaculated in her bed, came in her mouth and left with a warm bottom, cherry pink from spanking. They didn't seem like they belonged to me any more anyway. She was right; they were hers.

She keeps them in a clear plastic tube, on the bookshelf by her bed. They look like they could be brightly colored scarves, a variety of fabrics: cotton, lace and nylon. The tube once held the silicone phallus she bought shortly after we began making love. She asked me about my favorite cocks, and then sent me an email with an advertisement for just the right one. "Anything for my girl," said the caption. She didn't "need" another one; I believe she could wear a different one each day of the week. The hard plastic tube seemed too useful to throw away, so she didn't. Now it houses the museum display of my panties, visible from the place where she drinks her coffee in the morning. She can also see the portrait photograph of my feet – my Valentine's Day gift – and a big white cup with the word "DADDY" painted on it, which contains her hunter green bandana and a few love poems. She can see all of these items from the place where she drinks her morning coffee with extra cream. These latter items come from the previous girls in her life; the cup was a Father's Day gift from the girl who could never say, "I love you" even though Daddy already knew she was loved.

She sent me a cell phone photo of herself, in bed, with the red panties draped across her face; her eyes were closed. Below the photo, she typed the message, "Sweet daddy dreams." When the phone signaled me that I received a message, I opened it without a thought. I was standing at the farmer's market, ready to buy papayas. I was so flustered and mortified that I nearly dropped the phone trying to keep the photo private. Holding the phone to my body, though no one else seemed vaguely interested in my personal dealings, I deleted the photo as quickly as I could. My heart raced as I bought papayas, bananas and tomatoes. I regained my composure and bought a lemonade. My pulse slowed as I sipped and listened to the market band.

The multi-colored swirled pattern panties with a funny blue bow in back were delivered to her by post. I was away for a few months and she was not enjoying the best of times. Her pain returned; she sounded depressed and rather than tell me, she asked me, "Would you ever be able to send me your panties in the mail? I know you're shy, but you've been gone so long." She sounded sad, almost plaintive.

"Uh, no." I said right away, sure that I would never do such a thing. But within the hour, I was choosing those panties, for her. I was putting them on, still telling myself I wouldn't do such a thing. I sat and worked at my computer, nearly the full day. I made myself lunch, sat on the sofa and ate. I went about my day, wearing those panties. And then, without making too many announcements to myself, I took out a blue envelope, wrote her name and address, no return information. I pressed my legs together, as I wrote, to emphasize my scent. Then I stepped out of the panties, folded them into the envelope and headed to the post office before closing time.

Four days later, she phoned and when I said, "Hello," she said, "I just got an envelope from a very good girl."

And when I heard and recalled what I had done, my cheeks flushed and I could feel arousal scenting my panties yet again.

DADDY IN THE NEWS

Pedro Martinez' own statement defined the playing field for the jeers he would receive. The Boston Red Socks pitcher said, after a win by the New York Yankees, "They beat me. They're that good right now. They're that hot. I just tip my hat and call the Yankees my daddy" (Sylver, 2014).

In the 2004 American League Championship Series, Yankees fans chanted, "Who's Your Daddy. Who's Your Daddy" relentlessly as Martinez took the field. Martinez got the last laugh, however, as the Red Sox came back from a 3-0 series deficit to win the 2004 ALCS in seven games and went on to win the World Series.

Red Sox fans then began to answer back with versions of their own. When David Ortiz batted, they chanted, "Who's Your Papi." And when Jason Giambi or Garry Sheffield was up to bat, fans chanted, "Who's Your Dealer."

In the 2009 World Series, Pedro Martinez was once again the object of "Who's Your Daddy" taunting from Yankees fans. This time, he was a starting pitcher for the Philadelphia Phillies in games two of six of the series against the AL Champion Yankees. The Yankees would come through against him this time, as they were victorious in both games, including Game 6, which clinched the series for them.

PARENTING DADDY

PARENTING DADDY

Daddy and I went on a grand summer vacation in Europe. In Amsterdam, the day after the sex museum and the prostitution museum and the red light district and drinks at a bar called Cock Ring, we ventured to the Rijksmuseum, the Van Gogh Museum and then out to experience legal marijuana and a fine meal. Today is mine to organize. Today is my day to take the lead, and I do this gently of course, because Daddy is still in charge.

Daddy loves that I am cultured and well read. She loves that I know a few things about fine art and literature and that I make commentary on the paintings in the museums. I am the hostess, the courtesan, the geisha, and the well-trained mistress who can function in polite society. My real name is Mother, but we don't use that name. It bothers Daddy to admit to being mothered, even though it is so clearly what I do.

At home, I am the one who plans and hosts the literary salons, the small gatherings that we have constructed to focus on the inspirations of the muses, one at a time. This was Daddy's idea and I was happy for the prompting. She mixes cocktails and I channel the muses. I do the homework and make sure the guests are prepared to entertain each other. I make sure everyone feels smart and sparkly. They leave saying, "What an amazing evening – so thought provoking and so much fun" – and this pleases Daddy. It makes her feel smart and well cultured herself. Without me, she'd be having a few people over to play Uno or Monopoly. She'd be reading Entertainment Weekly and People Magazine and imagining the lives of people who summer in Europe, exude glamour and smell like money. Daddy loves people who look like and smell like money. Daddy loves an old-fashioned four-star hotel. And in the privacy of those hotel rooms, Daddy owns me. Daddy worships me. Daddy expresses appreciation for all I do. Daddy does this in private.

The museums were lovely, emotional. I wept through the Van Gogh museum – the passion of the brush strokes; Daddy put her arm around me. When I am in charge, I am still soft. Daddy's dominion does not cease; I give directions gently.

"What do we do?" Daddy said, looking a bit scared when we sat down in the coffee shop. She was so excited about smoking legal marijuana and yet, the cultural norms and standards were not clear to us. Daddy had only ever smoked marijuana a few times in her life and was scared, though eager. I could see this fear, the slight compromise in her stature, and that is my cue to take over. I am never to comment on what I see, just take over in a gentle, yet firm way. "Well," I said, looking around. "Let's go up to the counter and ask a few questions."

"I don't want to be too stoned." She shook her head slightly and I put a gentle hand on her forearm. "I know, sweetie, me neither."

"Well, you know, people talk about weed in Amsterdam as being pretty powerful," she said.

"I know sweetie, but let me just ask some questions and we'll get what we need." Daddy is articulate, a good communicator, an observer of people. This is one of the reasons Daddy is so superb at being my Daddy. She anticipates my desires and pays attention to my preferences. She says things that put me at ease. But often, out in the world, I am sharper, quicker, and more able to make everyone feel safe at once – and this makes Daddy proud. When Daddy is proud, she feels especially safe.

So, I did the talking. I asked for something with a mellow high, not too much kick, something that would help us enjoy a nice dinner. And that's just what we got. It was exciting to sit in a public place and smoke together, like we were doing something naughty in a private club. Daddy periodically said in a gleeful tone, "Baby! We're in Amsterdam, getting high in a café." I smiled at her, lovingly, and said, "Yes. But I think they call them coffee houses, if you're allowed to smoke pot."

"I'm so glad you know those things," she responded with pride.

And then we ate the best Indian food dinner we'd ever had and strolled back to our hotel with the cute little bar downstairs. Of course, I arranged this trip, our hotels – it's Mommy's job to make a home. Daddy carried the heavy luggage containing everything we thought we might need for a pleasurable stay.

"Clearly, the reason I incarnated into this body," she once said, referencing her impressively muscular frame, "was to carry *your* luggage." It pleased her when I had enough luggage to test her strength.

Back in the room, she was gentle; in exactly the same bed where she had been rough the night before. She kissed my face and thanked me for taking care of her. Sometimes, if I became too proud of her praise, she'd admonish, "Hey now. I'll deny everything publicly, if pressed." This was said in a joking tone, though I knew it was true. She could publicly praise my creativity, my talent, my beauty, but she remained in charge of the compliments and never let any slip regarding how I take care of her. Daddy must be seen to stand alone, rugged – the giver of real assistance, not the recipient.

That night, she thanked me again for such a great trip and after we made love gently, she laid down next to me, scooted down the bed and I nestled her head into the crook of my arm and pulled her body toward mine. As she had so often done before, she wordlessly raised her hands to pull my breast close and opened her mouth wide to take in the big nipple. As her eyes closed and she found her sucking rhythm, I stroked her head gently and saw her body relax completely. Daddy was resting, sated, warm and safe. She fell into a peaceful slumber.

PARENTING DADDY II

After she is sleeping, I pull away and adjust my bodice for my own comfortable slumber. I fall asleep and dream about the act of parenting daddy. In the house we have built, everyone needs a parent – everyone except Daddy. That's what we say. The Daddy is the top; the Daddy is in charge; the Daddy giveth and the Daddy taketh away. The Daddy requires lots of capital letters and semi-colons and archaic language and declarative sentences because the Daddy is eternal and unquestionable and supreme.

And human. So, who parents my Daddy? I do, of course. Though we don't use the word "mommy" because the mommy is always invisible and tolerant and long-suffering, I nurture. Mommy is rolling hills, blue sky, and the herd of sheep. Mommy is the rain falling on crops, the fertile fields, the birthing body, the body of the earth on which we walk without noticing her breath. She is no streak of lightening across the sky. She is not bold and entitled, but constant.

And human. I bring my Daddy into my arms and let her rest. I make her coffee in the morning and give her peace. I make the peace and give it to her. It is a gift, the only way she can be present and relaxed at the same time. When we talk about what is being given, we do not speak of the way I give her my breast, the way she nestles into the crook of my arm and relaxes her neck and nurses at my breast. We do not speak of this because what would we say? That Daddy is tired and sometimes cannot go on? No, we do not speak of this. When we speak of what is given, Daddy is the giver. Daddy is the one who has and chooses to give. She doesn't give to me only, but she gives to me best. She gives more to me because I am her own.

"Keep on moving – nothing to look at here!" Daddy calls out in the official voice. If the mothering were something special, something sacred, we'd be able to see it. We see nothing. My mothering is just something in the way I am. It's just something that some girls can do. End of discussion. It is hard for Daddy to yield and accept, so when someone safe comes along, of course Daddy will turn her attention sharply, snap her head in the direction of comfort the way a baby follows the scent of the breast.

Daddy doesn't yield nor accept help easily. That's the story, though girls like me know more. Help is so seldom offered – withheld from boys to make them men. Daddy can only accept comfort when the girl smells like mother and the scent feels solid and safe. When there is no safety involved, Daddy is impervious to the offering – chuckles as though the offer is absurd. Daddy pats the girl on the head and sits content in the truth of the story that Daddy doesn't accept help, ever. Daddy rarely feels safe and this is why the strong mother-girl is such a gift. She lets Daddy feel safe. This cannot be spoken. We don't talk about how girls become mommies because it is not a topic of any interest to anyone, ever. We keep our focus straight ahead on that which is bold and central to the picture: Daddy does not focus on the landscape itself.

And why would the process of girl becoming mother require focus? The mother is bred into the girl. It's simple. It is done. With a very young girl, there may not be a mother there yet; she is still the hard little wooden doll at the center of what will be a dozen dolls, nested, one in another. If she is very young, she may just be a hard little nugget, unable to break herself open to offer anything, able only to blink gratefully when Daddy takes care of her frail beauty. This pleases Daddy of course; sometimes there is no need for more.

But when a girl is sturdy, older, as I am, she can offer more. Daddy takes this soothing, with pleasant surprise. Daddy thinks nothing of it, but she is pleasantly surprised. And of course, the comfort, the rounded hip, the assistance, and the hardening nipple – these are for her to take if she can. Once I developed more layers, more selves inside of selves – I learned to break myself open. That's why Daddy can rely on me. At least a little, at least in certain ways, at least as it is contained in the ritual of the stories that Daddy tells to herself about why I am able to give comfort. I give what she gives: protection, comfort, validation, warm arms to come to, and a place to rest and feel precious. This doesn't mean anything about Daddy. Daddy is unchanged, but comforted, still in charge, but comforted, still on top, but comforted. How amazing to have the best of both worlds.

But this is so awkward to discuss. It isn't really personal, not really important; in fact, let's not even mention that it happens. Some girls simply have certain skills, certain experience, and certain abilities. Some girls simply know how it's done and what to offer and when. The girl can give, and Daddy can take, without ever mentioning (even to herself) that anything is really going on between them.

So, who parents my Daddy? I do, of course, until someone else comes along who can do it, then, who knows. We don't speak of it often, and not using the language in our throats, but the language in our skin, the language in the milk. I know how to break myself open and offer the sweet nectar of soothing that comes from somewhere deeper than myself: that hillside, that orchard, that flock of birds. But that's not really something important; it is just a fact of nature. I know how to break myself open, down to the smaller dolls within. And then I have trouble. I have trouble after a certain number of openings. I cannot find the hard nugget of the smallest girl by myself. That's where I have trouble. That's where my Daddy helps me find my vulnerability, my ability to be soothed.

My Daddy helps me. And that's what we can talk about. That is all that we should admit to.

SELF-AWARENESS

THE LIST

Daddy entertains me on a road trip. She can pick a topic of conversation and pursue it in entertaining ways. She is witty and knows how to turn a phrase. I enjoy Daddy so – except when she annoys me. Sometimes we are different in ways I can't fathom – except that I can listen and feel the fathom – I am already in over my head.

Daddy watches television with zeal. She watches the *Today Show*, every morning, and *Martha Stewart* and sit-coms like *Friends*. She reads People magazine and Entertainment Weekly so she knows about the people on those shows. She thinks it's cute that I am so clueless about popular shows – except when it annoys her. I sometimes see that Daddy's in too deep with me too.

Once, when we were driving, she took up a conversation about "The List." She wanted me to play along too and I just wasn't connecting with it. I found it really stupid, but she would not be dissuaded. The truth is, I sometimes carried on a conversation with Daddy that I wouldn't normally find interesting at all because I find Daddy interesting. She puts me at ease. We have fun. In some ways, we're a perfect match, Daddy and I. In other ways, we have little in common at all.

Here's the idea: You make a list of the celebrities with whom you'd like to have sex – the uber-hotties. And you share your list with your spouse or lover – the person with whom, of course, you have an exclusive sexual commitment. And both partners have made a list. So, the deal is, if you ever have a chance at sex with anyone on that list, your spouse has agreed to give you a free pass. Go for it! All is well.

Daddy had a list. She was talking about the list and wanting to talk about my list and why each of those people are on our lists. See, this is the thing – it's a getting-to-know-you tool. Why do you think someone's hot? I'm not totally dense. I know why people bond over things like this.

© KONINKLIJKE BRILL NV, LEIDEN, 2019 | DOI:10.1163/9789004383562_016

I don't have a list. I don't want a list. If I really liked someone well enough to want to have a romantic relationship with them, I'd probably find a way to meet that person, get to know her or him. Barring getting to know the person, why on earth would I want to have sex? Daddy guffaws at this idea – asks me if I've ever heard of the concept of "out of your league."

I stare incredulously. "I don't think anyone's 'out of my league.' I'm not even in a league!" I say this a bit more stridently than I had planned. This is honest. This makes sense to me and I find the whole notion of hierarchy of beauty and fame offensive anyway. Daddy rests on this notion like a brocade divan and often, I feed her grapes. She loves for me to be pretty, popular. Sometimes, I see this love and say nothing – pop another grape into Daddy's mouth.

So, Daddy could be getting to know me through my views about the list. But no, Daddy is annoyed.

Angelina Jolie and Catherine Zeta-Jones top Daddy's list. Well, of course they do. I yawn as the miles roll on. We pull into a gas station and Daddy says, "You have to come up with SOMEONE!" She throws the door open and extends one long leg from the vehicle. She leans back toward me, in the passenger seat, to give me a quick peck on the lips. "Now listen baby, while I pump the gas, you come up with someone to put on your list." She seriously wants an answer.

I sat in the car, beleaguered. Why does she need to talk so much about who's hot and who's not? Sometimes I think Daddy's a little dim. And I don't need to be relieved of responsibility for my actions by some list! If I wanted sex with someone else, I'd have it. The fact is, I don't want anyone but Daddy. I consider her views on infidelity. She'd definitely want the release of the list. There is honor to be upheld, after all.

"How about people who are small-scale famous, or theatre-famous?" I called out the car door. I could think of a few folks I'd met who might make the list, seeing as how I had to make a list!

"Nope! Celebrities only," she said firmly.

Let's face it, the kind of women to whom I'm attracted rarely get famous, except on a small scale. I racked my brain. Finally, exhausted, I said, "Okay, Laurie Anderson. Put her on my list."

I said it, not because I felt some sexual attraction to Laurie Anderson, but more to shut her up because Laurie was the only famous person I could think of who seemed remotely interesting!

"No!" Bellowed Daddy, "It has to be someone SEXY!"

"Well for pity sake, she's sexy to someone," I said, clearly missing the point. "Besides, the notion that famous people are more sexy, interesting or even more sane than the non-famous is poppycock!"

"Sane or not – Angelina Jolie is HOT," she said, climbing back into the car.

"Fine, put her on my list too," I said.

"Now we're talking!" She retorted. "Can it be a threesome?"

"Sure." I said, rolling my eyes at her.

"Hey wait," said Daddy, considering the possibility of this. "I don't think you get a list, baby. I think you just get me."

"Fine by me," I said with a flourish of my hand. "That's all I really want anyway." I smiled in her direction.

And Daddy was satisfied.

Later on, during that trip, I had fallen asleep in the car. I reclined the seat and used the pillow Daddy had packed for my comfort. In the warm sun with the movement of the car, I slept hard. When I awoke, we were Arizona and Daddy had pulled into another gas station to fill up.

I was disoriented from the sleep and the unfamiliar terrain. Then I saw Daddy walk in front of the car, open the door, get in and slowly, the slumber-fog cleared and I remembered where I was. Something about her didn't look fully familiar to me though. In the dream-place, none of our story was real. I was just a happy little animal sleeping in the sun.

Still blinking, I looked at her queerly when she got in the car. I said, "I almost thought I didn't know you when I first woke up. Everything seemed unfamiliar."

She smiled at me softly, like I was such a strange, precious little creature. She leaned over to kiss me gently. She said, "Of course you know me, baby. I'm yours. Of course you know me."

I had never heard her say it just like that before. And then she handed me a box of animal crackers from the mini-mart.

SEXISM

"The effect of opposites is equal." That's what the psychic said.

"What do you mean, I don't trust people?" I asked. "I trust everybody! I make a practice of trusting everyone." I said, stalwart and emphatic.

"Then you trust no one," she replied.

Daddy admitted to me that she fears she may be sexist. I suppressed a chuckle because of course Daddy is sexist, how could she not be? I asked simply, "Well, what makes you think so."

"I don't always think girls are capable of things, you know? I don't think they're as good at some things." She wrinkled her nose and said the word "good" in a whisper, as though she didn't like to admit it.

"I know." I said. "What else."

"I can't stand the thought of girlishness in me. I used to think it was just because I was more masculine. Because it didn't feel right, you know?"

"I know."

"But if it's just that I feel more like a guy, it would just feel normal to do guy things, rather than feeling wrong to do girl things, right?"

"Right," I nodded.

"This has really been on my mind, since you're so, you know, grown up. You're such a grown up girl sometimes, in addition to being young. And it's got me thinking. I love you so much, so I love all of you. And hey, I like a grown up girl! But I still think she needs a guy around. Is that sexist?"

"Yes," I said. "You still think you know what's best for me – better than I do, don't you."

Her brow furrowed as she looked into my placid face. "Well, yeah, kinda!" she blurted.

"But I love everything about your girlishness," she protested. "I worship it!"

"The effects of opposites, is equal." I told Daddy. She looked at me quizzically.

CHAPTER 17

LOVING MASCULINITY

MY LOVER'S WOUNDS

"But, I don't even remember being sexually abused," she'd say, on the rare occasions when she wanted to talk about it. Most times she didn't want to talk about it. She didn't want to hear my musings about our sex, and she didn't offer her own – unless to reminisce fondly about how hot it was.

What we did in bed was un-negotiated. It was not a kinky play-party scene, not a costume-party game. We were just living our lives.

"You're a sick twist, you know." That's what her ex-girl would say to her about her storytelling.

"Yeah, well I notice you're right there with me," she'd retort. As though the second observation negated the first.

"You can see it on people," she said to me. And she's right; I can. "Do you see it on me? Maybe it's just something I don't remember."

I don't say "Daddy" to a lover just for kicks. She has to want it for particular reasons. She has to make me precious, know how to take over completely, and – it took me time to know this – she has to receive with grace and gratitude. Many don't. Many big, bad, leather, butch, biker, aggressive, toppy-tops never stop doing long enough to be grateful for anything.

Reciprocity stands to reason: if you learn to take, you will receive. But it isn't so. Just because you take doesn't mean you get me to give. Doesn't mean you know how to receive. These are each separate parts of an equation so complex whole religious cosmologies of masculine and feminine forces were created to explain it.

My body knows how to explain it. My body teaches that there is a goodness that goes beyond reason, beyond necessity. I am a good girl – a rarity. I don't get off on being bratty, being naughty. I'm not seeking punishment – had enough of that for a lifetime. Shame is not

© KONINKLIJKE BRILL NV, LEIDEN, 2019 | DOI:10.1163/9789004383562_017

the main ingredient in my cocktail of desire. A splash perhaps, but not a taste that lingers on the tongue. Even though you don't feel you deserve them, I will give you amazing gifts and sweet abundance.

You know this in your DNA. You can be bad and I will love you. All the crime, the cruelty, the survival-responses that could've been more skillful; I will hold all of it without looking away. A Daddy who wants to fuck his little girl is bad. Let's face it; what could be worse? And I will give you sweetness anyway.

"No lover," I tell her, "I don't see my past on you." The incest, the shame, and the secrecy – my lovers are different from me, but they are like each other. Even the ones I don't call Daddy have things in common with one another. Almost all of them come from poverty and violence. They come from a fear of never having enough. More. They come from a fear of never being good enough to have enough, never being able to sleep in a soft curl with unballed fists. They have only cried in the cave of perfidy, pursued by those who smell weakness like it's an open wound. My lovers are fighters who either punch or burn, want to turn their bodies big and bad or smooth and fast – more muscle, more fortitude, more discipline, more speed, more winning than anyone thought possible. No, it's not possible in a fully female body. Who fights like that without a cock?

My lovers don't stay down for the count. I know how to hold that kind of damage, close those kinds of wounds. The actual healing, of course, will always be up to them.

I want to tell her that's what I see. I see many things. I see she doesn't want to hear that.

I am a girl who can play the role she yearns to play against but never fully trusts: mommy. I can be mommy without being woman. How seductive. Women may enjoy mothering and even be good at it, but they have so many responsibilities, so different from the girl playing mommy. I know how to answer silent expectations without a lot of language, without a lot of "worked all day," without a lot of "well, why didn't you" and "why am I always the one who." When the little girl is the mommy, she nurtures silently, grateful for the satisfaction she receives in return. All of her whys are about ponies and blue skies and cotton candy.

"Can I have cake for dinner?"

"Of course you can, princess. And then later, when we lay down, "you're going to give Daddy everything he needs. Aren't you, princess?"

"Yes Daddy."

My lovers are men who are women, struggling with bodies that say "keep away" rather than "come in." Receptivity is not natural to them, a boarded entry being pried open. "Try it and lose it," she says, and then wonders why I wait outside her gates. I love to wait outside, and then be allowed in.

I know how to let Daddy rest without making her give up her maleness. It's simple. I need Daddy to be hard. I know what she craves: always, I will give her my goodness. I won't always give her what she wants, of course not. But then, she doesn't always give me what I want either. But we're enough. Just enough. Our bodies choose one another, because they know better than the mind's prevarication.

"Do you see it on me?" she asked. And then she quickly grew tired of the question. She made this pronouncement instead. "I love it because of the drama," she said with a gentlemanly flourish of her hand. "It's all theatre! I'm NOT your Daddy. I'm not A Daddy. I'm not EVEN a man!" she exclaimed. "It's all theatre and I love that." She concluded firmly.

And I nodded silently, wondering if she would ever notice that she is always acting. There is nothing left to go back to when she leaves the theatre each night for sleep. She is the frightened child I hold at night, in the dark, blinking, wordless and waiting to be loved. I love her so consistently, provide such a reliable softness against which to rest, some of her fear subsides.

I didn't say this: What I see on you is why you chose me. And why you will choose me again. When I look to know myself, I look to my lover's wounds. I look to whom I have chosen. Again and again.

THE FIGHT

Daddy is down on the mat. He's heaving blood; it's pouring from his face with every gasping breath. His ribs have cracked and sweat stings his eyes, his gashes. He's drenched and throbbing, swollen blind. Daddy's struggling to get up. He's going to get up. He's the little guy, the young guy, the puss, the woman, the girl. He's going to get up because the body can take a lot and still remember its yearning to be upright. Daddy's coming up. He's coming up and that takes guts. Battered and rising, not lying there needing a stretcher, not needing a hand like a girl, like a woman, like a puss, like a boy. He's getting up after all that. Daddy's tough.

Daddy is up on the ropes preparing to jump. He's the big guy with the fierce mouth and the hard eyes. Daddy's muscles are bulging and his skin is a tight suit around his hulking mass. Daddy turns green and huge and his anger rages when someone's in danger, when something's not right, when someone needs saving. Don't make Daddy mad. He's the big guy and he barrels through; he pushes through; he uses his big shoulders and his strong hands. Daddy horns in, busts out, steamrolls the competition.

Daddy is smart and brutal. He's got the goods, the strategy, and the bankroll for the back up. Daddy is buying more thugs, more weapons, more armies, more strategic locations from which to strike back, strike first. Daddy knows what move you will make before you make it. He's got infrared, night vision, and techno-spies. Daddy takes no prisoners. That means he kills them on the spot. That means no one gets away; no one lives to tell the tale. Daddy gets the job done and lets God sort 'em out.

Daddy only gets one metaphor. Just one. Daddy is never baking a cake or building a school or perfecting a dance or writing a sonnet. This hero has one journey. Daddy is not climbing a mountain, unless to conquer it. Daddy is not tracking the deer unless to shoot it. Daddy is not taking a woman to lunch, unless he means to have her.

Daddy only gets one metaphor. The Fight. Do you love Daddy? Then you look at the metaphor from all angles, in all seasons, clothed and naked. To witness Daddy, you examine the fight. To love Daddy, slow down the action so that each frame holds for a full second. Rope bondage becomes artwork. Burns and cuts create patterns. Do you love Daddy? Slow down and take the pleasure of the beatings with awareness. Give Daddy the sweet, slow intimacy of the violence – what it feels like to spend out, rest himself against the human punching bag. Give Daddy the chance to take it and triumph. Let him stand up to the barrage, bite his hanky and take it. Do you love Daddy? Let him rest, release. He has so few ways to do this.

Daddy only gets one metaphor.

BE GRATEFUL FOR WHAT YOU HAVE

When Daddy is a woman, I can curl up next to the warm, hard body of masculinity and rest without fear twisting my sleep into tight little knots. I can rest while my feelings of love for Daddy soar through my dreams like fireworks on the fourth of July.

Daddy and I are watching the fireworks from the beach, amidst all of the other families assembled for the Independence Day display. We are sitting close together under a blanket. Though we are at a community event, Daddy and I are alone, her hand on my knee under the blanket. One arm behind me, I can lean easily onto her shoulder. Children are everywhere, their voices making them sound big and powerful, whiny, tired or frenetic. Fathers have been playing catch with their children, some celebrating the patria with drink, slurring their words in amplified conversations with one another. Some Daddies yell menacingly at children who will not stay close, or who will not stay away. Stay away from the water. Stay away from the cooler. Stay away from the fire.

"Didn't you hear me say to let your brother do that?" one Daddy bellows at a little girl who is trying to heave a log onto a crackling fire.

When Daddy is a woman, I can handle the fire of masculinity and not get burned. I am the girl by the bonfire who was told to leave it, told not to get dirty, and told to stay out of the smoke because it will make my hair smell bad. When I was small, my father tended the bonfire. He made a good strong flame. And then he stood alone in the smoky air, arms crossed, no jacket against the chilling breeze as the sky darkened. I sat under a blanket, my book still in my lap; too dark to read. He squinted through the smoke and I wondered what he was looking at, alone, alone. Always standing alone with a glass of wine, with a glass of vodka. I did not sit close. I did not warm him with my small flame, lean against his body. He did not put his arm

© KONINKLIJKE BRILL NV, LEIDEN, 2019 | DOI:10.1163/9789004383562_018

around me. I never knew what my father smelled like. I stayed away from the fire.

Sometimes we do not know enough to be grateful. Feminism allowed the men who already knew love's value to walk into their roles as fathers. "You have a place here, you should take it," said the feminists. They said, "These roles you were handed are not rigid. Women are capable; men are caring; we are all so much more than culture allows." And for those men who knew how to love already, who knew what they had given up, along with the jacket by the seashore, there was no hesitation. They walked silently into the hallway and bent to one knee, arms open to welcome their children in. Perhaps with tears in their eyes, they embraced and softened, just a bit. And maybe they were grateful to feminism. Maybe it felt like too much to say so, or maybe they still didn't have the words or the practice to discuss it. Just let me love my family, the fathers thought. That's enough for now.

Sometimes we don't know we should be grateful – things are simply the way they are. In some past era, perhaps boys and girls had trouble knowing their fathers. In some past era, perhaps, those fathers were rage wound around a spool, tied to the kites of themselves that fluttered, far, far away. Watch the line. Always watch the line. A person could strangle in a line like that. If the children feel loved, that's enough. Who would know to be grateful? It's as natural as having clothes to wear or food to eat. We can take love for granted. And because it's never perfect, it's easier to find fault. There is much to improve, so much for men to learn about themselves without admitting that they lack anything, ever.

When Daddy is a woman, at least I know she remembers having been a little girl. She may remember the taste of her own anger at being told to sit far away from the fire. She may have felt more boy than girl – but all children need the soft hand of love.

My Daddy remembers something of girlhood fondly – if not her own, then someone's. She remembers enough to adore me. That's how it is with my Daddy – but not all Daddies are the same. Some girls play out another script – seek a Daddy who takes pleasure in loathing them, a Daddy who wants to eviscerate girls, filet them and eat their pink flesh with cream cheese and capers on a chewy bagel. These Daddies

132

exist – male and female, and they sharpen their kitchen knives on shrill demanding voices, pornography and pageants of perfect dependence. They don't see what's to be admired in femininity, so they slice and slurp and chew.

But when Daddy is a woman, something is kinder – at least with a Daddy like mine. She loves the fireworks and wants to make sure we have a big enough blanket to keep us both warm. She brings hot chocolate in a thermos for us and she doesn't mind when I get sand in the car. Daddy is kind. And I am grateful.

DELIBERATE POWER

WOMEN AND WOLVES

The docent on the architectural tour of the Denver Art Museum pauses in front of a statue of St. Genevieve with a May wolf. She calls the artist, Kiki Smith, born in 1954 "a feminist artist from the seventies." To my knowledge, Kiki Smith is still a living, working artist. Why place her, static, in that decade? How easy for feminist sensibilities to be stuck in time – a past time. The docent said the sculpture contained a message for women not to fear the brutal forces. The woman depicted in the sculpture is nude next to the docile wolf. She is unafraid. The docent added, with a flirtatious cock of her head, that the wolf represents men.

On the phone this morning, I told my Daddy I felt a big love for her and that I felt very protective of her. After her silence, I added, "I know I'm supposed to think you're dangerous. But often, I feel protective."

She was still silent for a moment, then, she said, "You don't have to think I'm dangerous all the time. But I want the danger to excite you."

"It does." I said.

She added, "When we're in public, you should be excited about my adoration, at ease. You should just enjoy being pampered. At home, you can protect me. At home, when no one else is around, you can help me rest." She paused. "I appreciate that," she concluded.

I didn't say anything for a moment – too long a moment apparently, as she seemed ill at ease.

She said, "Well, it's not like that really, but you know.

And I do know. I said, "I think that's a good depiction." I was thinking things I couldn't convey – thought fragments in my mind about the 1950s housewives and the men who stayed out at the bar long hours before going home to be cared for, managed by their wives,

© KONINKLIJKE BRILL NV, LEIDEN, 2019 | DOI:10.1163/9789004383562_019

transformed into their home-selves. I was having thought fragments about women in Taliban Afghanistan who never left the house – never. Who, when poor and abandoned by men who had no further interest in them, were barred from going out to beg. I thought about how women's lives were imprisoned by Taliban rule. And yet, there was less rape, less violence committed by strangers. Does the origin of the violence matter? I thought about women consigned to poverty in the U.S. because they have children and our culture does not support child-raising as a useful activity. It must be privately supported, by men, docile wolves who don't eat their own young. I thought about the many women in the world who wear head-coverings by religious choice, who release their hair when they arrive home.

Across cultures, across time, some call these ways foolish, unequal, and unliberated. Even within our culture, when a couple names their roles – let's say they call themselves "Daddy" and "girl" – it's easy to think, oh, how gross! How different from *my* smart ways.

What is safety worth? What worth, belonging?

My Daddy wants me to feel pampered in public, honored, and beautiful.

"Why would I burden my wife with grocery shopping?" said the Taliban Muslim shopkeeper in the interview I read. "She is precious; she stays at home."

I am on my knees for my Daddy at home. My throat is open and there is so much adoration to swallow. Where women are liberated publicly and we have no men with us, to shield us, we are defiled by men who don't know us. My lovers are not men, and yet I live with masculinity. The masculinity, in my home, is trying constantly to sort itself out. My Daddy is gentle and kind. My knees are sore, raw, and this feels normal. Some part of me loves the wounds, wouldn't want them to heal. I love her and feel I want to protect her.

"I think that's a good depiction," I said to her again, with finality.

POWER

I am the chocolate covered cherry in the center of the box of Bordeaux crèmes. I am the reason Daddy planted the fig trees along the north side of the house and the pink hibiscus by the bedroom window. I am the glittery pink flames airbrushed along the sides of the silver coupe that will reduce its resale value. Resale value be damned!

Don't act like I'm the only one who wants to be adored. Every girl wants it. It's proof that we are not as disposable as we feel when we aren't allowed into the conversation, can't get healthcare, won't earn enough money to pay for baby formula and can't nurse the baby in public because of the cost of impropriety. Who's got the time to be buttoning and unbuttoning one's blouse all day anyway? Women have to work for money or be cute enough or sweet enough or young enough for someone to give it to them.

I am my Daddy's own and I get my power from doing what others won't do – from making Daddy think she's worked for her reward. I preserve myself for Daddy. I struggle through shame for Daddy. Daddy gets a rock hard boner from feeling my peril and protecting me. Daddy takes my intimacy and wraps it around her fist, in her pocket. It feels so good.

Daddy carries my panties in her pocket. Only once did she take a clean pair from the clothesline – the one with the stripes and blossoms – these have special significance to us anyway. More often, she leans over in the car and tells me to take them off and give them to her. "Hurry up now, we're going to be there soon." And I do as I am told, before we reach our destination. My thighs slicken a bit as Daddy presses my panties to her face and inhales deeply, a look of true contentment on her face. My thighs slicken a bit with no fabric to absorb the moisture of my pleasure and Daddy smiles a grateful smile because she knows this. "What a good girl," she says as she stuffs the panties into her pocket and tells me to wait for her to come around and open my door and take me out to the party, the grocery store, the bar. Wherever we are, Daddy wants to open my door, be my savior. Sometimes this slows me down, but I let her do it. I love her for it, if not always, then certainly.

Is it natural to be turned on by the exchange of power mixed with intimacy? Well, who would know? Nature and culture merge. It's the way we know how to do it – we were born into it. We can find other paths to turn-on, sure, but even if we fail to name it, the model is everywhere. And so it is.

I don't like for anyone to be too cheeky about what I give to my Daddy and my Daddy alone. I can grow up fast in a pinch. Once, someone who thought she knew us, someone who had heard stories and thought she knew my Daddy spoke to me in a private corner of the nightclub.

"So, are you wearing any panties tonight?" And I whirled right around without thinking and struck her face with my open hand. Her cheek reddened and she gasped as I stared icily, stunned by what I had done. I did not let on that I was stunned by what I had done, but she sputtered, and her pride looked wounded. I can grow up fast in a pinch.

"I can't believe you hit me," the woman said, as though I had been the one to breech propriety, as though she could intrude upon my person with her words in any way she pleased. Or perhaps she does not know that story carries intent, that words carry intent, like the cat calls and the hollers from men on balconies, the subtle grunts of men on sidewalks and street corners – all of whom think themselves polite or complimentary. They do not know – that which is given breath has power to it. An intention is released into the air and its trajectory toward the female body has meaning. I tried hard to feel as though I'd done something wrong, the palm of my hand still tingling from the contact with cheek.

"That was not a blow; it was a reprimand. May your innocence be preserved by never having to learn the difference between the two." My mind juggled the possibility of remorse with the hot leaden feeling of outrage, but the juggling was just a game. I put down both remorse and outrage; they are just a game, meant to distract one from the truth. The truth was in my marrow, pooling like the blood in the lower regions of my lungs as I took a deeper breath. Do not toy with the adoration my Daddy gives me. Put that down foolish child – that is not a toy! Without my Daddy's adoration, I am nothing but a slave, nothing but a wanderer and none of the heavy keys I carry fit the locks of any houses in the finer neighborhoods. At least I know why I am allowed to sleep in a soft bed, why I am allowed to shop for fine lingerie and jewelry and fancy chocolates. You are the one who is deluding yourself, sister. I have power in this place. And I enjoy it.

WHAT DOES A GIRL WANT FROM DADDY?

From the online Daddy-Girl Question and Answer Forums (names and locations have been changed)

Girlygirl in Des Moines IA says:

I like some rules. I walk on his right side, unless we're out on the street, then I have to stay on the inside so Daddy can keep me safe. I'm required to say Daddy at the end of "I love you," which is quite fine by me. Ummmm, mainly just rules that keep me safe. There are a lot of things I love for Daddy to do. I love hearing him call me his kitten. I love snuggling and such. Sometimes all he has to do is grab my hand and I just melt for him. At that point, I can only think about being alone in our apartment instead of out and about. Anyway, I love that he exists for me.

Pouty1 in St. Louis MO says:

I like rewards, and attention and hugs and cuddles and stuffed animals and approval from my Daddy. I know security would be another, knowing that I can come back to him with anything, and things will be all right. Daddy should be generous with affection, praise and attention.

Cuddles, Draws (when Daddy draws pictures on my back), hand holding, good night kisses, Praise (always always always praising, I love to be told I'm a good girl! It makes me soooooooooooooo happy to please my Daddy. I would almost do anything to be told "You are such a good girl, Princess") playing, tickles, forehead kisses, presents (nothing big, just things to put a smile on my face), wiping tears away, kissing ouchies better, teaching, worldly guidance, and love, are all musts from my Daddy.

Chaoskitten in Bakersfield CA says:

I like to be daddy's inquisitive, yet bratty, not so little, "bad" kitten. My daddy disciplines me when I disobey his wishes. I'm feisty and stubborn in my submissive/little girl side. I love to keep it playful and

139

on the purely incestuous level psychologically. He doesn't know it, but Daddy is there far more for my enjoyment than his own. I like to be punished more than rewarded. Sometimes I like to be coddled by daddy and treated like his little princess, but most of the time I prefer being his slut. I enjoy daddy acting out his role in a cathartic way as well. I like the structure of some rules, but mostly I enjoy letting daddy embrace the illusion of him being in control, when all along I'm getting my way. :::sticks out tongue:::

Fussybaby in Fargo ND says:

I love it when I get to lie in daddy's arms and hear his heart beat knowing he is there for me. I also love it when daddy calls me "kitten," when we hold hands and when he brushes my hair and then spanks me with the brush when I act up. I enjoy making daddy mad a lot to see how he will punish me next. Mind you these are purely loving punishments. Nothing too over the top. My fave thing is when I feel daddy's loving warm big hands wrapped around my throat when I look into his eyes. Yummy!

Daddysgirl023 in Las Vegas, NV says:

I like the rules that Daddy has for me, they are simple and mainly just cute and meant to keep me out of harms way! Like holding his hand in parking lots and basically anytime we are out so I don't get losted or wander into oncoming traffic (bad habit of not looking before walking!!) And we love to hold hands anyway, constant contact, we're very touchy feely with one another.

I have to go to bed when Daddy tells me to so I won't be too tired to enjoy our evenings off together but when I nap Daddy normally holds me and naps with me :-)

I'm not supposed to put items in our grocery cart (we do the shopping togethers always) when Daddy isn't looking ... giggles, but he just laughs and normally lets me keep what I put in anyway <3

Daddy treats me like the most special, prized, and loved little girl in the whole world. We're cuddle bugs, we love to snuggle and just be close, lots of petting. Even when Daddy has to do something college related while at home he loves for me to be close by, especially when it's curled up at his feet or resting my head in his lap. Daddy is my safe place, my own personal heaven. (I second fussybaby's hand around the throat thing. – *melts-*)

Silvertears in Houston TX says:

More attention than he has time for, more cuddles than he has strength for, more validation than he has breath for, more play time than he has patience for, more discipline than he has imagination for and more love than he has heart for.

KEEPING DADDY IN LINE

MISTRUSTING DADDY

I am waiting in another hotel lobby – this time for my room to be prepared. I am watching another silent television and George W, the Daddy we elected for eight years running, is speaking. He is speaking in a familiar way in his well-fitted blue suit and red tie. He is familiar with us; we are his children. When he became our Daddy, he took on a different way of speaking, a more down-home tone and way of pronouncing words. I can't hear the words right now, but I can tell how he talks. I can tell it's him and what he's probably saying just by looking. It's hard to know whether his simple way is an act, but one thing is certain, his Yale education is not on display in his vocabulary. Words he pronounced just fine before his presidential campaign are now countrified in his mouth.

The sound is off now, and I'm watching him without pronunciation, without content. I am curled up in the corner of the sofa, my shoes off, my feet tucked under me. I still wear my coat and my suitcase leans against the sofa as I wait for my room to become available after a long day of travel. Daddy is on the TV and the sight of him always brings up a tiny bit of nausea, light-headedness. I am outraged each time I see him – surprised that he is still around, has not faded the way a bad dream dissipates, throughout the day. In the morning, I can feel a dream so vividly, then it starts to dissolve and by lunchtime, who's thinking about dreams anymore?

He is talking and sniffing, silently on the TV. I am watching as though in a dream. He's speaking but I can't hear him and someone inside of me is rearranging the furniture as I watch, but I too am silent, sitting alone, but in a public place. Wordless music is playing through the lobby, accompanying the television silence. Something about his grey hair and the movements of his shoulders remind me

© KONINKLIJKE BRILL NV, LEIDEN, 2019 | DOI:10.1163/9789004383562_020

of my stepfather – suddenly I recall the way he'd get in bed with me at night when I was twelve, shove me over just a bit, as though we always shared a bed and I was in his spot. The slight nausea makes my coat warmer. Why is this Daddy on the TV again? He has been more blessedly invisible near the end of this unpopular term of office. Entitlement and dignity each look slightly different on a person, I think; as I watch him, sound off. I can see how people mistake one for the other.

Perhaps I always mistrusted this Daddy, because of his Daddy before him. Perhaps I always felt suspicion, and I know what it's like to mistrust a father, a Daddy, a patria. He is the father of our nation, commander in chief, the man with the answers and the veto power.

Daddies can lie. Of course they can, as everyone can, but Daddies do it with more impunity. His job is to make us feel safe, not to make us feel well informed. Daddies can lie and we give them permission; we give them creative latitude. I have done it myself – encouraged lies. I can't always admit this to myself, but it's true. I have done it myself in my own bed, in my own home. Tell me what you will; just don't tell me what I am afraid to hear. But I never wanted the lies to be untrue. I wanted them to be real. I wanted Daddy to help me make them all come true.

Daddy is all about spin, and it's for my own good. "We believe they have weapons of mass destruction" is not a lie. We do believe this, even without evidence, even without analysis of why we keep our weapons. So many weapons. There are ways to tell a story that conceal what is salient because when Daddy speaks, he speaks only to me, speaks only the story that I would want to hear. And truly, I have no skill for hearing other stories.

Getting up from the lobby sofa, putting on my shoes and trudging toward my newly prepared hotel room, I feel my young self. I am going to my bedroom after dinner. My stepfather and I get up from the dinner table and I go to my bedroom; he stays in the living room watching television. I leave him there and move on, though I am still aware of him, always nearby. I leave the president on the television, but he is always nearby, making decisions in my name. My stepfather and the president are busy. Perhaps they are doing something that will affect me, perhaps their movements and thoughts will be benign. I remember how it felt, as a child, to feel that someone is entitled to use me. Perhaps my stepfather will come to my room later and leave his rubbings on my skin. Perhaps he will be occupied elsewhere. I glance back at George W, in his blue suit, talking on the silent television as I leave the room. He may come into my dreams later to shake me with images war or torture. Is it my torture or someone else's? The images vacillate between the two. His face talks in that down-home way. This is my home too. His face smirks and his eyebrows rise just slightly as he nods. This is my home too. I have left the room, but I know he's still there.

KEEPING DADDY IN LINE

Daddy wants to be good. He wants it with all his heart.

"No matter how many times I lie, you just keep calling me on it, baby." That's what he said to me. "I rely on you." He added with a furrowed brow, a nod of concession, as though he was giving me a real gift by letting me ferret out his lies. "You're the only one who can hold me to my better intentions."

Daddy wants to be good. He wants a house in country, a girl who knows how to drive a wheelbarrow, and then later, put on rhinestones and a silky gown and dance for him. He wants some chickens in a predator-proof coop. Pretty chickens in a coop painted to match the house in the country. He wants me to make scrambled eggs for him every morning – except when he's making me waffles, or cereal for Saturday morning cartoons. He wants a simple life with a good girl. Weekends in the big city at fancy hotels. He likes my hair curled, my heels high and my lipstick dark. Simple love. That's all he wants. No more sex parties. No more online trysts with tattooed redheads. No more Internet porn. All Daddy ever wanted was a good girl and now that I'm here, everything will be different. All Daddy ever wanted was the girl that would let him settle down, settle in, feel loved and comfortable. (Maybe a little porn. What's wrong with a little porn once in a while?)

I am the one who listens, the one with good ideas, and the one who's hot beyond belief. Sizzling hot, can-you-believe-what-I-got hot, lets me do it all night hot. "Sorry buddy, no time for the stripper bar – remember what I've got at home!" I am the sensible girl, the reliable girl. I say, "This feels so right." When I gaze into Daddy's eyes. I say, "There's no one like you, anywhere." I give Daddy permission to be good.

I don't let Daddy get too far off track. I keep Daddy on the straight and narrow. I make sure he eats his vegetables and gets enough sleep and calls his mother on Mother's Day. I am the kind of woman who's dangerous, because I'm so hot, I'm so sassy, and I'm so freaky in the sack. Daddy will do what I ask, show some obedience because I'm just that good. Daddy will say to his buddies going out to the bars, "Naw, I gotta go home." And they'll nod and say they understand. One will shake his head and say, "You've got a dangerous woman at home." And Daddy will feel proud. Daddy will feel worth something because of their envy and because I have prompted Daddy to do what he really wanted to do – go home, read a book, turn in early. With me, Daddy doesn't have to put out the effort to seem like a Big Man. It all happens at home, in private. Daddy does not have to say he wants to be quiet, docile, and grateful. It's all because I'm dangerous, I'm hot. Watch out. I'm on fire.

It's all about the attitude. My beauty is not about having long hair or wearing sexy clothes, or always having a fresh manicure. Those are just what I want to do. I want to wear stylish clothes. I want to have lots of shoes. I want to have tight jeans. I want to wear my hair in pigtails when I put on some overalls to work in the yard. It's not about that. It's all about the attitude. It's the way I beckon with my eyes, with my fingers; shoulders cocked forward, pendant resting on the smooth skin of my chest, hair falling gracefully around my cheek. It's not about that though. It's about the attitude.

I am every girl who's ever been a pretty bride. I lead the Bible study, I cook the fry bread, mix the potato salad, bake the casserole. I am the Women's Temperance Union and Mothers Against Drunk Drivers. I am waiting in front of the White House on a hunger strike. My sons are already dead, but I will wait until the president brings back all of the other sons too. I am holding up the signs, I am sewing the flag. I am waiting by the phone. I am on call. I am the last one to know and the first one to bring a hot dish to the house after the death.

No, that's not me. That was some other version of me. I am the hotter, sexier, woo-hoo version of me. I am keeping Daddy in line. I have so many Daddies to keep in line. I have started wearing them on a charm bracelet. This one is the Daddy that goes to work every morning with a perfumed note from me in his lunch box. This one is my father that never calls, never writes – I make the contact. This one is my congressdaddy to whom I send emails every week. I click on the boxes for healthcare, for poverty, for children's issues, for education. Sometimes I am too busy to keep my nails done. But I know I should. I know I should. I put on my pink rhinestoned running shoes and I go.

My first priority is family. My first priority is in my own home. I am putting a good meal on the table. I am asking what Daddy had for lunch. I am reading the phone bills, circling numbers in red that Daddy will have to account for later. This is what he wants from me. He's done it again. He said he wouldn't talk to her anymore. He promised. And this is what he wants from me. Keep him in line. I have to speak up. I have to say something. I am Daddy's conscience. He has a better self; sometimes he just forgets. He says, "I didn't lie to you because I didn't call her – she called me." He says, "What am I supposed to do, be rude to someone?" He says, "Why does it matter. You know I'm here with you. How long have I been here with you?" Daddy says, "You know that our love is bigger than anything I've ever known, right? Why does it matter?" But I know my job. Sometimes I think Daddy is weak and pathetic for not holding back his baser urges without my persistent reminders, but I know my job. This is part of the reason Daddy loves me. I am like the pretty, bossy girls that Daddy knew when he was young. I feel entitled to the truth, entitled to an expensive necklace. I will wave the phone bill in Daddy's face and say, with exhaustion, with diligence, "You're at it again, aren't you?" Daddy used to be afraid of the pretty bossy girls, but now he's more confident. Daddy is remorseful, apologetic. Daddy learned how to handle girls like me. And I do my part to make sure he doesn't handle me poorly. When Daddy flies right, I feel a sense of mastery.

It's amazing how I find time to live my own life, know my own interests. I put in so much effort, keeping Daddy in line. It comes so naturally to me though. I just love him. I just love him, so it comes naturally to me. And I have my own life. I have a job and interests. I have friends. It just comes naturally to me. And Daddy knows that I deserve nice things, a nice ring, and nice gifts. I know he loves me and values me and he decorates me because I deserve it. When he treats me well, I do him right tenfold. He deserves it. I deserve it. We deserve just what we get.

CHAPTER 21

INTERGENERATIONAL INCEST FAMILY

My mother said they lived together for years, and that something just wasn't right about that – siblings living together like they were a married couple.

"He beat her just like she was his wife." That's what folks used to say, and it sure cleared things up saying it like that. She took care of him of course – did the cooking, cleaning, washed his clothes, whatever else. Nobody ever commented about that. He'd get drunk and beat her like she was his wife. That was my grandfather and his sister.

My grandmother had divorced him for that same drinking. I don't know whether he beat her too, but he moved down the street when my father was eight years old. It was odd to divorce a man for something as common as drinking, or even beatings. It was strange in 1943, but my grandmother was a bossy Baptist and wasn't going to put up with that. She stayed living in their home with just my father as the man of the house. Boys grow up quick, become men of the house.

She cooked for him, cleaned his room and washed his clothes. He mowed the lawn, picked and shelled the pecans that littered the backyard. My father loved his mama's pecan pie. He still saw his father, when the drinking would allow. The sexual abuse started when his father moved out. Becoming the man of the house meant moving in to sleep with his mother. Boys grow up quick, when a man is needed.

My grandmother wasn't ashamed of the new sleeping arrangement – strange for a mother and a son that old. She was more proud of being in charge, outright told anyone who'd ask that she made the rules. Where her son slept was one of her rules and my father's rage raised his shoulders right up to his ears, muscles and tendons tense as piano wires.

Mother and son spent time at church, preparing and eating meals with aunt and uncle. They were always close, my grandmother

© KONINKLIJKE BRILL NV, LEIDEN, 2019 | DOI:10.1163/9789004383562_021

and her two siblings, one sister, one brother, the youngest. He'd go off, my great uncle, drinking or traveling. Odd jobs, building jobs never held him and he'd travel for a while. He stayed in his sleeping bag at the side of the road and at roadhouses, anywhere he pleased. He never mentioned the dishonorable discharge he received for homosexuality after thirteen years of service in the Marine Corps – how that would've affected his employability. He felt better moving, he said. He felt better on the road.

When my father's uncle was home, he lived with Sis, the middle child in the family. Her job paid the mortgage and kept things together, being that his jobs were odd. Sis is what everyone called her. She never married and was always just Sis. That's what my father called her too, though she was his aunt. By the time I found a place in the family, my grandmother had married her second husband; Sis was old. All of the family relationships were re-arranged again.

Where a person slept, whose clothes a person washed and to whom a person was married – these defined one's position in the family. My grandmother was bossy, concerned with daily life. Sis was spiritual – and a pleaser. She lived to serve others. She learned Hebrew to understand the bible better. She read the bible every day of her life and was tormented by the incestuous relationship she had with her brother. All her life she hated the things she let him do. She didn't know why she let him, knowing it was wrong to God. She just knew that her job was to put on a smiling face, a bright face. I loved her smile – I think she actually found the way to smile herself into being truly happy.

I have never lived in Texas. My father left at sixteen with no intention of returning. His Daddy-Uncle Sam gave him the GI Bill and college. His new stepfather encouraged a fib. My grandmother didn't want him to leave, but with a home birth, her word set the formal paperwork right. Sixteen became eighteen and off he went to the army. My parents started taking me to visit when I was young because my grandmother had to get her hands on the baby. I remember her loud, big, enthusiastic. As I grew up, I resembled her. I resembled my father.

I started saying that I come from an "incest family" long before I knew just how much of it we had. I started saying that because it seemed more honest, less like it was about my looks or actions or the way I "related" with my stepfather. It seemed more honest, though he was clearly the responsible adult when I was just twelve and he fifty-six years old. Something in our family held his actions still and dear. Something bigger was taking care of incest, cooking its meals, washing its clothes. I squirmed beneath the sheets of a tidy incest home. And mine was not the only bed in which it paced its circles, shook off its fleas before sleeping soundly.

My father never sexually abused me. He drank a lot instead and remained stoic and self-punishing in his corner den of my childhood home. Some days he acted like he deserved lead in his pockets in the swimming pool, some days, like he deserved to fly his kite in the parade. He stayed quiet. His intimates – not his daughter – felt his pain most. I knew it, but wasn't made to hold it: dark, brooding, inebriated, animal. His glance could wither me and all I ever wanted was to please him.

It wasn't the Christian part of my Texas family that ever dug into my drawers, laughed at my shame, or made me want to murder or die to find freedom. And yet, I came from an incest family, part of which was Southern and Christian and white, despite not being all white. My family was proud of its ways. A family that knew how to keep its secrets. Or maybe they weren't keeping secrets, just not speaking what no one wanted to hear.

I have chosen my father again and again in my Daddy-lovers – kind, though just as broken, deceptive and cruel when no other action would serve. My father – who never hurt me as a child, other than through absence and disapproval – left me when he went into himself, out to the bar, into a silent rage. He kept drinking – though less as his life neared a close. I can't say whether he ever found peace.

I miss my Daddy so much each time she leaves me. She cannot love me out loud, unconditional, proud and beautiful. I miss my Daddy – even the way she becomes needy, cruel and at times, pathetic, a bad liar who persists nonetheless. She is intoxicated by her own story about the world. She is not bright about anything when she is drunk on her own story. She is as dull as the garden hoe left out in the yard in the rain, pelted by pecans falling from the trees.

TRUE PLEASURE

Dear Daddy,

I want to be pleasing to everyone, all the time. I stand in front of my mirrors in the morning, planning and practicing to be pleasing. I read magazines and buy products and listen to others' advice about being pleasing as though it's a lifelong project worthy of attention, worthy of investment, worthy of sacrifice.

There's just something about being pleasing that brings pleasure. Everyone wants to feel that they are worthy of someone's praise and admiration. Everyone wants to please – even you, Daddy. I can see it on your face when you have made me happy, when you have made me dinner, when you have made me come. I can see it on your face that you are pleased that I am pleased. I am aware that being easy to please is one of the ways that I become pleasing.

Could this awareness possibly affect my pleasure? I wonder, but not for long. Surely all that pleases me genuinely pleases me; otherwise, how could I seem pleased without planning? I am not planning my pleasure, I'm just stirring the cake batter, feeding the dog, buying the groceries and being sure to get enough cream for your coffee, Daddy, enough butter for your bread, enough milk to drink with the cake I am baking for our dinner, Daddy. I am not planning to be pleasing, but I am expecting pleasure. I feel a bit tense, because the pleasure doesn't always come. Daddy, you might shake anger off your coat when you walk in the door. You might not be able to shake off the cold that lives in your marrow; you might not want cake; you might not notice my new blouse. Daddy, what if you have other things on your mind when I need you to be pleased? But, still my hope rises like the cake, turns the corners of my mouth up when you are in the room. My hope is as red as the cherries on my apron fearing you might be blue.

Daddy, you are my favorite person to please. You are the pinnacle of my pleasure-giving. You are both the hardest to please and the easiest. This is indeed a pleasing paradox. Daddy, you love me no matter what and will always be pleased with me, at least in small measure. I have to believe this, even when I can't feel it. And you are the hardest to please, the easiest to disappoint. Pleasure doesn't come easily to a Daddy and it makes me want to try harder, offer more, give and give and give pleasure. If you didn't love me so, if you weren't supposed to love me so, perhaps I wouldn't try to please you. I wouldn't slice the cheese thin, like you like it in your sandwich; I wouldn't put a cherry on top of your perfect scoop of ice cream and tug my blouse down just a bit in front when I hand it to you, so that my breasts are round and pleasing. Oh, how I crave the confirmation of your love! I tingle when I receive it. By pleasing you, Daddy, I become worthy of all good things and I never once have to focus on my own life to do it.

Daddy, I know how I please you. I know that you see my chest and want to fuck me. You see the round scoop of ice cream with the cherry on top, presented in front of my breasts. It's like a music video. It's liked the scene in the porno right before the action starts. After your ice cream, you will fuck me. Spent, you will be pleased. Spent and sated, you will never have to know yourself. I know what respite I offer. You just look over at me and know I know you. And then you sleep. (And Daddy, I know you better than this, even. I know that in your darker moments, my knowing you makes you want to smother me with a pillow. I am always looking at you, anticipating your next need. In your darker moments, you do not want to be seen; you don't trust me. You keep yourself from picking up the pillow, you don't stop my breath.) And I keep looking, unflinching. My eyes are dry but if I take them off of you, even to blink, how will I know you so you don't have to know yourself?

Poor Daddy! It would be awful to be so alone, and so I watch. I watch the coffee as I pour in the cream so that I get it just the right color. I still carry the paint chip you gave me so I'd get your coffee just the right color. Clever Daddy. Why am I so poorly rested? What is this tension in my neck? I read that anger makes a home in the jaw. Surely, my jaw hurts from smiling, not anger. It's amazing that I can be so pleased, so often, just by being pleasing.

I don't know how to take my coffee. For a while, I took it with a little cream and sugar, but then just sugar because the cream could make me too plump for Daddy's tastes. Then I drank it black, but this felt austere. I like to take a few sips of your coffee when you offer it and I enjoy this, but perhaps it's the offer I enjoy and not the coffee. I keep changing my mind, finding new information, trying new things, adapting. I am an adaptor. I am a sturdy steel, beautifully embellished adaptor between your thick pipe and the threads of the outside world.

When I first heard that I have no self of my own, it was hard for me to take. I think I heard it on the TV, but the woman who said it wasn't on for long and then the program switched back to something more pleasing. I think I read it once in a magazine, but the message seemed so implausible and then my eye wandered to the ad for skin cream. I like that skin cream in the softly curved bottle with the words in pretty rolling font. That cream smells good. It was hard for me to grasp: "defined by men's desires." How silly! What do I care for most men? I care about family, about you, Daddy. I care about making a good home and that's what's right. I have a job. I have friends. I raise children. I like to go shopping and I love red boots! I am taking a cake decorating class and trying to get to know my aunt Trudy so I can scrapbook the story of her life. She was a dancer. I have interests.

When I first whispered this into my own ear, I scoffed. "Poor individuation." I am definitely not just like all my friends! And who uses language like that anyway. Psychobabble. If I had a personal problem, I would know it. To whom would it be more personal? If I had a personal problem, you would see it Daddy. I would stop caring about my appearance. I would forget the cream at the grocery store. I would eat too much cake and plump up around the middle. You would see it if I had a problem. You would intervene, wouldn't you Daddy?

You are not in charge of my life! Why did you smirk the last time I said that, Daddy? Some girls have their lives ruled by men, some stupid, vapid girls. That happens to the girls the feminists speak of, to the young ones, to the older ones from another generation. That happens to some of them, but not all of them. I guess it happens often enough that they talk about it in books, in magazines. It's so sad when that happens. So sad, when someone's intimate partner smothers her in the night with a pillow. How could a person not see that coming? That happens to some girls – but not to me. Where is my cup of coffee? It's been a busy morning. No matter. I might not even like coffee.

    I work at a job. I raise children. I contribute to society. I do all of these things and everyone loves me for them. You love me for them too, don't you Daddy? If something were wrong, you would say so. But maybe you aren't paying attention. The feminists say that the patriarchy is hurting you too. When did you last speak as though your work was pleasing to you? When did you last speak of being pleased by your friends? They laugh and joke and you have the same conversations again and again. That makes it easy. That makes it predictable. It's good to be able to predict pleasure. They're having a sale at my favorite shoe store next week.

    I told myself this unpleasing bit of information again. I told myself again and slowly, and my own awareness began to dawn. By pleasing you Daddy, I become worthy of all good things and I never once have to focus on my own life to become that worthy. Could this be true? You want me to work and be productive and to learn and be smart, and to strive and compete and to make you proud. You want me to be my sweet little self, darling, honey-bun, sugar-boot, and pumpkin schnookums. You are happy with me just as I am, aren't you Daddy? I am just as Daddy is happy with me. Happy is just as with me as the way I am Daddy. What? What? Daddy wants me to be strong and to accept that he is stronger. You love my grace in accepting being less. How can I not be living a full life?

    And what would my life be like if I weren't striving to be pleasing? I could fail to be pleasing! And then what would happen? I don't know. I don't know. I am wearing my favorite red boots, sitting at the kitchen table for a moment before going to work. I am sipping my tepid coffee with skim milk and sugar and if my brow furrows for too long, those lines on my forehead won't go away. Have I poured my pleasure into the mold of Daddy's needs, misshapen by misogyny? Have we both become distorted? That word, misogyny, makes my head hurt – such an exaggeration. Daddy, I know you don't hate me, only sometimes. I'm starting to wonder.

    But I can't be late for work and who wants to wear the mask of worry? That's not pleasing to look at! I don't want this coffee.

I set the cup in the sink and I know I should wash it, but I'm going to be bad and leave it. Still I wonder. What is my life? For whom is my life?

If I weren't already so busy, I might find out.

Love,
Your Girl

INCEST CULTURE

I started fantasizing about strangling my stepfather with a piano wire, putting rat poison in his food, waiting until he became old and pushing his wheelchair to the edge of the cliff to get a nice view of the sea and then whoops! He'd just slip on the sand, his body parting from the chair in slow motion as both fell out and down, the gentle parabola disturbed only by his waning screams.

My first urge for a kiss prompted my seething. I became smitten and attracted to someone, as we mammals do when the body ripens. That urge was nothing like a compromise, a calculation, a theft, and a silent deception. That urge was desperate in my blood, every bit of my body yearning and moistening, reaching forward for her kiss. And it gave the lie to every bit of frottage, sickening domination of flesh, twisted manipulation of wanting. Suddenly, I knew what wanting a kiss felt like. And that had been the worst of the incest: the kisses. He forced them into my mouth and I dreamed of leeches, like his slippery tongue would detach and slug-slide down my throat. It wasn't what he did with my genitals or wanted me to do with his, it was the kissing that threatened internal bleeding.

But those thoughts of death and murder made me the madman, the waste case, the internal space waste. Pull the plug. She's twelve and nearly a vegetable already! My mother sent me to counseling for my "abnormal" dislike for my stepfather. "There can be animosity about the father being displaced, the mother loving someone new," the Doctor-Daddy explained. But anyone who can't love *this* man, now that's strange, sick, queer, and unnatural. Nurse! Teacher! Newscaster! Saturday morning cartoons! Someone must intervene. If it can't be spoken, you must be smokin'. Officer! Lifeguard! She's going down and doesn't even know she's in the drink.

© KONINKLIJKE BRILL NV, LEIDEN, 2019 | DOI:10.1163/9789004383562_022

I live in an incest family and in an incest supporting culture. The evidence is everywhere, but it's all inconclusive. The ripening of my body into the curves of a woman was my first advance. My next flirtation was an eager mind and a shyness that caused me to watch people, learn them. Of course, he might've been turned on by reticence or simplicity. There are so many ways a man can read a girl. So many types toward which he can be attracted – the substance of our selves reduced to mere typeface.

I hoped he would just go ahead and fuck me, with his penis, in my vagina. I knew that was called rape and that it was illegal and that I should not be made to endure it at my age, period. That was the only act I could name.

What he actually did to me was illegible and he had so much more credibility than I. I didn't really feel to blame during those three years of sexual abuse, but I felt blame-worthy. Feminism had not visited my suburban San Diego neighborhood. I was astonished later to learn that some women never wore make-up, always cooked what they wanted to for dinner and survived the act of taking out their own garbage. I couldn't fathom the flamboyant queers, the university educated women of color who were creating language for why I was white to my mother, brown to my stepfather when he wanted to hurt me. Because my Texas family was mixed race – Indian, poor, who knows what else – he called me "savage" and "squaw" when he wanted to make my twelve-year old body sexual. In my neighborhood, everyone visible to my eyes was white. Women were defined by their beauty and behavior, men by their power and money and no one had yet invented an alternative vehicle to take us through our days.

My stepfather's blood-daughter, nearly twenty years my elder, confided once, on a visit home, that her divorce had been terrible. She looked at me, sisterly, and said, "You may be the only person on the planet who can understand this, but I loved him – even though he humiliated me. He humiliated me like Dad did," she added flatly.

I nodded, because I did understand though we had never spoken of our common history with her Daddy. We had never spoken of it, but she assumed it. And she was right. Plenty of girls, women, would've understood. They may not have been supportive, but they'd have understood. We all recognize predatory sex, the need to guard the mouth from the intruder who could suck out the soul. We all understand, but women are part of incest culture too. I might've turned away from my sister's troubles. She took a calculated risk to tell me and she was correct about me. I looked her in the eye. I didn't turn away.

My first consensual lover taught me, with her attention, how to give a kiss – not just how to get one. Over time, I understood that "incest" was not between my stepfather and me; it was an act of my culture. Though Daddy can be a victim – someone's Daddy is always in charge. My act of growing up triggered his act of looking; my curiosity triggered his need for dominion. This is just the way men are – my culture told me so. There were more views and values nestled in the blankets of my childhood bed than I could name. Telescopes poking out of the pillows, yardsticks measuring the length of my nightgown, microscopes, pondering the pigment in my skin. Where is that heavy breathing coming from? Oppression is researchable; now I know.

"If you touch me again, I'll kill you."

There, I said it. Fourteen. I said it, not about him, but to him. They had failed to protect me: the officer, the nurse, the teacher, the therapist, the mother, and the culture. So I said it myself. I meant it. He knew it. He told me I was worthless and that no one cared about me. He had gone too far. I had her kiss in my mouth like the sweetest truth I'd ever tasted.

I still visited that incest family for years after I left it because it was mine. He'd smile politely at me, as I arrived in the driveway for Thanksgiving dinner.

"Aren't you going to give him a hug?" my mother would admonish me, though he also made no affectionate move forward.

"I'm okay," I'd say with a smug smile and a wave in his direction. He feared me. And she couldn't understand why.

Those who throw away a mother will suffer greatly. I came home on holidays. Both my stepfather and I kept an eye on the knife, as he carved the turkey.

Oprah.com
May 14, 2009
Facing Freedom (Freed From Prison After Killing Her Father)
The Oprah Winfrey Show

Growing up, Stacey Lannert seemed to have the perfect family. Her father, Tom, was a financial consultant, and Deb, his wife, was a stay-at-home mom. But as Stacey and her sister, Christy, got older, their picture-perfect life began to unravel.

***

Stacey says she was especially close with her father when she was young. "I was daddy's little girl. ... He was like Superman to me because if there was ever a problem, he fixed it," she says. "I always felt like everything was right in the world when he was there."

***

When Stacey turned 8 years old, she says her father started molesting her. It started with a game called "touch tongues," and quickly progressed to genital touching and oral sex, she says.

***

Stacey says her father raped her for the first time when she was only 9 years old. "I felt like he was just tearing me apart," she says. "It felt like I was literally being ripped in half, and he was saying such hateful things to me. I didn't know what to do."

***

Stacey says she didn't tell her mother, because her father said she already knew. "Somehow in my mind I blamed her immediately," she says. "Like it was her fault."

***

When she was 12, Stacey's parents got divorced. "I became resentful even more so of my mother for leaving my dad and almost even took his side in the whole divorce," she says.

***

Despite the abuse, Stacey decided to live with her father when her parents got divorced. "At some point, I separated my dad into two different people," she says. "My dad, and then Tom, the man who would abuse me. Sometimes it would be anywhere from three times a week [to] all five days of the week."

***

Years later, Stacey moved in with her mother, but Christy stayed with their dad. One day, Christy called for help and Stacey decided to return home. "I walked in the door, and there he was," she says. "He wound up throwing me down and he raped me right there."

***

The day Stacey went to help her sister was the last straw, she says. "When he got done raping me, he kicked me, and I got smart probably for the first time ever," she says. "I was going to fight."

***

One month later, Christy sneaked into her father's house. Stacey says she grabbed his gun while he was passed out and shot him in the collarbone. Stacey says he then sat up. "All of a sudden, he just started yelling," she says. "I remember thinking, 'He can't get up, because if he gets up he'll kill us.' So I picked the gun back up and just closed my eyes and pulled the trigger."

***

Stacey and Christy waited hours before they called the police, but when they finally arrived, Stacey confessed immediately.

***

Prosecutors said they didn't believe Stacey's claims of abuse. Instead, they thought she murdered her father for money. They said she had been forging his checks, using his credit cards and stood to inherit nearly $100,000 from his estate.

***

Stacey was found guilty of murder in the first degree and was sentenced to life in prison without the possibility of parole. Christy pled guilty to conspiracy to commit murder and spent two and a half years in prison.

***

In January 2009, Missouri Governor Matt Blunt commuted Stacey's life sentence from life without parole to 20 years. After 18 years in prison, she was set free. Stacey says she has a lot of people to thank for her release. "[I was released] by the grace of God and the perseverance of two wonderful attorneys, a police detective who never gave up and a governor who had a lot of courage," she says.

***

Her own faith and patience helped her survive the past 18 years, she says, but her attitude couldn't always be positive. "There were times I gave up," she says. "I really believed I would spend the rest of my life in prison."

***

While it may seem strange that Stacey chose to live with her father after her parents' divorce, she says it made sense to her when she was 12 years old. "We got sent back and forth between the two of them a lot, and there were times that he didn't hurt me," she says. "My father loved me, not the abuser who would rape me. They weren't [the same person] in my mind."

***

Stacey says she is often judged by the decision she made to live with her dad. "A lot of times we wind up seeing more victimization because of the choices we make," she says. "My life was hell, and I was struggling just to be able to survive every day, and then after the fact I have to face answers of why I didn't do this or that – it's harsh."

***

Stacey says her father only physically abused her sister. "I felt like I was protecting her by taking the sexual abuse," she says. "If he'd hit her, I'd just thank God that's all it was."

***

On the day that Stacey shot her father, she says she was determined to scare him into stopping the abuse. "I had this mind-set, 'This is going to end,'" she says. "I wanted him to stop. I wanted him to know we're leaving and I can stand up to [him]. I didn't ever really make a conscious choice. I guess somewhere in my mind I did, but I wanted him to know that I could fight against him."

***

Stacey says she believes it was right that she served time in prison. "I did break one of society's rules," she says.

***

Still, Stacey says she didn't feel she had any other options at the time. "There was nowhere to run to. I didn't feel like there was anywhere I could go that he couldn't find me," she says. "He would tell us how he would find us – the car was registered in his name, he could track me through the social security card number, and he would tell me how he would find me and I believed him."

***

Stacey is telling her story in hopes of empowering other abuse victims. "Secrets lose their power when they're shared," she says. "I think that every woman who's been abused thinks at one point in time, 'I'm going to kill you.' There's power in the thought but not in the actual act itself, and I don't think people understand that. Now not only do I have the shame and guilt of what he did to me, I also have the shame and guilt of my actions."

***

After years of learning to deal with what happened to her, Stacey says she's finally felt some closure. "I finally have been able to fuse [my father and the abuser]. I had to in order to forgive myself for the action that I took, because there were moments that I missed my father," she says. "I had to forgive him in order to be able to forgive myself, but there's a difference between forgiving and forgetting."

***

Stacey says she forgave her father because she didn't want to face the alternative. "If I don't forgive him, then I'm in prison—it might not be a physical prison, but it's a psychological prison. You know, I was incarcerated and I was free in my heart. The rest was geography."

***

Though she's thrilled to be free, Stacey says prison was one of the best things that happened to her. "It made me face myself. I couldn't run away from my past at all," she says. "The compassion and encouragement and support that I have been met with from other women who went through the same thing just really made me feel like I wasn't alone."

***

Stacey recognizes that prosecutors believe she killed her father for money, but she says it's untrue. "I had his permission to use the account.

I wasn't working at the time, and he didn't want me working," she says. "It was a way of him isolating me."

***

Stacey doesn't hold it against people who don't believe her story, she says. "Every person in America is entitled to their own opinion," she says. "I can't judge them."

***

One of the hardest things to adjust to in her new life is having the freedom to do what she wants, when she wants, Stacey says. "I ask for permission all the time," she says. "I need to learn how to break that. It doesn't seem real to me yet. But I'm working on it, and I'm so happy. I can't believe I got this second chance at life, so I'm just excited."

***

After spending 18 years in prison, Stacey says she wants to work with fellow abuse victims. "I want to help end sexual abuse in America by putting a voice to it and talking about what happened to me, so I make it okay for others to talk about what happened to them," she says. "I've been pretty busy, and hopefully we can make a change."

DO WE KNOW OURSELVES IN
EACH OTHER'S EYES?

TOO YOUNG

I used to wonder, how old am I to Daddy? Where does Daddy go, in her mind, when her cock is hardest, when she comes so fast just by pushing her fingers inside of me, at the drive-in, her tongue invading my mouth, other hand squeezing my breast hard? Who is Daddy with? Who am I? If we could see a film of each other' fantasies, would we recognize ourselves?

Daddy said not to worry. She said she would never fuck a little, little girl. When she says this, I always think about the four and five year old girls in the Little Miss beauty pageants. The ones who wear the heavy make-up, curled up hair and pouty lip-glossed lips in fancy gowns. They look like dolls, or tiny glamorous women at first glance. Why does that image always pop to mind when she reassures me: I would never do it with a girl who's *too* little.

When we have a slumber party, it's not about sex. She just wants to paint my toenails and brush my hair and then eat cereal and watch cartoons in the morning. It's just a slumber party. Even though I'm hot and naughty and Daddy still has a boner for me, she won't do anything sexual when I'm wearing my frilly butt jammies and letting her brush my hair.

"It's just sweet Daddy stuff at that point. I won't do it when you're too little." She said. "Don't worry."

Daddy has certain boundaries – everyone does. For some, biological age is the ultimate cut-off. Laws are made for good reason. Some guys need to see ID before the date. For some, an adult face, flirtation and an enticing figure are good enough. He wouldn't want it if she couldn't handle it, right? For the rare fellow, the grown up woman with the shaved armpits, legs and pussy is too much. It's age-play to

© KONINKLIJKE BRILL NV, LEIDEN, 2019 | DOI:10.1163/9789004383562_023

those guys – they want a real woman. Daddy's boundaries are different, but they exist. And they correlate with certain ethical codes, just like everyone else's. Boundaries are movable. But who moves them?

Daddy knows I don't like to feel too young during sex. And in Daddy's mind, she says I'm most often a curious, naughty, very willing teenager. I think of how adult I felt already as a teen. Already this story doesn't match with Daddy's. Perhaps I am fourteen with her, just not the fourteen I actually was. Or is Daddy revealing parts of myself I didn't know, couldn't allow into the narrative of my life, the self that had to be in charge? Why does Daddy prompt so many question marks in my text? Perhaps the boundaries shift depending on who's in control. Sometimes I want to be in control.

I've considered trying to push the boundaries, trying to provoke sex when Daddy doesn't want it – when she sees me as very little. It's a bit twisted, but that's part of our story, right? When I surrender to her, do naughty things that would seem wrong if we said them out loud, that proves I love her. When she sets boundaries, and I get her to move past them, that proves Daddy loves me. It might be something like when she let me drive the truck she's never allowed any other girl to drive. It might be letting me put the frilly apron on her while she makes me waffles in the morning. It might be refusing to go to sleep after the hair brushing and toenail painting unless Daddy kisses me goodnight, real sweet, in a special place. She would shake her head, purse her lips admonishingly at first and say, "Now, that wasn't part of our deal."

I am too little. Then I'd see Daddy's frustration rise as I reach around in my pajamas impatiently, coquettish, innocent eyes demanding. And then, finally, she'd look around, as though for witnesses, take down my pants, pull my hands away and tell me "Shhh." She would soothe me as I hold her head and wriggle and moan and say, "Good Daddy." In the little girl voice, I say, "Yes, you are my good Daddy," when I can tell she's doing it real gentle, just for me, not for herself.

I might convince her to do this, though she thinks me too small, because in her mind, she's just taking care of me. At least it's not fucking; at least she's not hurting me. She's giving me what I wanted, and no one else can do that for me, though it's wrong. She still knows it's wrong. I might convince her to do this, by pouting with my lips wet and parted, with my cheeks slightly flushed by my own hot desire to force a bit of the surrender she gets from me.

It would be my Daddy's flushed cheeks that reward me as I push her away, having had my pleasure. "No more Daddy!" I would admonish sharply, entitled petulance dripping down my thigh, wetting the bed, hot and satisfying. It would be my Daddy's flushed cheeks that reward me as she sits up, sheepishly wipes her chin, tells me to pull up my frilly-butt jammies and turns out my light. She still has her boundaries, though I've bumped them out a bit in a way that shames her. She knows I know that she'll go in the other room and stroke herself to pleasure. She knows I know.

And she adds, with a voice that sounds as though tears are coming, "I love you sweet girl. You go to sleep now."

DOMINATING DADDY

Daddy wants me to dominate her sexually. This feels peculiar to me at times, because my job is to be submissive, but I am starting to learn: my job is to be all things – each on cue. She loves my effort in submission. I have to reach into myself and find the part that wants to please her more than anything else. But it's not enough – I have to play all the roles.

Daddy wants me to dominate her and this will be harder still. I understand what Daddy sees in me. I understand that I have beautiful shiny bossy boots and my tongue is like a riding crop to keep the dumb animals in check. I do not believe in dumb animals; would not want to whip or beat any creature. The thought of it makes me sad, and strangely, lonely.

I know what she sees in me. I am in control of so many things. I am in control of my home and my work and my bank account and my future. It looks like I am in control of my future, though that part is an illusion. I know what she sees in me and she thinks that surely I can give her just a little bit. Surely, I can dip my golden ladle into the glorious well of structure and intentional pain and let her drink. Surely, I can do this.

My Daddy wants me to dominate her and I can barely make love to her. I can't just want to "do it." In a simple way. Sometimes, something in her eyes goes young and scared and I don't want to be the one who pushes through that. Suddenly I feel like a Daddy, like bad Daddy, like my stepfather or one of the men on the news, shown in profile, one of the men on the Internet, shown having fun with a young girl that couldn't be his daughter. Or, is she? I don't want to feel like those men and I tell her, "I can't do it, if I see you get small." And she says, "Maybe we should only do it in the dark."

This solution does not satisfy me the way it satisfies her. Her young part is scared and she wants me to make her like it. My young part is not that way. My young part just wants to be adored, worshipped. My young part just wants to be precious, especially when she's as petulant as she can be.

Sometimes, Daddy is not scared. Daddy knows what she's asking me to do and she understands why she likes it. And yet, I still can't do it – even then. Why can't I do it? Is it because Daddy wants it so much and I don't want to disappoint her by doing it once and then never doing it again? Or do I fear doing it, but not to her satisfaction?

I don't want to hurt Daddy, ever, at all. And yet she wants this from me. I know why she sees it as a gift of love. I know what she sees in me. Sometimes little girls grow into Daddies, or mommies who punish. I would rather stay young forever than to be the kind of Daddy that hurts someone, the kind of Daddy that enjoys causing pain. Sometimes girls grow up into Daddies. My Daddy did. And nothing is sweeter than a Daddy who knows how it feels to be treated real special. That's how she treats me. So, I would be really good at it. My Daddy is certain.

WRATH

My Daddy is afraid of my wrath. I have the ability to stomp my little foot three times when I'm in a rage and a wind gathers around me like a hurricane. I am the eye of the hurricane, unmoving, and my hair comes untied and dances like snakes. My body grows twice my Daddy's size and fire comes off of my tongue when I speak and my eyelids bleed. The wind that gathers around my body is full of dirt and dead leaves and bugs and it carries the scent of rotting flesh. A vortex opens at my feet and it is a black and roiling sea full of anguished faces, parts of sea creatures and if Daddy looks for too long, it's as though he's being beckoned in. A strange rumbling pulls him into the depths of my Mariana's Trench of grief and despair. Suspended above this vortex, I wail and my arm floats up, pointing a finger at Daddy, accusing.

Daddy had no idea I possessed this ability at first. And indeed, neither did I. Before I knew Daddy there was no smelly hurricane, no black pit of sucking sea. I was just as surprised as Daddy when it first happened, and I too felt as though I was being sucked down, never quite descending, but unable to move from my wailing, nonetheless. I longed for Daddy to save me from this evil wind, but when he made no move to help me for fear that he would be destroyed, I began to mistrust Daddy, knew that I would be left alone and writhing in pain. Daddy's heart would pound with mortal fear and he would run away and let me sink to the depths.

Before Daddy, perhaps I had only ever stomped my foot once or twice at a time. And I was a full size woman anyway, not a little girl, not something that needed to grow up out of itself to be heard, so maybe that's what made the difference too. But when Daddy makes me small again – and then angry – oh Lordy, the winds blow!

Maybe it's not fair to say that Daddy makes me small. I play a part in this process. I participate and enjoy it, but then what happens next takes hold of me and shakes and I am too small to fight against it. And Daddy loves this when it's good – when I am an earthquake on a sunny day. Daddy loves the way the feelings overpower me and I am held safe and ecstatic in his arms. I participate by allowing the transformation, but Daddy is in charge.

At least that's how it seemed before the winds and seas whipped up. During the storm we wondered who was in charge. Daddy pointed back at me, accusingly, as if I was doing something to bring on the foul winds, the sucking sea. But I was not doing anything I could discern, other than becoming angry and stomping my pretty little foot. It happens when Daddy's stories don't match up and I become confused. They seem like deceptions and placations and then I do not feel at all precious any more. And the wrath comes on. I accuse Daddy of angering me, of betraying me, of humiliating and disrespecting me. I accuse and accuse and accuse as though the fire in my mouth has its own will. And all the while my mind knows that these are things no one can do to me; I must allow them, arrange them, produce the show and sell the tickets myself. And still my finger points and my eyes bleed. And Daddy can no longer see how wounded I am – only that I am dangerous.

Sometimes Daddy will dive down around my feet when I have only stomped the one time. Daddy makes jokes and tickles my ankles, or he rubs my feet and kisses each of my toes until I calm down. I long to be soothed, to be calmed, to feel loved again. I long for this more than anything. That's why I have a Daddy after all, so that when I fail to love myself, soothe myself, someone is there to do it for me. But I fear Daddy too. Daddy has too much control, even though supposedly I am in charge because I am so precious.

Sometimes Daddy is able to soothe me, by leaping forward around my ankles on that first stomp, the second stomp. And we feel relief and become playful once more. Sometimes, my foot is in the air for the third stomp and Daddy dives to let my foot come down wherever it may rest – on his hand or face or shoulder. I see Daddy wince in pain, but danger has been averted and the pain was worth the outcome. And then after the tickling or the stroking, Daddy kisses my knees and then my thighs. He lays me down, dangerous feet no longer on the floor and Daddy slips down my panties. Though I am petulant, I yield after swatting him once or twice and Daddy smiles, tells me what a good girl I am. I am demanding as Daddy licks between my legs. I hold his head and press my soft flesh forward for his suckling. Then Daddy takes hold of my ankles and pulls them up and back, as though I'm being diapered. He licks the sweet hole that still echoes with the moans of the black sea. And Daddy is once again in control of my seasons, the climate pleasant. As he feels his mastery, his hunger grows and he drinks the beautiful sea that is for Daddy alone. I am both giving and taking as I hold Daddy's head and feel the power of his hunger. He grunts and eats, swallowing all of the anger and ill humor I have. It turns to sweet nectar for him, transformed by Daddy's love and Daddy's strength. I simultaneously fear and am soothed by Daddy's ability to avert my wrath. He transforms my wrath into sweetness, and sometimes this takes great effort, great courage. He swallows it and I am pleased that Daddy seems nourished, strengthened. And then we can both rest.

KNOWLEDGE IS KING

THE MOST POWERFUL POSITION POSSIBLE

When I was twenty-two, I started to attend a peer support group for "women-survivors." That term was loosely defined – pretty much anyone who identified as female and presented an experience of sexual abuse and/or violence could participate. We had a set of guidelines we read, but there was no therapist, no social worker present. We supported each other, according to a basic twelve-step meeting format.

It was important for me to keep the professionals out of it because they'd really been idiots before. When I first told someone about my incest experience and "the authorities" became involved, it was like being on trial. I don't know what my step-father's experience was like exactly, but I know mine. I had difficult conversations with therapists and social workers always ending in questions I couldn't answer about him because I didn't have enough language for the creepy things he did. Those meetings always ended in questions I couldn't answer about my own fetishes and deviant behaviors because they clearly thought I was a pervert and fuck you anyway. Just fuck you. My stepfather was a quick talker with a lot more credibility than me – a pink-haired lesbian-leaning trollop in funny clothes.

In the game of credibility, he won. Look, therapists are great, if they're great for you. So is prayer or any strategy that helps a person come to a fuller life after being hurt, but for me, keeping the "professionals" out of the picture was a big help.

I met some amazing women in those groups – some real wingnuts too. A few things become clear when you get a group of women survivors together – we have things in common. We felt silenced on many of the same issues. We felt shame in many of the same ways. We all had trouble talking to our mothers about the abuse. And without exception, the men who abused us knew that what they were

© KONINKLIJKE BRILL NV, LEIDEN, 2019 | DOI:10.1163/9789004383562_024

doing was wrong – or would've been wrong if only we had not met the requirements for abuse-excuse. If only we had not been dressed that way, looking that way, saying those things. If only we had been their blood relative, or not their blood relative. If only we'd been a different race or a different gender or raised in a different home. Every perpetrator knew what he did was wrong – but something happened to excuse his behavior under *those* circumstances.

One of my support group friends told me that when her brother started raping her, even though she was only seven years old, she felt powerful. She did not understand sex; she was still a small child. Her brother was eighteen. She didn't fully understand about sex, but she knew about power. We all do. As children, we may not be able to assemble all of the information on why the feeling is happening, but we all learn the feeling of being able to control our lives – often by controlling others. That's how we do it in Daddy's house.

My friend said she felt important – that she had information no one else had and that this allowed her to control others' perceptions and therefore their behaviors. Knowledge is power. Most importantly, though he was abusing her, she used sex as a tool to make sure she had a voice. She was not a Kleenex, a disposable plastic zip-loc bag; she was not a bottle in a no-deposit state. She believed she had knowledge and voice; power.

Daddy does not stand for open communication. He must be the one with the most information about what's being said and done. If all communication fails to flow through him, everyone will be in big trouble. BIG TROUBLE. He throws up his hands and says, "I don't need to tell everybody everything! Who's the Daddy here?" He says this jokingly. Only, this is no joke. Every incest survivor I've ever met was told not to tell what was happening to him or her. They were told in one way or another – usually in more ways than one.

The slightest scent of deception, of withholding, makes my stomach turn with fear. Someone is entitled to hurt me soon, and I won't even see it coming. My intuition for deception is like the air bending around the arm that's moving too fast to be seen. The skin anticipates, even before a bloodying contact is made. My intuition about deception is always true, always correct, and I have to be careful because it sometimes causes me to take a speculation too far – make things up that might only exist in the realm of possibility. The Buddha said that worry is like praying for things you don't want to happen. Sometimes, intuition turns into prayer.

My mother always thought that she could stay on top of knowledge. She would get on the phone and gather as many views and opinions as she could about a thing – ask people if they heard what he said, or if they knew what he meant, or what they thought he might mean. She exhausted herself trying to be the king of information, but silly mama. She is just a woman. Not a king. Still, she had more information than I did at times. And she thought it right not to share. I learned this too – with her at least. I longed to share with her, to trust her. But my truths always felt dangerous in her mouth. My words would drop directly from ear into mouth where she would re-shape them for re-issue.

I understood what my friend said about victim-sex making her feel powerful – I could identify with that view right away. Perhaps it's because women are competitors and the doting Daddy is the prize.

Knowledge is currency, and withholding it made me feel rich, despite the impoverished condition of our family dialogue, trust, openness. I wanted a different kind of family and I believed I could grow up and make one. I can invent whatever I lacked as a child. So I planned to create a family where I could have trust, and honesty. I will offer – and receive – good communication. With my new Daddy, things will be different.

But you can't choose an apple and expect it to taste like a peach by just renaming. Even if you did spend your last dollar on it. You can't get the taste of chocolate from a pickle any more than you can get open communication from Daddy. S/he has too much to lose by sharing, by being transparent. Because if s/he descends in rank, and I ascend, there will not be equality: I will win. Everyone knows that. And Daddy's just not going to let that happen.

DADDY SICK

Dear Daddy,

Do you know that I have started having panic attacks?

I thought this was just for fun, something special, an amazing match to enrich my world, not imperil it. But another truth has begun slithering up next to me, sliding quickly into a cupboard, under the bed. Whenever I turn to see it, it's gone. I know something is there and I can feel it slither up my belly, between my breasts and over my shoulder and into the covers again. I am half-waking; I lay stiff, still, terrified.

Daddy, I am short of breath; I am watchful; I feel suspicious of everything. I can hear my high shrill laughter and I am pushing your hands away, looking away from your ever-swollen cock. I can hear my laughter, once lilting, now lunatic. I love you Daddy. I still want to give you everything you want.

Help,
Your Girl

(Psst. Hey. This is a secret – don't tell Daddy.)
I started planning ways to leave him. I was astonished at first that Daddy could be bad for me, bad for my health. How could this be: the painful deceptions, the pointless dominations – they're all for my own good. How could they not be good? I am not well. Daddy is all I can smell. There's no other answer.

I am something gone awry, the head pulled off the centipede, the legs still walking, moving like a mechanical toy. Daddy is still fucking me. I keep giving sex, not admitting that I don't want it. I am still gasping and moaning with pleasure. There is pain but the brain doesn't yet know. Pain is in the room with me. What is in pain? Who is in pain? Is it the chair, or the desk? Is the wallpaper hurt, or the notebook? I am hurt. Everything is closer than I thought. I love Daddy's dominance and encouraged his deceptions. Where do I go now? My mouth forms an O.

Nothing is as interesting, as intimate, as satisfying as being with Daddy. Nothing.

The mind does not hold one's best interest the way the body does. The mind will take an addiction like Daddy and tell you why it's a good idea, why you need it, why you won't be any worse for shooting up some Daddy, why you might miss out on a lot of fun if you don't smoke a big Daddy. The body will throw you down and give you some time to think. The body says it to you, straight up, "Don't make me do this. But know that I will – because I love you."

I've tried to leave Daddy before. I cried for six days and then the mind said, "Well, just look at it this way." The mind said, "Crouch down and get the right angle on this. Really." "Why would you throw that away?" "It's just for fun, for comfort. It's just hot sex. It's just ..."

The mind said, "Re-negotiate your terms. Be a little more generous. Daddy needs some help."

And so I did. I wrote to him about how I could still allow the tear-rusted hinges on my heart, my pussy, my ass and my mouth to open to his vivid penetration "if only ..." and that's how the letter went. If only this, if only that. I proposed generous terms – a treaty that would cede more of my lands, but still ensure me a favored spot at the table next to Daddy. My dress is shabby around the hem. My jewelry is on loan. I will still be sitting next to Daddy for dinner. And of course, Daddy was always only too willing to say, "Yes baby. I love you baby. Yes baby, if that's what you want." Because that's Daddy's job. The compromise was all mine.

As soon as I had written this letter, I put my hand between my legs to feel my own slickness, the hunger that prompted the mind to write, the hand pushed into service on the page, pushed into service in the pulsing folds of my pussy as I came once, then twice, then four times that night – each fantasy of Daddy becoming more and more twisted – the love and the revenge, the love and the recognition, the love and the validation. You make me do things I can't console, Daddy. I will make you suffer too. The body comes easily to orgasm for Daddy, whether or not he's in the room. The body also sends painful alerts.

The letter betrayed me. The part of me that wants to be cared for betrayed the part that wants truth. I fell into a deep fever with chills. Fever and chills, interrupted only by my hand reaching between my legs to come again and again. Maybe if I just hurt Daddy a little for his wrongdoings. Maybe if I just let Daddy hurt me a little. I will feel loved. The fantasies raged as I rubbed my engorged, slick, sore pussy. The fever raged and I lost track of myself, almost as though Daddy was in the room with me, telling me the stories that soothe, the stories that strangle.

I could hear the change in my own voice. Shrill hysterical laughter – sometimes a maniacal guffaw – too much laughter – no fun to make or hear. The body has given me fevers. The body has given me pains. The body grew me a huge tumor in my uterus and the psychic said, "That part of the body is about a lover's betrayal. That part of the body is about your betrayal of yourself." My uterus started armoring itself with muscle and I bled and bled. Big and fast – that's how my tumor came when Daddy left me – he saw me planning to leave and he left me first. I held the tumor like a baby, breasts full and aching. I held it like a lover while Daddy was away at night. By day, I was courting Truth with an open palm and tear-stained cheeks.

I let a doctor take it. Not a Daddy-doctor, as many are, I chose a surgeon who does not collect women's uteruses as prizes and when she said it needed to go, I agreed. Six hundred thousand American women per year lose a uterus. Lose it on the bus, in a parking lot, leave it at your boyfriend's house and never go back for embarrassment sake. Those organs don't grow back. Six hundred thousand more American women each year lose a uterus. I was not alone. Me: in a silent crowd of women who have betrayed themselves for "love," many women never articulate the word "Daddy" in their own bedrooms, but they bear the scars nonetheless. They grow around the missing parts.

In her essay "Working Class Incest Survivor Femme," Tara Hardy believes she is hard-wired to want Daddy (Hardy, 2009, p. 160). "We were programmed for it. My father saw to it, crossed and soldered my wires early, so on a lot of days there is no difference. Desire and shame run the same circuit ... Those who know shame as it lives with want will seek each other like water seeks to level. There is a sameness, while there is also containment by the opposite, the other. Water to bank, femme to daddy."

My body has something to say about it. It says "yes please, more." It says "harder, bigger, longer." It says "take it, take it, take it." Sometimes I am giving when Daddy takes; sometimes I am demanding. The body has something to say. It says lose blood. It says fall down. It says burn, burn, burn.

It's not that all women who've had hysterectomies have Daddy issues. It's that all women have Daddy issues – the patriarchy is all around us, in our lungs, lining our mucous membranes and everything looks so normal. Some of us name these issues. Some of us get sick.

Some of us go to the mall or eat lo-cal linguine and call it just another day. Some of us get wet between the legs and call it a blessing that Daddy will always take care of us. Some of us don't know. Not yet.

Tara Hardy says, "This is my normal. What is freakish and horrible made me. I formed around it. And I am nonetheless extraordinary. I wouldn't be the same without it. But I am supposed to be polite, not to reference it but obscurely." (For Tara and me, this simply will not do. I will take a role to its natural end, affix the wallpaper in every room to see the full pattern, feel the brocade under my fingertips at the light switch. I will live in that house and learn.

We have all been touched by Daddy. Our bodies know.

CHAPTER 25

DON'T MAKE ME LEAVE YOU

TEXT-FREE LOVER

I decided not to sleep with Daddy anymore, and I took a new lover – not a Daddy, a lover. We are both grown-ups and that's how it should be. And still, I miss Daddy's special ways and I wonder what would happen if my lover and I put on the daddy-story. That's how a lot of couples do it, right? They put on one story and then another during sex, but they stay themselves. It's fun. That's what they claim. My new lover is open to trying new things, and she's got a pervy streak, so why not?

I said to my lover, "Why don't you try this: tell me what you want to do to me in bed and then, don't wait for me to respond, just do that thing. And while you're doing it, do it zestfully, and tell me what a good girl I am. Say: 'ooh, you're such a good girl,' and 'what a good girl.'" I modeled these phrases for her, in case it was difficult to tell what I was getting at.

My lover shrugged and said, "Okay, I'll try that." And she did, but it rang hollow. And I forgot to tell her about the part afterward where she needs to hold me tight and stroke my hair and make contented noises. The part where she needs to seem deeply fulfilled. Instead, afterward, she just said, "How was that? Did it get you off?"

"You know, getting off is hardly the point," I said to her, irritated. Why was she talking to me? Why was she out of character? No, this wasn't going to work at all. And so I said, "Yeah, well, no. Never do that again." And she shrugged and said, "Okay."

It was like the time when she became fascinated with my multilingual abilities. She asked me to speak German to her in bed – just say everything in German that I would normally be saying in English. Then, the next night, she said, "Now do it in French. Say everything to me in French while we're doing it, okay?" I did and afterward, she propped herself on one elbow in bed to make comparisons. She said,

© KONINKLIJKE BRILL NV, LEIDEN, 2019 | DOI:10.1163/9789004383562_025

"I liked the German, but the French didn't do a thing for me." She scrunched up her face and shook her head. "No, I definitely didn't like the French. Don't do that one anymore, but do the German any time you want." She never asked for multi-lingual sex again and it just seemed silly to me, so "anytime I want" was never.

I mean, what was the point in that? I couldn't tell. And she didn't seem to be passionately involved with the German anyway. It was a lark. Nothing was different in the way she fucked me. Everything was the same. When she likes something, she just grunts and likes the sensation of it. There doesn't seem to be any compelling sub-text, hypertext. She's a text-free lover.

Daddy is all about the story and I miss that sometimes. I don't miss it all the time. Sometimes I got lost in the story and my head would spin and I'd forget who I was, my age, my name. Daddy said I was the little girl at the birthday party. Daddy said she was taking me to the world's fair and I was wearing knee socks and black patent leather shoes and it was 1904. Daddy said she'd push me on the swing set and I always pictured 1972 in my own backyard – the swing set under the fig tree where I'd swing and swing and eat figs until I was stuffed full. Sometimes I got lost in Daddy's stories.

Like the time when Daddy and I were in Amsterdam and all in one day we visited the red light district and the prostitution museum and the sex museum. We had a drink at the bar called Cock Ring and I took a photo of Daddy standing outside with her arms folded across her chest, looking very smug indeed. And then, that night, as she held me down and fucked me, that night as she clapped her hand across my mouth to keep me from making any noise while she fucked me, she told me a story so twisted I cannot even recall it to relay it. It was a story so woven into the ropes that have bound bodies like mine through the ages, so tanned like the leather of whips and masks and harnesses, I couldn't contain it. Daddy gathered that fucking story – the *fucking* story – from every corner of our historical memories and my experience became fueled by the pictures at the sex museum. I couldn't contain it. All of those pictures – ranging from naked bodies, smiling and coupling to bodies being beaten and racked, to open mouths drinking piss and licking dirty assholes and being impaled by horse penises and bodies and bodies and bodies with the faces not showing. She fucked me and I was lost and becoming nauseated by the story she was telling of how she possessed me, how I belonged to her and how she would do as she pleased with me until the day she died and no one else would ever have me, ever. I was lost in the story – and not in a good way – bound by her strong hands as Daddy poured out the centuries of domination we had witnessed into my little body, my little body becoming smaller and smaller with each thrust as the many Daddies of the ages fell into me and into me and into me.

Sometimes the story is not a good thing. I should feel safe in Daddy's hands – that's what I count on – but not that night. I was the immigrant in the window box selling my sexual services to pay my way. I was the slave in the back room, shackled to the bed. I was the woman in the picture, paid too little to do things in front of a camera that would leave me diseased and barren. These were not stories we invented for our entertainment; they come from real life, current life. This is not 1904. This is not the world's fair. There is no birthday cake being served. And she was every Daddy who had ever owned a girl, ruled a land, commanded forces, marshaled resources. She owned the land of my body and the mind of my patria. She was all of the Daddies and I felt so ill, I came close to vomiting. If she hadn't held me so firmly and fucked me so hard, I might've rolled over to vomit off the side of the bed. But I didn't. Like all fucking, eventually she was done and I could love her once more. Usually Daddy and I are enjoying ourselves in the story, somehow, some way, our stories intersect so that she wants to take exactly what I long to give. Not that night; the story became bigger than I could handle. And I had already renounced the voice that could change the course of the action.

Even Daddy has to come up for air though, pause for a meal, go have a piss. Eventually, she was done and I could love her once more. I always loved her of course – so fiercely that I became a container for her madness – the swollen, throbbing madness of Daddy.

And mostly, that's what I remember: how much I loved my Daddy. I miss the way she kissed me goodnight, like she meant it. Good night. I miss the way she loved my surrender. The way she could tell a story like she really meant it. Because she did.

Dear Daddy,

This is no way to live. For your sake, I want to tell your secrets and show you how wounded you are by your own silence. I want to tell your secrets – even the ones in plain view – how you make me precious by filling the mouths of those who are different with dirt, kicking until blood and filth fill their lungs. You take sadistic pleasure in hurting anything that is not strong, not white, not fierce, not local, not manly. I am not manly. You make me precious by diminishing others, then hiding the ugliness from my vision.

Our fates are bound. Daddy, you are bigger than I can hold in my arms, in my mouth, bigger than any house can contain. We have formed around each other and you have spent so much time making me precious, molding my body around your will. You have taken so much time protecting me, forsaking the others. We both forsook the other girls. To find our own home, we turned away from their blue bodies in the alleyways; poor strays. There are so few words between us; words are leaving – a few more each day. Some words are taboo and I hold them in my mouth so secretive, my tongue is black with ink. They poison and I am restless. For fear of others seeing my blackened mouth, I only open it for you.

I want to tell your secrets so that you can be free of carrying them, you are like a beast harnessed to a carriage carrying carnage. I want to kiss your mouth Daddy and it is not free for me to kiss. Drop the bit, let your tongue wag – your jaws go slack. Drop the club, Daddy. Let your jaw go slack.

You control the boys by making men of them too soon, Daddy. I will say it. They have bottled their demons waiting to explode in whichever direction you hurl them. You have made grenades of my sons. Ruthless, rustic grenades. They don't know what they've become and so they play with fire for fun. They have given up on love. I could not love them and love you too. So I chose you. I chose you. My father never knew me.

You know me. And you know I know of reciprocity. Though we do not speak of it, I know best what you need. I came to this silent house because I loved you. You needed to rest in my soft stillness. I know best what you need, even still. What you need is to grow up – up toward sunlight, turn your face toward the light, up, Daddy, grow up. Take this last bit of guidance from me Daddy. Grow up.

I know of reciprocity and our endless taking and giving should make some kind of expansion in us, but it doesn't. It isn't. How can we give away the big house and free the captors with the captives? How can we cut collusion from our names and make humans of these boys once more? I want to be free, Daddy. Not just from your bind, but from my own. I want to be free from my own actions that cause such pain. Our fates are bound and I am still your girl. Free you with me.

I love you,
Your Girl

CHAPTER 26

POSSIBILITY

INCANTATION

I can look at my relationship with Daddy in so many ways. I can see it differently. That will help.

Our love is an incantation. Words and rituals create reality; cause healing, open our hearts to greater possibilities. This is not play – it's not just some kinky way to get off. I get sex just fine. I don't need to call someone Daddy to have good sex. It can happen through touch, through sensuality, through a slow breathing focus or a laughing urgency.

With Daddy, the sex is not really about the sex, though the turn-on and ecstasy are profound. With Daddy, it's about the ability to open, to nurture, and to love. It's about strength and vulnerability, about the union of opposites, the balance of male and female energy in the cosmos; it's about divine love. We practice through the ritual of role because so much of culture tries to make us forget that we are already loved – by the big love, the enduring cosmos, the god that is not Daddy.

We are each trying to remember that we are still now and always have been loved by the only love that can love. There is only one love. We practice channeling it and receiving it in our precious little animal bodies, in the world around us. We are already loved by the only love that can love.

When I call her Daddy, we are not playing a game. I am looking for truth and beauty and balance in the universe. It's already there, but I've lost it so I look for it in Daddy's eyes, Daddy's love. The word "Daddy" is an incantation. The balance of masculine and feminine energy in the cosmos does not have anything to do with whether one is of male or female sex. The biology is incidental; we are always, already both genders, searching to find the union of our opposites, searching for nurturing, for an ability to nurture. We give birth to each other again and again, an undulation of infant and parent, growing up and dying away.

But Daddy and I are operating on a flawed principal, though we're striving, always striving. We cannot find the divine in each other – only in ourselves. That's the paradox – we find the god in ourselves, then share it.

Some people don't seem to understand this. They think it's a game, just something kinky to get off. They use the word Daddy as a joke. They say, "Who's your Daddy? Who's your Daddy?" And they think they are joking. They are fools not to hear what they're asking, not to answer their own questions. When I call my lover Daddy, and she calls me sweet girl, some people think it's grotesque, a twist in the garden hose caused by a rough tug early in life, caused by a jagged terrain over which the hose has been pulled. They don't see their own rough terrain and the ways they have made a pact with their culture never to see. They have agreed to live in the false security of gender roles and marriage agreements and misogyny and the practice of male dominion over female. They have agreed without agreeing that boys will be boys and girls will be girls, and that a wedding is a transfer of goods. Daddy gives away his possession, smiling. Some people decide never to look closely.

At least I know how to unkink my garden hose, let the energy flow. At least I can see the rough terrain I travel and I have respect for flow. How could they know until they know? When I call her Daddy and she accepts my sweet yielding, when I become a vessel and allow her to fill me, when she honors my fullness and allows herself to be nourished by me, the world is repaired. When we enter into mutuality – a creation of energy, a giving and taking and giving and taking and giving and taking – never out of balance, the world is healed and we right along with it. This is not a game. I don't need to play games to get off, have an orgasm, make lovin' fun. I am not interested in kinky relationships where people negotiate each activity and memorize each other's danger zones and safe words. I am not a player at lovemaking. Love is my serious occupation. The world is dangerous and there are no real exits. I have to learn to give and accept real love, learn to make my own safety, learn to trust that all is well. Truly, all is well. Our love is an incantation.

This is how I feel and what I believe. Words and rituals create energy. Energy creates reality. Believe me, I am aware of the problems here. How else do we become aware of problems but by opening our eyes to see them in our behavior, opening our ears to hear them in our speech. I am aware of what needs to be healed exactly because I have not made a pact to honor the false security of standard relationships. My ears are open and I can hear what I'm saying, what's being said to me. "Come here sweet girl, Daddy loves you." "That's good, put my cock in your mouth." "You're all mine, sweet girl." "Daddy needs to fuck you. You're the best girl."

I know what I'm saying. "I want to make you happy Daddy." "Yes Daddy, fill me up." "You are my good Daddy. I will let you." "Please don't hurt me too much Daddy." My ears are open and I can hear the problems here.

When it is time for me to mother, there is no language, just expectation. And I fulfill it. When it is time for me to mother, there is nothing but a mute and need-filled grasping at my bodice, or a pulling under the covers as we get in position to do what we do. The boy is mute and the mother continues to allow this. The boy is mute and at times, the mother approves of this. She does not know the language either and sometimes, she thinks, who needs language for mother love? We've done without it for millennia already.

Some days, I am illuminated – the light shines through every poorly closed seam. Some days I am ill-contained and all I can do is remind myself: I am now and always have been loved, by the only love that can love.

DOLLHOUSE

I still love Daddy's rescues, but I have grown weary of feeling imperiled. Surely we both want to grow up – metaphorically ascend – become more than we are. I ask Daddy to comfort me so that I can relax enough to grow. And yet, any comfort he gives me stifles. I am mistaken about which balm will soothe, but still Daddy rubs and rubs. I become logy and dull.

Daddy, in his turn, asks me to show him enough sweetness to prompt the loving, smiling heart he hides – he asks me to crack his stoic mask. At first I crack it and we laugh and make a game. Daddy seems so happy when I take pleasure in his indulgence. We play pony and I ride him and he trots around the room, my head back laughing, my arms flailing. Daddy seems so happy when my tears crack his stoic mask, but it is not breaking. We both know that the mask is not breaking and Daddy is asking for more and more force. I am exhausting myself, becoming fearful that I will put out his eye when the mask breaks, that I may run my sparkle spurs through Daddy's temple and put out his lights. Rather than liberating him, I could saddle my blood-lust, ride and ride, slip Daddy's spinal cord through his wound and use it as a whip.

We are each looking to grow up, past the petty competitions of patriarchy, of dominator culture. There's something beyond the wall, if only we could get high enough to see it. Daddy likes to corrupt me by giving me puffs from his pipe. He smokes and chuckles, bends my head forward to take the sweet smoke from Daddy's lips. We get a little high and I reach for the wall. Then we just fall down laughing in the cuddle puddle of our love.

We fear the change so much that we resist the help we seek. I wanted to move into the dollhouse because everything is so perfect there and it seemed that if only I could touch the perfect, breathe the perfect, sip the perfect from my morning teacup, I could finally attend to what I've been neglecting. I could grow up. In the dollhouse, surely I could stop searching. The bed is made with the tiniest pink coverlet and there are matching curtains – pink with yellow flowers – on our bedroom window. I wanted to move into the dollhouse where our shiny plastic faces are always smiling, and the table is always set for dinner and there's never water on the bathroom floor. Daddy is always clean and he takes care of me. Daddy never smells like anything and his shirt is always pressed and he punishes me when I am bad. He always makes me know what I've done wrong – and right.

I wanted to move into the dollhouse until I realized that our bed was so hard, and I don't want plastic turkey for dinner. Everything is so small, so small and I am always seeking. There are no pans in these cupboards. The hose is coiled so tightly against the side of the house, nothing can get water. Our lives are so small and I just wanted to grow up. I want Daddy to see how sad his little plastic face looks here in our dollhouse life. I know Daddy treats me better than I've ever been treated before. The rules are so clear. Yes, I am certain that I want to grow up – even if it means I have to force my little plastic legs to walk away from the turkey and the pink coverlet, and the forever green-with-no-water yard and the big hand that moves us, moves us.

"This is what Daddies do." "This is what girls do," says the hand. It tells us and we fly into motion without even thinking, without even knowing what we want for our own little plastic lives. Oh Daddy! Oh Daddy-boy, do you want to grow up too? My Daddy-man, my Daddy-

President, my Patria. Do you want to grow up – see what could be if we came up above our small selves? Who bought the pretty red plastic corvette convertible that the hand delivered today? Who pays for the electricity that keeps the sun shining here, day after day after day and sometimes through the night?

I know you want to grow up Daddy and I know how you fear it. I can see it on your little plastic face. I do too, even though you are a living, breathing, soothing promise. You are the promise that I can be taken care of and made special and thought pretty for the rest of my days. How have I come to leave that? How have you loved me so much, despite your training to be rough and tough and never falter? You are my living promise. And I have promised to make your dinner and give you respite. We have touched the promise and we are still turning away; there is no room for resting in this hard little bed we've made.

What if I go first? Will that help? What if the next time you tread across our bumpy green grass and open our little plastic door, I am gone? What if I am no longer in the dollhouse and you search and search, and I'm nowhere on our whole plastic block? What if there is no other Daddy tucking me in, or buying me popcorn at the movie. What if I never live in a dollhouse again and I get bigger, bigger than our little hard plastic world? Will you wonder where I've gone and try to find me? Will you try to come with me? Even as the girls begin to line up around the block for a ride in your red Corvette?

PART 3

TRANSFORMATION

CHAPTER 27

THE TURNING

THE COLLAPSE OF THE BIG BUILDINGS

High romantic drama: I walked out on her in a restaurant – left her sitting there with lasagna on her fork. She said something cruel and I began to cry. I tried to hold it together in front of the server, but then I thought, why not just go? I didn't want to be there, didn't want to ride home with her in the car. I had become someone I didn't want to be in our home: was it going to happen publicly too? Just go.

Rather than come right out and tell me she didn't want to be involved with me anymore, she became cruel in pedestrian ways, less enthusiastic about spending time with me. Her narrative about my harpy ways won her over. She was respectable and self-sufficient and didn't deserve the likes of me. She deserved to be happy, that's what the new girl said to her over tea on the cozy sofa in the living room of the firehouse after dinner. They spent time together at work and in that profession, co-workers never rat to your wife when visitors come to call.

"I know you want to uphold your commitments," said the new girl. "And that's really honorable of you." She nodded with understanding in her eyes, "But you deserve to be happy." She nodded some more, her eyes moist and sparkling with understanding. "Take care of yourself."

Daddy couldn't tell me she didn't need me around until a commitment was cemented with the new girl. That would be awful – and unwise. She couldn't tell herself that she needed the adoration of lovers like a transfusion to her own emotional hemorrhaging. She couldn't say the new girl was more suitable. She fit like the dream-suit of devotion and adoration. And she always brought dinner – and dessert. The guys at work all thought she was hot, and cute, and girlish – without being too full of herself about it. Oh yeah, that's the way. She couldn't tell me that she wanted someone more malleable than me, more durable, less questioning. I was the suit she needed to grow into and how long can one cuff ones pant legs without feeling inadequate? She deserved comfort.

I didn't know it at the time, but we were about to crash and burn. She was on her way to work at Fire Station Five. It was a sunny summer day along the front range of the Rocky Mountains. The light was just teasing the window blinds, thick velvet curtain swags trying to seduce a few more moments of darkness. At seven a.m. I sat on the sofa blinking as she made coffee. I would drop her off for her twenty-four shift and then take the car in for brake repair. She rose from bed with purpose, as usual, turned on the *Today Show*, put on the coffee and started rummaging in the refrigerator, assembling food for lunch. She liked to keep her meals in order and was already chatting absently with me about what the firehouse team might make for dinner, when the first plane hit the first tower.

"Was that real?" I said, mouth agape, not sure I was focused on a news story or a movie trailer. Everything on television seemed the same to me. I wasn't sure, but all the information was there. The faces of surprise told that the story was not fiction.

She was asking me what. And I sat staring.

"What?" and prompted by my lack of response, came into the living room and looked angrily at the television. "What the fuck!" she said as the smoke billowed from the building's wound. The news people speculated and reassured. And then the second plane hit. We were watching in real time and I began to cry with the weight of the suffering, with a sorrow about what might come next. We just watched and soon, the buildings were collapsing.

Immediately, my mind moved toward the revenge my nation would likely enact against someone. But whom? I could not trust my patria any more. I had begun to suspect it was up to no good because of its cruelty and lack of enthusiasm for me, my peers in the nursing homes, in the hospitals, the segregated schools, the overflowing landfills. I had begun to suspect that my patria might start looking for something else to do with its time. All of the information was there. And now this. No details. Just images. I called my mother. "Put on the TV. Just watch."

Daddy is a rescuer. She wanted to get to work for a different support than I could offer. After the buildings fell she said, "The firefighters would be all in by now."

Firefighters joke about their own sanity. They say, "I run into burning buildings for a living." She said this to me once in seriousness when I called her a coward because of some half-truth about a recent intimate encounter. Her chest puffed, "I'm no coward. I run into burning buildings for a living." I had simply stared at her, one hand on hip.

"Overcompensation." I countered.

For most urban firefighters, the calls are mostly medical. Some require only community management skills. Burning buildings are the exception, but the possibility is real. I joked, because emotional pain often requires joking, that she was a rescuer – didn't know how to commit to the kind of relationship she so clearly craved. She used her skills to get in, save the day, and get back out again. Standing on the sidewalk, breathing hard from the exertion of causing another woman to swoon, she didn't know what to do next. So the swooning women sometimes piled up. She was happy for this proof of her prowess. But the life of the rescuer is devoid of follow-through. I opined later that she had to dump me for a more compelling damsel in distress. That's part of the job description.

The first plane was just stunning. The second plane made clear what none had hoped. This was someone's plan. And then the buildings fell. Few things were clear. We drove to the fire station without speaking to one another, the radio turned on the whole way. Her co-workers looked somber, familial, as they welcomed her into the firehouse. She kissed me goodbye with a look of fear I couldn't reach to comfort. The men sat together, in front of the television, my Daddy included. They had entered a mythic trial and I was an outsider. Shields and arrows poised, they sat helplessly around the television, waiting for information.

I could do nothing, so I drove on to the brake repair shop where I stood, watching the collapse again and again on the news. A woman said to the man behind the counter, "Well aren't you glad we didn't end up with that Al Gore now!" He nodded slowly and his lips stiffened.

I didn't ask about her reasoning because another man, white, about fifty, said, "Yeah, Bush is going to take care of this. He's not letting anyone get away with this shit. I liked Gore, but he'd have been a pantywaist right now."

The woman nodded and said, "Yes, our President's going to take care of us."

I wept silently with strangers in the brake shop, our white SUV up on the lift, abandoned. Workers and patrons alike stared at the television. I watched, as we became the evil we claim to deplore.

"Sorry, we'll be running a little late today," the man behind the counter, said to me. "But the boss just called and we're getting in some American flag stickers this afternoon, so everyone will have one of those, free of charge." I was stunned. "Can I give you a lift somewhere?"

"Sure," I managed. "And I don't need a flag. Just the car would be great. When you can." I added, wiping my eyes. He nodded. Tears and anger, countrymen still. We treated each other gently.

I could feel them cranking back the catapults on either side of me: Fort Carson to the south, the Air Force Academy to the north. So much male energy in America, bottled up for just such a purpose, under pressure, our adolescent weapons walk the shopping malls, stand in silent, stoic groups around the convenience stores, alone at computers, play stations killing and killing and watching fucking and killing and thinking about fucking, killing, fucking killing. Disconnected, each loaded into his own cannon, waiting to release, waiting to explode into the one emotion available to young men: rage.

I feared loss. Of what, I could not have said, but as the New York City Fire Department became a recurring focal point in the television stories, I started to feel anxiety. I could lose my Daddy. She was my partner, my friend, and my spouse. I had not yet allowed myself to feel what her loss would mean to me and then there it was. She was unbuttoning the loose fit of our relationship and I knew what I was allowed to fear: the job. There was so much more.

Each of the three days she worked that week, I felt almost angry. "You are not allowed to die at work, do you hear me?" This made no sense, but I said it. "I will be so mad at you if you don't stay safe."

Years later, she told me a story about her new partner, her new wife, the new girl in her life. And how she watched that woman collapse in grief one night when her daughter went missing and abduction was feared. When the daughter returned, after a mere adolescent lark, Daddy was angry with the child beyond belief. She had seen her girl-wife fall apart and she had felt the depth of her dependence. I listened with compassion, remembering my moment of collapse some years earlier, the beginning of the end of my belief that another human being can take care of me in the world. The slow, bright dawning of the understanding that cruel circumstances as well as cruel choices can cause the edifices of one's imagined stability to fall.

No matter how good a couple looks in a photograph, no matter how charming the family seems, we are just human. We are just human and we will preserve ourselves as we think best. We will sacrifice each other and the things we have built will come tumbling down around us, sometimes taking the janitors and secretaries and artwork and fancy machines with them.

This is the moment of opportunity, if we can rise to meet it. Just after terrorism was blamed for the airplane bombs, I prayed our nation would look to mending global policies and embracing peace. But no, we are too slow.

I was slow to forgive when Daddy broke our union, by phone three weeks after the buildings collapsed. On our anniversary, she told me she was seeing the girl whom she'd lied about seeing. I sent verbal firebombs into the home from which she exiled me. I surprised us both with my rage. The narrowness of my role with Daddy had put me under pressure too. I became a firebomb with a specific target. I had not yet, in the whole course of my life, let myself know that I was capable of rage.

And somehow she liked it. Like when I called her Daddy for the first time, and she told me all of the ways she owned me, my body, my future, my soul; she liked it. I was reaching to give her something I had never given this time too: my rage. If she couldn't have both the new girl and me, she'd take my rage and carry it in her pocket like a stone always ready to warm her hands. She once told me, when I had reached a point of calming down, letting my life move on, "I actually prefer it when you're angry. At least then I know you're engaged. I know you still love me."

Selfish need. We are just human, after all. And we are learners. After September 11th 2001, the psychics and seers, astrologers and clairvoyants were making meaning along with everyone else. My Daddy loved the guidance of seers, me included.

"We're all psychic," I'd say, shaking my head at her seeking. Though at times, I was pleased that she used me as an oracle.

"How hard is it to see the future?" I sometimes asked her. "You just change the channel, tune into a different frequency and you can know things. You might not get the clear picture we've come to expect with television, but you get a picture!"

"Baby, I don't see anything," she'd say. "But that's why I have you." She'd smile and hug me.

"The great shift is coming," said the psychic. "Some Americans are using these upheavals to move toward the light, some are digging their heels into the lives they think they want – the lives that make them feel safe."

I was throwing open the shutters on all of Daddy's declarations. I was growing a tumor of discontent and would not be soothed. It's no wonder she had to leave me. I was airing the house of her utterances. I was making phone calls to all the prophets and singing from the rooftop. Everything became clear, but I couldn't believe it. I would rend our house to free us. I became a hydra screaming for nourishment I couldn't name. I tore the house apart looking, and she couldn't give it to me, so I gave her rage.

She left me for a littler girl. And at first, I didn't recognize the girl as sibling, thought she came from another family whose traits did not resemble mine. She was not quick-witted and grand and yet she was my own kin, my own blood. She was younger, sure, and cuter and smaller and all things desirable. And in that youth, she did not even name her girlishness, didn't call my Daddy, Daddy. We were sisters and she couldn't even pronounce the word: Daddy. She knew she was baby, sweetheart, gorgeous, but she just looked at our Daddy with her little sparkle-eyes, wordless. She thought she was a grown up and I scoffed when my Daddy said, "We don't use words like that. I've outgrown the whole Daddy-thing."

"You fool," I told her. "You've moved into the dollhouse and won't even talk about it!" I paused for a moment; couldn't stand her self-imposed ignorance. "You do know that, right? You've chosen a little girl who doesn't even know what roles you're playing out with her! But you and I know what you think of her big-eyed innocence, her shaved pussy and drive to please. You've moved into the doll house and you know it!" I shrieked.

"Yes, I know that." She said it quietly, shame in her voice. We didn't speak again for weeks.

A few months after they moved in together, my Daddy called me to tell me she knew that this was not her real life. She had to find out for sure by getting everything she ever thought she wanted and still being unfulfilled. She said that my vision and love and compassion that transcend petty affections and appearances – these were her aspiration. They moved in together when Daddy broke her leg. It was the day I told her I had started having sex with a new lover. She said she couldn't believe it. She didn't think I'd do such a thing. Then she went out to the street, fell down and broke her leg. Of course she had to let the new girl take care of her. There was no other way.

"It doesn't matter when one chooses to leave the illusion," said the psychic. "We're all on our way toward the light; it's just a matter of time. A few years difference, later, won't seem like the huge amount of time it seems now." She used an analogy that lingered in my mind, my dreams.

"Think of revelers leaving a stadium during a game. Some of us will leave the stadium first. We will seem to be alone – odd, because the game is still happening, still fun. Many will leave together at the end; there will be a bottleneck and people will be fearful. Perhaps some of those who departed early will still be around to help with traffic. There will be some who linger long, reminisce about the game, pretend the game is still happening."

After my Daddy leaves me, I am disoriented and I fall a long way from the stadium balcony onto the cement of the outer arena. No one saw her push me and I am not prone to dizzy spells. I am disoriented. Hot-dog and beer vendors stare at me as I lift one arm and then the other from the trench my body dug in concrete. They snicker like the roadrunner watching my coyote head puff again after being squashed flat by my own steamroller. It's not supposed to happen like this.

The girl is supposed to leave home and always send gifts on Father's Day, write fond cards and visit her Daddy occasionally. It's not supposed to happen like this, but in an incest family it always does. Growing up breaks the pact, frees the girl. But freedom and destitution are the same for the trained parrot who's grown accustomed to the leg band and food bowl. It's not supposed to happen like this.

I shake off the fall and feel elated with the elasticity of my body. My body walks, mind floating down like a leaf to join my heavy body. I am out in the parking lot before the mind can choose which direction to walk. There might've been a free seat next to some nice fella in the stadium. The game still moves in full force. I could've looked for a free seat, and as the headache set in, I almost wish I had, but that is not the direction in which I was turned.

I feel alone in the parking lot full of cars. Everything scares me and I slowly realize that I want to be alone despite the way everything around me seems built for tandem use. There are a few individuals wandering the parking lot, looking for the exit. One of these seems angry that she can't find the way out. She is very handsome. She is tall and, though somewhat aggressive, the bulge in her pants entices me. I know how to climb that tree, I think as I catch her eye and wink.

In a moment, she is wrapped around me, her hands groping my breasts, squeezing my ass; she is sucking my neck and nearly lifting me off the ground as she grinds her raging pelvis against me. I feel confused at first, but happy. Was this a new Daddy? Outside of the stadium? Wasn't I looking for a way out?

For a moment, we both forget the exit and climb into the back of a nearby pick-up truck. She strips me naked, leaving her clothes on. She licks the sweat from every part of me, savaging me in the sunshine. Vitamin D is soaking into my skin as she finds my persistently moist places and applies herself like a balm. I salivate as she unbuckles her belt, pulls her cock free of her jeans. But then she re-fastens the belt just below her dick so that not even her ass is exposed as she pushes my legs open and fucks and fucks, pouring sweat into her own clothes, keeping it for herself.

We are having our own tailgate party in the back of a big blue Ford pick-up. Standard size. She is not my Daddy. Definitely not, but she fucks me just as gorgeous. I marvel at this at first – that the difference between a Daddy and a lover is what I give back, not what she gives me. She doesn't allow me to soothe her. She doesn't fully let me please her – holds my wrists, fucks me hard and I go to my contentment. She has fun; she enjoys this. But she is not my Daddy.

Stunned and soothed, I put on my clothes, leave her behind, and continue to look for the exit. I run into her again. We are both circling the parking lot. We have crazy-great sex in five more truck beds as the game rages inside. The last two times, her shirt is off, jeans still on, but the belt buckle is wounding me so she discards it; leaves her ass bare. As soon as sunlight hits it, she is fueled. Her ass is a full solar array and I am amazed by her athleticism. I scream and claw her back in my ecstasy as the crowd cheers. In the last pick-up truck, we collapse into sleep and I realize I am starting to love her. She is so openly wounded; she is searching and howling her pain at being lost. I fear her wolfishness, but I am beginning to love her. She is not a Daddy. I don't know what to make of this and curiosity causes me to linger, watch her. I am amazed that the game is still going on when we wake with dew on our clothes and fairy dust in our eyes. At least I'm out of the stadium, I think, as I watch her pick the lock on a nearby recreational vehicle and start to make coffee with the supplies she finds.

A NOTE TO MY PREVIOUS DADDY

Hey There,

Something's been on my mind. Maybe now that we're just friends – just careful, kind acquaintances with an intimate history – maybe I can mention this to you ...

You know how hard your girl is working to make you live up to all of those promises you made to her? You know how she keeps track of what you've said you'll do to make her feel safe? You know. Like, how she doesn't like you talking to me, writing to me, how you're forbidden to see me?

You've got a very smart girl there; let me tell you. She chose you for a reason and you can really help her out, if you want.

She's waiting for you to fail her so she can live her life, bust the chrysalis, and emerge from the muck of hoping for safety through

203

another's obedience. She's waiting for you to do as you promised, without words, without contracts, without witnesses. You promised, when you first began together, that you would do it, like you did it to me. That's why she still tries so hard for safety, struggles for it. She's in a bind. You made a promise. You just didn't know what it was.

She saw how you did it to me and she wanted some too. She saw and she coveted, and then she angled to become your girl. She won the prize and now she waits. She knew she wanted all of it – not just the gifts, the adoration, the pretty-making, and the hot sex – all of it. She knows she wants it – not with the part of her that thinks, the part that talks. Other aspects of her are aware. She knows you are capable of throwing the match into the crucible that will burn away that which she cannot discard of her own volition.

You've got a smart girl there. And she's waiting for your help.

Love,
Me

CHAPTER 28

DADDY'S VESSEL

Daddy moved into the dollhouse with the new girl. We met just once more, in Hawaii. It was a home we had never shared, though shortly, the volcanic island would become my home alone.

I wasn't thinking of meeting up with Daddy on that trip to the island at all. Indeed, it seemed that she had followed me there. Suddenly, quite by coincidence, she claimed, she had booked a room at the same inn where I was spending my visit. I was planning to stay a few weeks, look for some property to buy. I had been called to the island by an otherworldly force a few months before but my friend Pammie – the voice of reason – suggested that I not buy property in the middle of a break-up. "Wait three months, honey. If the volcano's still speaking to you, go back." That was her advice. And indeed, three months had passed and I was back on the island. Then suddenly, there she was – that Daddy – moved into the same inn for a few days in the middle of my stay.

Perhaps she wasn't stalking me – said it was a coincidence. Daddy and I were no strangers to cosmic coincidences. It's amazing how many signs people can find when they're looking for them. Daddy consulted psychics, astrologers. She had already moved into the dollhouse with the other girl and I wondered what she could possibly want with me at this point – so remote seemed the possibility of coincidence.

I had become Daddy's oracle. In addition to the help of the psychics and the seers, I told Daddy what I could see. Sometimes it seemed that she had purposefully blunted her sixth sense. She had purposefully set herself up as needing guidance so that she didn't need to do anything else on purpose.

I became Daddy's vessel for understanding. It seems so strange and brutal now, that Daddy would use me like that and love me as much as she did. And yet, so natural that we would arrive there. It was the destination for the train we boarded, after all. I used her too, in my way. One who cannot find gentleness within herself, has a hard time fully extending it to another.

Daddy felt that she should be sexually faithful to the new girl and she told me so. Daddy loves the idea of honor and still, she had conveniently not mentioned to the new girl that she was with me in Hawaii – what a surprise! And somehow the girl found out – heard my voice in the background on one of their daily phone calls – who knows how she knew. Daddy didn't like to tell an outright lie – her specialty was deception, sleight of hand, and clever language trickery. Daddy chooses smart girls, intuitive girls. Perhaps she just felt my presence, and asked.

For my part, I was not interested in deceiving anyone – except maybe myself. For my part, I felt sorry for the new girl, but she was not my job. She had, after all, angled for my Daddy's affections during our romance. She angled and she won them. Now she was getting her prize. I had my own business with Daddy to attend – begun long before the new girl ever met us. Run along, pesky girl. Daddy and I have business here.

I became Daddy's vessel for understanding. Daddy wanted to be true to the new girl – made sure I knew, in those first days, that she intended to return to the new girl. Nothing lasting would happen here between us. And still, Daddy felt compelled – compelled to fuck me, compelled to nurse at my breast. She felt compelled and yet could not accept what she was doing. Daddy's attention became diffuse and trancelike – her affections for me as a person, as her family, her blood had been trafficked away and sold to someone else for the promise of greater gain. Daddy was not connecting with me as a human being during those days. She was alone inside herself.

We had horrible, confusing sex. After her orgasm, she'd snap to her fears and leap off of my body, go to sleep in the other room. She turned her head if I tried to kiss her, as though that would keep me from accessing her soul while her body writhed on mine. We kissed only once, for an extended period during that visit. We were standing on lava rock at the edge of a rainforest jungle, nude in the outdoors beneath a shower of water. We were standing on lava rock under the night stars and she had just poured oily sugar over my body, scrubbed me up, tenderly, as she had done in the past, looking after me as precious. She had just exhilarated my skin and when I turned my face to her for the kiss, I saw her retreat and then reconsider.

When she kissed me, with the moon as witness, I was surprised by how her mouth tasted like fear – a sickening metallic taste – like fear and shame. Who was this Daddy and what was I in her eyes? I was no longer her beloved; I was her vessel. The kisses tasted like fear and they imparted fear. Fear was sliding down my throat and I could feel it burn my stomach. I didn't yet understand what was happening between us, but very quickly, I turned my face away from those kisses, opted instead for her warm, wet, oily embrace.

I didn't understand what was happening between us. When I learned that she would join me on that trip, I didn't know what to make of it. It was my second trip to the island since her decision to take another girl shot me like a bullet out of the safety of our mutual delusions. I decided that I would simply be open to whatever happened between us, to what I felt. I had come this far with Daddy and I hadn't fully let go of her as family. Though she'd moved away from me, she hadn't let go of me either. Something in my evolution frightened her – and she picked up the other girl as a human shield at first. (Who knows what they later became to one another.) I decided to leave myself open to whatever happened between us.

Daddy brought a tarot deck along on that trip. She had been learning new ways of casting and reading the cards for different occasions. She took out the deck one night and said, "Here, I'll show you how we can ask one question together and then cast the cards and read them separately. Two people can have different outcomes for a question that concerns them both, right?"

"Of course," I agreed, wondering what question she would ask the cards. What question could possibly concern us both at this point?

"For example," she said cautiously – for all of her bravado, Daddy was emotionally cautious – "let's ask about the outcome for our individual spiritual development and soul evolution if you and I were to get back together again – carry on as we were, in relationship." She looked into my eyes truly for one of the first times on that trip, but only briefly.

"Okay. Good question," I said, knowing that it would put Daddy at ease. And we prepared the cards according to her training and slowly, I read them. She was busy reading them too, out loud. She was telling the story of this card and that one – in that way she does, looking for the good story regardless of how the cards actually lay.

I looked at the cards and suddenly, everything became clear. Daddy would be best served in her life's trajectory by staying with me. I would be best served by staying away from Daddy.

The card layout was complex – I can't begin to recall it – but the message was suddenly so clear. The cards were laid out for each of us, and for each possible scenario – if we carry on together, if we carry on apart – both trajectories for each of us, laid out before us on the big bed where I slept, the big bed where she could fuck me but not look at me, not kiss me.

The ceiling fan hummed overhead, casting a light breeze onto our bare shoulders as we sat on the bed, staring at the cards. Her voice droned on and I lost track of her interpretation. I didn't need to hear her; could see it all for myself. Finally, I tuned back into her speaking just as she said, "See, baby. This is not so good for you to stay with me." It made her feel better if leaving me looked like she was doing some good. Of course she couldn't see the rest – about her own spiritual development – soul evolution. She was purposefully blunted on these themes.

"I know." I said simply, and then added, "Darling, I'm tired." And we went directly to our separate rooms.

The next night, she wanted to give me a massage and I agreed. I lay on my back, nude, on the bed, as she instructed and as soon as her hands were on me, I could feel her breath quicken. I could feel her trance-like retreat to the place she goes when she doesn't want to remember or admit something to herself. Does everyone know how to go to this place? I could feel something dangerous, though it felt so normal. My awareness was heightened; I was like a small animal in the forest at dusk.

Suddenly, her hands were on my skin more firmly. She was pressing one hand into my chest, not so much to hold me down, though that was the effect. It was as though she was trying to steal my beating heart. She was pressing down and grasping at my skin and her other hand dove down and roughly spread my legs, my labia. She was pushing her hand inside my vagina, holding me down and while this felt so clearly dangerous, I had too often been rewarded by her aggression in the past to move away too quickly. I had promised to remain open to her – I made that promise to her when she was still my Daddy. I made that promise to me, before seeing her on this trip. At first I was stunned – then wounded.

She was hurting me. And I began to cry. Daddy was raping me and I had become her vessel, her silence, her oracle, the fetish she hides beneath the bed and pulls out to fondle in a private moment. She can orgasm just by thinking about me, just by seeing the symbols of our union. We are united in the act of filling and being filled. I became her vessel, but now her deception was hurting me. I was not available to her rape without tenderness, to her pillage and revisions without the security of being called her own. And more than that, I had glimpsed the future in the tarot cards. Although I didn't yet understand what was happening, I could feel the truth: She could no longer pour herself into the vessel of my body, my spirit, my psyche, because I am already full.

My vessel is already full. How had I missed that? How had I yearned for so long to be filled by my lover, by my Daddy?

I am already full.

She was raping me with her hand, reaching in to pull out the heart in my chest and the one in my pulsing womb. I broke the silence with my sobs and I clamped my legs together – ending my openness to whatever she chose to perpetrate. Daddy had gone mad and would use me for whatever she thought necessary. I clamped my legs shut and sobbed, and I used my arms to try to wrestle her closer to me. I tried to hold her, make her hold me. She pulled her hands away from their intrusion, pulled her body away from my grasp, and left the room.

The next day, she had reframed her intrusion as "some weird energetic between us." It wasn't her. It was never going to be her, unless there was glory involved.

CHAPTER 29

THE END

DADDY'S GOODBYE

I moved into the little cottage by the sea and mostly, Daddy let me be. I could see no hope for change in Daddy, and I had to sort my head, so I said – please don't come to visit any more. Daddy had taken to visiting my house when I was away – we didn't see each other, but somehow she was still occupying my spaces. She took pleasure in touching what I had touched, being where I had been. She prompted me to take the same pleasure. She always left me gifts – sometimes I'd find them for weeks after her departure. She left me little notes. Once, after Daddy had been there, there was a note in my bed that said, "Do the sheets still smell like me?"

She had gone too far, and I told Daddy not to visit any more. But before she left, she planted fruit trees. She planted corn and sunflowers and a pink hibiscus outside my bedroom window.

I told her I didn't need a Daddy any more – not in the way it had been. I had grown up and things had changed. In my mind, the story went like this: We will remain friends. Of course we will because I could never stop loving her. A Daddy becomes Dad, then father, perhaps even a man with whom one is on a first name basis. Why would I ever stop wanting to be around her? I will always want to call her sweetie and kiss her cheek. I just won't curl up in her lap the way I used to, pull back the covers and join her, naked, as I once did. In my mind, the story went like this: I will be forever grateful to her for loving me so much and I will always send a card on Father's Day. I will thank her, every moment and in (almost) every way for being such a good Daddy, for being such a good friend. I will bless her being with my gratitude.

That was my story of parting, of continued love, changing love. But though my Daddy treated me like the only star in the sky, this is not so. Daddy's story is different; we each enjoy the free will of our different types of departure. I did not count on the sadness I would feel – being grateful without seeing my Daddy accept my gratitude.

My Daddy always accepted my gratitude with such joy! How could I know that it would be like this? I did not count the number of ways I would want to say thank-you and how much I would miss the shining joy in her eyes as she watched me receive those gifts. Daddy, did I always receive you in order to feel your precious pleasure?

I still want to say thank you, Daddy. Thank you. You. You. I am still speaking to you Daddy, even though you are gone away from me now, taking your solitude, licking the wounds you gave yourself, daily lashings for my leaving. I did not do this to you, but I can still feel your gaze in my direction as you break open your skin. I still want to talk to you, kiss you, and give you my love, just not my sex. I am not yours for sex anymore. But you are gone now, and maybe forever. I did not know about this part of growing up until it arrived and introduced itself as a tidy row of fruit trees: avocado, tangerine, sapote, lychee, orange and fig. I cannot say thank you. You. You are not listening to me any longer.

I can only remark to myself how much I appreciate her goodness – no longer miss her pressing need.

Before my Daddy left, she planted trees and had a small garden built with a passion fruit vine standing alone in the corner. She left me a bin full of worms to make the tea and castings that will nourish the plants. She explained how I should feed them with leftover food and wet paper and keep them in a nice shady place. She was worried that the sun had shone too much on the box she left – between her departure and my return to my house after travel. I moved the worms back into the shade and I picked up the phone to call. I asked, "How do I know if the worm-friends are still alive without putting my hand in the muck? I shook the box, but no one surfaced. I'm worried about them."

And she said, "Just keep feeding them and if the food disappears after a week or so, they're still alive. Now, try not to call me anymore, okay?" Her hands are out of the muck and I am talking to myself. She had left me, now I left her. Now she's leaving me again. Separating from Daddy took longer than I had hoped.

She had my house cleaned and the oil changed in my car. She put in a new battery because I had not done this, even though she had been telling me I needed one for some time. She told me I needed one and predicted that I would be stranded one day with no charge, unable to start the car. She smirked and said, "Don't worry. I'll come get you."

She put a new battery in my car, placed a stone Buddha in front of the garden with the single passion fruit vine and then she wasn't my friend any more.

THE BLADE

Daddy holds my head in her hands. Her touch is so tender and yet so firm and I love how she guides my head. It lets my body relax and open up. I love how she takes what she wants with such a firm gentleness. She turns my head and runs her thumb along my lips, parting them, moving her thumb briefly inside, just enough to wet it in the eager warmth of my mouth. She smoothes my hair away from my face and then, using the hand that's just a little bit wet with my spit, she pulls my hair firmly to turn my head even more sharply toward her. With purpose and a steady strength that I have come to love, she pulls my head down, down. One knee comes to the ground and then the other. My body is bent and giving. My head is in Daddy's hands.

My head is resting on the big wooden chopping block now. I look up at Daddy, with love in my eyes, just the way she likes it. I look up at Daddy and then look away, not sure how to hold the intimacy of this moment in such a small body. Daddy loosens the blue satin ribbon that she tied around my neck. I am wearing the pale pink pajamas with the little red flowers on them. My breasts are unbound, moving roughly with the gravity of Daddy's smooth tugs. My knees are digging into the ground where she has placed me. I am wearing the blue satin ribbon around my neck but I didn't know its significance. It's not really bondage, just a ribbon. I let it happen because Daddy wanted it and I love my Daddy. She said I was beautiful. She said I looked beautiful; that I was beautiful.

I am beautiful in Daddy's eyes. She tied the satin ribbon around my neck because she liked how it looked. The soft satin and the pretty bow against my throat sent a shiver through Daddy's body and I felt my own goodness vicariously. I felt my own goodness, my godness, the goodness and the godness that I can only see reflected in Daddy's pretty blue eyes. I didn't know why Daddy was tying the satin around my neck but it felt soft and I felt pretty and Daddy was showing me to myself in her eyes.

Daddy loosened the ribbon around my neck, my head held firmly against the big wooden block. There is a blade up above – parna – the flash of enlightenment from the corner of my eye. The flash of something from the corner of one's eye that is gone the moment one turns to look at it. It's the thing I can't see if I'm looking right at it, but at the angle when the eyes stretch, at the moment when the mind is distracted by something like a blue satin ribbon, there it is. I see the blade. It's silver and glistening and then I see nothing else but Daddy's blue eyes. I see Daddy's blue eyes looking at my throat adoringly, looking at the blue ribbon as though she had planned this moment. Daddy loves the softness of my throat, so I give it to her, willingly.

Daddy is an excellent planner. Of course she planned this moment. The satin ribbon against my skin, the soft stroking of my hair, the pajamas. I am ready for bed. I am ready for our slumber party. I am ready to go out into the world and say I love my Daddy. I love my Daddy. I love my Daddy. I will do this without my head on my shoulders and with my blood soaking my jammies all the way down to the ruffled cuffs that Daddy likes so much. I will do this with the smell of brains seeping into my pajamas. I will not sleep. I will not sleep. Daddy doesn't like the smell of brains, but it is such a familiar smell, she could not help but smell it again. Daddy is in charge of the wars and the carnage. Daddy is the victim. Daddy blames me for having the brains. I am too smart, Daddy says. Daddy blames me for having the reeking, smelly brains. I can't see the blade when I look directly at it. But I know it's there.

I look up at Daddy lovingly and she is beginning to cry. Daddy tells me to be patient, and my knees are starting to hurt. It's taking Daddy too long to either drop the blade or lift me back up into her arms and hold me, stroke my cheek and kiss my forehead. It's taking Daddy too long. She just keeps staring at my pretty neck where the ribbon lays loose, not tied anymore. There is nothing that ties us anymore. I can see her adoration out of the corner of my eye and the tie has come undone. Daddy is pulling away from me and I know this isn't personal;

the carnage is inevitable. This isn't personal; the war has to come and my blood knows how to flow; my brains know how to leave my head. I am the obvious choice. I am the perfect girl. My womb is aching, my breasts are hanging.

My neck is exposed and Daddy's hand is lingering on the side of my head, even as she pulls away to make space for the blade to fall. I can't see the blade if I turn and look, but the silver flash of its brilliance winks into the corner of my eye. I can feel the blade. Lately, all the time, I can feel the blade. I am looking into Daddy's blue eyes with love, just like she likes me to when she holds my head. The high sharp sound of the blade surprises me as it slices through air. It slices through air and a swift little puff hits my cheek.

Am I still pretty, Daddy? Am I still precious? Am I still your sweet girl? My head is turned away from myself and the smell of brains sickens my Daddy. Once she smells the brains on the block, (blood and brains will never wash out of these pajamas) once she smells the blood in our bed, the brains on the block, she'll have to turn and go. The stench is too horrible. Daddy is no stranger to this stench. Daddy is the victim here. Daddy is the victim and I help her play out her helplessness over and over. Her hand still gently touching the side of my head, until my eyes roll back, lifeless. I cannot look up at her lovingly, like she likes. Daddy turns to go.

CHAPTER 30

THE STORYTELLER

STORYTELLER ME

I am a storyteller too. The Daddies love my stories as much as I love telling them. I am lounging on the bed in my leopard print panties and bra while Daddy fixes my computer. I am practicing the dance I will do for Daddy's birthday wearing the schoolgirl outfit she likes so well. In the last moments of the song, I tie my panties around Daddy's wrists, playful-like. This will make a good joke of the way we pass dominance back and forth, back and forth like a hot potato, but Daddy always has it for dinner, wipes the butter on my skin. I am hiding my black lace bra under Daddy's pillow just before we leave the house for the airport. She will find it later and miss me. I coo my approval softly into her ear when Daddy tells me she has purchased a pacifier, to remind her of me while I am away. She misses me in certain ways and I cultivate the story that allows this to happen.

When it ended, I couldn't understand why Daddy had to break the story of our love so completely. Why did it have to be irreparable? At first, she threw down our specialness and broke it with her deceptions, but that wasn't enough. She had to stomp on it and break it into a million pieces with the boot of her revisions – revisions of the beautiful stories she had told me. Suddenly, in her stories, she was never attracted to me; she was never really my Daddy; I was always on the outside of what I thought to be home.

This is how I have interpreted what she said. I invented the broken relationship metaphor – said it could be repaired with a little attentiveness glue, a little apology glue, some precision and devotion. I came up with the metaphor of her boot coming down upon the precious vessel of our love, smashing it to indistinguishable bits, making powder of the pretty patterns that adorned our days. These are

© KONINKLIJKE BRILL NV, LEIDEN, 2019 | DOI:10.1163/9789004383562_030

my stories, now that I am wounded. And the Daddies had to wound me – that was always part of our deal.

I am in charge of the story now and I manipulate it to my greatest pain. There are other ways of telling the story – don't think I'm blind to their possible unfolding. I am a master storyteller too and I know my own masochism. The Daddies and I are alike in our love of a good story but at the end, I tell the story of my own righteousness. I have been wronged and this hurts me like a guillotine chopping off my head. It hurts me like the fear of public ridicule and revulsion, every secret revealed to unforgiving audiences. I am the one who is vulnerable: the girl who longs to please her Daddies, the benevolent controlling mother who knows just how to soothe the little Daddy-boys.

When the stories please me they are powerful metaphors; when they displease me, they are powerful lies. Daddy told me once that the girl is always in charge. Daddy adores her, but must have her permission. That's one of the Daddies' stories. It seems to me that the girl is vulnerable to the whims of Daddy's adoration. That's one of my stories. Both are stories of potential betrayal and pain and we wallow in these shallow muddy pools alternately, according to our needs. I am sullied by my own understanding of things that would be simple, if only we weren't telling such tall tales.

I am no stranger to my own shortcomings – don't think I truly believe it's all the Daddies' fault. I am holding up my wrists to be bound, loving the pressure of the ties against my flesh. I am pulling down my brassiere in order to free my breast when my Daddy-boy's brow furrows and she looks helpless. I am pulling her to me, looking lovingly and giving. I choose to give – and get something from it in the process. I am not selfless, but who is? I am not loyal only to love. I give allegiance to the stories I create. I write love with my left hand, recreating the universe in perfect balance. With the right hand dominant, I prepare the legible writ of oppression. The Daddies will betray me. That's what the script says. And so it is done.

The Daddies reel me into their confusion and deception again and again. I am outraged. This is also in the script. It starts to sound like I will be soothed and so I forget my troubles, pull back the covers and open myself for the Daddies' stories. I can't always tell when I have sold my integrity for comfort. I can't always tell, until the blood flows out of my eyes into the tissue as I listen to the story shift toward horror and betrayal. I can't always tell until the story that soothes me becomes a lie and I throw it back in Daddies' faces. No, I don't want it! I yell, I just want the truth, but the sticky sweet soothing has tarred me like molasses. I want the truth more than I want to be taken care of. At times this is so, but not always.

I ask for it and I give it. The Daddies are not alone in creating the universe through stories. I am making the world spin too.

ONE OF THE ODDITIES IN THE CURIOSITY CABINET OF KIMBERLY'S PSYCHE

Step right up, ladies and gentlemen! Behold the wonder! Preserved for all posterity, this image of Kimberly's Daddies is carved onto nature's perfect canvas: the peach pit!

This peach pit carving may be the artist's finest work. Often worn as a solitaire pendant, or as a personal ornament, hanging from the end of a fan, peach pit carvings were sometimes strung together as a chaplet in the Ming and Qing Dynasties. This particular specimen in on limited display only, is the curio cabinet of Kimberly's psyche.

The artist's previous works were stunning indeed – his rendering of President John F. Kennedy on a peach pit was also a marvel: Kennedy, wearing a veterans hat; encircled by the inscription "President John F. Kennedy of United States," an eagle on a shield to Kennedy's right, a depiction of St. Christopher below the eagle and shield, foliate patterns below and to the President's left completed the scene. Now, it seems, that thrilling peach pit carving was but a warm up for this rendering of Kimberly's Daddies, here now, for your viewing pleasure.

First, this amazing peach pit was formed by nature into the shape of a phallus. It's unmistakable! Note the sleek and classic curve, the gently sloping bulb at the top. The engraving is an improvement on nature's skill. This stone called to be the canvas for Kimberly's Daddies! Never before assembled in one place, the Daddies sat for this engraving, many long hours in stillness without a quibble or complaint. Two even returned from the grave for this unique opportunity to be immortalized in fruit stone.

Close examination will show that two of the Daddies are male; two are female. Four Daddies, you say? Look closely; the two female Daddies are actually conjoined twins! We aim to enthrall – this is a circus side-show after all!

Only one of the Daddies is actually a blood relative to Kimberly. Indeed, he is her biological father. Marvel at the physical resemblance! Note his relaxed though sophisticated stance, cigarette in one hand, he leans on the edge of the table on the viewer's right. He is wearing a sport coat and slacks and the engraver has been kind to restore his full head of hair. Even with age, his down-tilted head, up-cast eyes and sucked-in cheeks have not changed from the photographs of his youth. He gazes coolly at the carver, un-troubled by the company of the others. A half smile on his lips, he accepts his place in the picture as he accepts his maturity – alongside a vodka martini – straight up with a twist.

Seated directly behind the table, flanked by the other two, are Daddies Deux and Trois – the conjoined twins. Note the one on the left – her dramatically outstretched leg, downcast glance; she appears at first like Hamlet pondering the demise of human reason. Upon closer examination, her fluffy locks and ruffled poet's shirt cause her to resemble Oscar Wilde after a weekend in the country with the boys. She is a bit disheveled, her long hair obscuring part of her face. Or perhaps she appears to the viewer more like a mid-life Natalie Barney? She is lecherous and brilliant, condescending and benevolent – somehow charming in spite of herself. Conjure any grand and ridiculous dead literary figure and impose him here, dear viewer. You cannot go wrong. Does she lean on the table for balance or theatricality? This is up to the eye's discernment, but a few things are clear: She is cocky in spite of her compromised condition and she has breasts. Take note; this is one of the females in the image.

Just next to her (of course, and always) Daddy Trois is seated forward, facing forward. She is leaning both elbows on the table and her steady gaze engages the viewer. What is she thinking? What would she be saying? Her stoic, steadfast eye contact seems to follow you, does it not? She seems unaware of anyone else in the portrait. Her beautiful eyes are actually blue, should the viewer wonder. And despite her thick body, crew cut and masculine constitution, she is indeed the other female in the carving. Again, the sculptor is to be lauded for rendering the numerous and intricate tattoos on her forearms so accurately. A black swan graces the left arm and the benevolent Virgin Mary adorns the right. The female Daddy-duo is joined, indeed, but at the hip – which makes this particular rendering tasteful indeed.

To the viewer's left, the final Daddy in the scene is standing, leaning away from the other three. Does he find them, ironically, distasteful? That will be up to the viewer to decide. Note his somewhat bored gaze. Perhaps he was interrupted in the afterworld when asked to join the portrait-party? His hand is planted firmly on the table. The sculptor is to be commended for the graceful arc of the Daddy-pack – what symmetry! This Daddy's head turns to face forward and his grey hair is mussed, lips parted slightly in a practiced smile, so that his short front teeth, dull from years of grinding, do not show in the photograph.

A simple pitcher of water on the wooden table and a glass for each are the scene's only embellishments and, rest assured, these are a utility, provided for the Daddies' comfort. Again, the artist is owed kudos for capturing each detail, including thirst, on this peach pit phallus – nature's perfect canvas – in the curio cabinet of Kimberly's psyche.

(Note: *On the back is shown an unusually grim Crucifixion, with a soldier on horseback, Longinus piercing Christ's side with a lance, the cross is surmounted by a titulus inscribed INRI. Imbricated foreground.*)

CHAPTER 31

MY FATHER'S TIME

REALIZING

My father spends a lot of time sitting on the black leather sofa in his sparsely decorated living room. His back's been bothering him. His feet are numb. Sometimes he falls when he stands to walk to the restroom. He figures he's in good health, considering his lifestyle over the years, the extra weight, the drinking, and the smoking. He figures he's in pretty good shape. No high cholesterol. No sign of lung cancer after sixty years of filterless cigarettes. He's taken off the weight. He listens to the show tunes station on cable TV. Pictures of the singers and their most notable performances remain on the screen while the music plays. My father has time to think.

When I was a child, my father came home late from the Cotton Club almost every night. Sometimes, if he picked me up from an event or an appointment after work, I went with him to the bar. He ordered me Shirley Temples, without asking what I wanted. He reached over the bar to swipe an extra cherry for my drink, and then he'd wink at me. Three, four years old, I sat up on the ledge that surrounded the piano, the giant brandy snifter filling with dollar bills as the night progressed. My father loved the sound of his own singing voice after a few drinks. His eyes would soften and he'd sing "Raindrops Keep Falling on My Head." I'd sip my syrupy soda and I could see in his eyes that he loved me too.

The Cotton Club also had a steak restaurant, adjacent to the bar and sometimes my family ate dinner there. It was not a place for kids; I didn't like how dark and quiet it was and I didn't like the food. But I wanted to go. I felt special as I passed under the wood-vine trellis at the entrance, looking down at my shiny black patent leather Mary Jane shoes on the brick walkway. I wasn't often allowed to go out with my father. My mother was frequently cross with him, so I preferred she weren't around, but better her there, than not going at all.

© KONINKLIJKE BRILL NV, LEIDEN, 2019 | DOI:10.1163/9789004383562_031

The meat was flame grilled and it arrived on the plate with blackened lines across it on each side. I didn't like all the food crowding up the plate and the tin foil around the baked potato. My father would shoot me a stern look, as we'd sit down, indicating that I would not have a fit about the fire on my meat again tonight. My mother would ask for my plate to come with just the meat on it. My father ordered my steak medium rare. I hated black lines on my meat and I would pout. My father drained his second martini, ordered a third and he'd look at me with affection, my brow knit, sitting in my plastic molded-butt booster seat, looking like a cross little princess before a blackened lump of meat.

"She looks like me," he thought. "She looks like my mother, but prettier," he thought. At home, on the rare occasions he'd sit at the table with my mother and me and watch me eat, he worried that I would grow too fat, like his mother, like him. He'd comment to my mother, "If it's baby fat, why isn't it gone yet?" Then he'd add, "She's three." Or "she's five." Or "she's six," as the years moved on. Gazing at me in the Cotton Club in my white bodice dress and my hair pulled up in little white clips, two martinis down, he felt the joyful burden of parenting. "She is my own," he thought. "And that's pretty special."

He leaned over my plate with his knife and fork in hand. He said to me, very quietly, "I'm going to scrape the black off of the meat. See, it's just a little bit. And then it'll be gone and then you're going to eat your steak." His black hair fell down over one eye as he leaned forward and began scraping. His proximity rendered me completely still and breathless. Other than carrying my sleeping body in from the car at night when we'd been out drinking, he was almost never so close to me. When I was awake and able to look at him, he was never so close to me.

"What a strange little creature she is," he thought to himself. He liked me quiet, but without the piano playing, or my mother around, he would never know what to say to me. I seemed to have my own internal life anyway, he thought to himself. Without speaking any more about it, I ate my meat slowly and swallowed hard, still tasting the black lines that he had scraped and then wiped away with his napkin.

My father has time to think in his seventieth year. For a few years after leaving, he still worked occasionally at the college from which he retired, but then his health slowed him down. He sits and listens to show tunes and eats scrambled eggs and toast for dinner. He sits on a barstool to make the eggs, wash the dishes. He chuckles to himself that he is still sitting on a barstool. Some things never change. Doing pretty well, considering, he thinks to himself.

He spends some time looking at the polar bears on the front of the Christmas card I sent him. Those bears are so beautiful, he thinks to himself, and he feels a sense of connection with me because I sent him the card. Those bears are so big and can be so mean, but they're fragile too. They sleep so long and wake so hungry. He calls to let me know that he'd sent money to adopt a polar bear. He'd been giving it some thought and global warming was going to hurt those bears. He said, "It's a beautiful picture on this card." And he sounded like he might cry.

"I agree." I said, stunned at his philanthropic outburst. "They're very special animals, and so close to extinction."

"I have the picture they sent me here – when I sent them the money. And now your card," he said. "It's from the same group. You got this card from the same group I gave the money to," he added.

He sits with his pile of special things on the table by the sofa where he can reach them easily – his reading glasses, the black and white piece of round, decorative pottery I brought him from Peru, the pictures of the polar bears, cigarettes, ashtray and the jar of cat treats. He listens to his wife talk about her day, what's new at her condo, across town. They have a better relationship now that they don't live together. He listens to her talk about her day and he feels grateful for her companionship. He has time to think and has started wondering about how they act differently with their children.

"Hey, this is your Dad," is his typical conversation opening on the rare occasions when he phones. "Hey, I just wanted to talk to you about something. Do you have a minute?"

I can't imagine not having a minute for someone who calls me no more than once a year. "Sure, what is it?"

"You know, I was noticing that Joan talks on the phone to her kids every day. I mean, she calls them." He says this with surprise in his voice at this discovery. "Well, not so much Michael. I mean, she calls him. But Stacy. They talk pretty much every day."

"Wow. Right." I say it in anticipation of the next thing because I'm not sure what he's getting at.

"You and I only talk once a month or so. You call when you're in town, but …" If he could see me, he'd see my eyes widening, my jaw dropping. He adds the direct question, somewhat flustered by whole matter. "Do you want me to call you more?"

"Well," I stammer. "If you'd like to call me more, that'd be great. I feel like we're okay though."

"That's what I thought too," he says hastily before I can say anything else. "That's what I thought. If we have something to say, we say it. But when I realized. I mean. When I thought." He swims around in the thoughts like he'd never heard of water before being immersed in it. He doesn't seem to be drowning though. He continues. "So, I just wanted you to know something else too."

Now my interest is piqued. He really has things to say. Conversations with my father during the past decade have evolved into a predictable collage – a reporting of doctor's visits, stories from his life of work, updates about his grandson, reminiscences about my childhood – moments of engaged parenting he seems to carry like a deck of cards – a small, finite group of images over which to linger. This conversation is not of the usual batch.

"You know, I've been thinking about the kind of parent I've been, the kind of parent you've been and I just want you to know that I want to help." His only grandson is nearing college age, and he has already alluded to his desire to help financially, but here, he seems to be moving toward specifics.

"I never really realized it, until I saw the way you parent, but I could've done more for you than I did. I could've – done more." The words hang there for a moment and tears fill my eyes.

"You really support him," my father says. "You make sure that he's getting everything he needs for a really good life. I could've done that for you, but you just always seemed so – so, fine. Like everything was going to be okay. You always seemed like you just had your own life and everything was going fine so I just didn't – Hey. I just want you to know that I want to help now – help get him a car. I could've done that for you, but – I don't know. I just didn't."

I hold the phone away from my mouth, still pressed to my ear so I can hear every word, so he can't hear me beginning to sob as he speaks. He is speaking more words together in a stretch than I've ever heard him utter about me, about our relationship, about anything at all personal.

"I just want you to know that it's not because I didn't – want to. It just didn't occur to me to do it. It's not because you weren't important to me. I just didn't realize, that's all. I just didn't think to – well, I want to help now. I just didn't realize – hey, you just let me know if he needs anything. I don't have a lot of money, but I'll – hey, you just let me know, okay?"

"Okay, I will. Thank you. That's really great to hear." I manage these words with even breathing because I don't want to interrupt his moment with my emotion. Though this sounds like a different father than the one I've had, I still know that emotion can ruin a thing for him. I still want to take care of him, not make him feel uncomfortable about all he's said.

Once a month or so – that's enough. I visit, and we talk – mostly about our list of pre-approved topics. He doesn't think much about what he said to me. He doesn't drink as much as he used to and he has time to think about things.

When he loaned me money for the first time, after I got up the nerve to ask, the note with the check read:

Hi –

Nice talking to you the other nite – hope you used your cell phone – we must have talked 45 minutes. Check enclosed. If you need more, just call.

Love you very much

Dad

IN THE RECKONING

It turns out that my stepfather was just an asshole among assholes. A pretty common, run of the mill misogynist. He was a pedophile sitting on a pillow of privilege and not a very nice guy. I tried to overdose on pills; I stopped eating to gain control of my body; I smoked a lot of pot to get away from the reality of him, but mostly, I just endured him until I could leave.

I feel compassion for his biological daughter. He loved her when she was little, but then what? Then what? She tried to tell me once that we had it the same. But I didn't really have it the same as her. She was his flesh, his little girl from the beginning. But in the end, we're all the same to some men once we start looking like women.

My father affected my life. He was not an asshole – not to me anyway. He was a pretty nice guy, according to many – still misogynist, especially at work. Sometimes when he told a story, it was clear that he used shame and rumors to undermine women – and felt proud of his own cleverness. Some women also spoke well of him. I only know what I heard and what little I witnessed; I never really knew him very well. He's the one that I wanted to please. I wanted his warmth, his approving glances, and his love. I spent a lot of my life trying to hold him in all of the gentle forms of masculinity I could conjure.

It sounds so simple, but when he really started to act like he loved me, tell me he loved me – when I really started to feel it, it changed my life. Like a flower that's lived to see the thaw, I started growing up again.

He started taking the time to know me near the end of his life. He came to my events; he read my publications. He paid attention. Before he died, my father's became the loudest laughter in the theatre when I was on stage. His applause was the longest. He began to care about the polar bears, about the planet. He never liked the beach or the mountains, never took me camping. Now he is re-thinking things. He is trying to un-endanger me.

Barbara Deming wrote about her father dying, her sorrow that only in death did his body become touchable, holdable (Deming, 2004). She loved him, but he was unapproachable, like my father. She was able to caress him as she would caress anyone she loves, only in death.

We find surrogates.

My father conjured love with his laughter and it flew around my head, amplified by applause. I didn't know what it was, at first, what to make of the strange, joyful fluttering. And still, when I think about it, it makes me want to gasp and cry. I am coming to the pleasure of it, still stunned by the truth of it. His will to know me began fueling the crucible in which he could recast himself.

CHAPTER 32

PLEASURE

PLEASING DADDY

I have put aside my pleasing face. I don't read the news of the Daddies' expression in the morning and make my face to suit them. If what I have pleases, this is coincidence – an unexpected pleasure.

I no longer look at the tension on the Daddies' faces and entreat them to lie in my arms. I no longer give a soothing glance that allows them to lay down their burdens, allows them to accept my respite without requesting it. I look at them with understanding. I listen like a person who's interested in another person. And I empathize. I do not mother. I am not their mother. We know it because I no longer throw milk-scent around the room. The Daddies must eat the solid food of self-awareness. They may learn to like it.

In fact, it's starting to feel strange to call them "Daddy" these days. Just strange. I am changing and somehow, so are they. The Daddies outside my home do not shift so perceptibly as the ones I know personally. And still, the world as I see it becomes different even though headlines have not radically altered.

I have put aside my pleasing face. When my face is pleasing, I accept it without nervously studying the contours of my expression, cataloging my face for future pleasures. I wear the face that is there when I wake each morning without consulting the news of Daddy. Each morning is different. I am no longer the recorded, edited, airbrushed version of myself that comes out of the album jacket the same every time. I am different, day-to-day. Some of my performances have been previously released, but no longer rehearsed. I choose which performances are private, or public. The Daddies are not my agent, my publicist. They do not hold and edit the questions to which I will respond, the topics that must not be mentioned. In order to respond,

© KONINKLIJKE BRILL NV, LEIDEN, 2019 | DOI:10.1163/9789004383562_032

first I listen. I do not try to be perfect. I listen and respond from the place where I sit, wearing the face with which I woke that morning. And slowly, others, even the Daddies, are not expecting different from me.

I have put aside my pleasing face. I am not always productive. The Daddies wanted me to drink the coffee, drink the Red Bull, and take the energy shot. The Daddies wanted me to swallow the pills, breathe the aromatherapy, and take a twenty-minute spa vacation. The Daddies wanted me to keep working, though I was horribly sad. Clean the house, take care of the children, correspond with the relatives, plant the garden and still do my job and pay the bills. The Daddies have to buck up, why not me? The Daddies have their roles to maintain, why not me? They wanted me to call this just.

I have begun practicing new words. Since I have divorced Daddy's pleasure, I am free to swallow what I want. I am not wed and can make my own declarations. I open my mouth to call out injustice wherever I see it. It is standing in doorways, leaning out of windows, waving from a passing car. I open my mouth and slowly now, words are coming out, making messages. My hearing becomes keen to the sounds others make against injustice as well.

I look for domination because it has been lacquered into the wood grain, raked into the leaves; fish are swallowing it in the sea. Injustice has been hidden by the painter in the magazine picture of everyday life where you have to look closely, sometimes turn the page upside-down in your lap. Sometimes you take another view and you see it. There's one! There's one! Circle them with a dark pen or they'll blend right in again. There's one – in the flowerpot, in the girl's hair, in the cloud, on the man's shoe, in his hatband. I am not wed to the Daddies' pleasure any longer and I carry a black pen with me everywhere I go.

I have put aside my pleasing face, but I am still kind. I do not want the Daddies to suffer any more than is necessary to become fully aware of themselves. I still love the Daddies – maybe even more now that I know their humanity, maybe even more now that I believe they can be my partners. I am kind and it takes effort sometimes. I am so used to habitual kindness, placation. I am learning to be kind, not as a façade; it is real. I know this because I show kindness to myself. Often, I open my closed palms and smell the scent of sweetness there. I cup my face and give the beauty of kindness to me. I know it's real and delightful, amplified by forgiveness.

CHOOSING TO CHANGE

WHY SHOULD DADDY CHANGE?

Why do I think the Daddies will ever listen to me? Believe me, I've been asked that question – and I ask it of myself. Well, for the same reason that I and those like me have not simply defected, moved away from men, renounced our sons and fathers and established a sovereign island nation. My girlfriends – lots of women in fact – joke about this. It's not like we couldn't do it – we could. Stranger things have happened. Was the isle of Lesbos really once a sanctuary of women-loving-women only? I don't know. But we could do it if we wanted to.

And look, there would still be at least two genders present if all the woman-bodied people went away. There are always two genders present – more, some would say – within each one of us. What is this two-gender business anyway? An obsession with dichotomies, that's what I've always said. A way to punish the other without seeing the other in ourselves.

Why do I think the Daddies will listen to my plea for change? Well, it's because they love me, that's why. They love the girls and women in their lives as best they can. They have all the toys, sure, but it's no fun to play alone. There's so much pleasure in the tension of everyone playing together. Hard to know, if you've never played that way, but look. Men have also not renounced their daughters and their mothers – not totally. Abuse them, sure. Subjugate and relegate them to meager resources – but leave them behind? No, it hasn't happened. And it could. Men could do it if they wanted to.

No, despite the unfairness of the game, the Daddies love us. The Daddies sometimes admire us even. There's evidence of that too. And insomuch as they have asked us to look after them, asked us to give them pleasure, there is a precedent for us helping them to try new ground. There is a precedent for us having an effect on one another.

© KONINKLIJKE BRILL NV, LEIDEN, 2019 | DOI:10.1163/9789004383562_033

That's why. The Daddies are suffering too. And they love us. That's why they may choose to change.

Patriarchy is the single most life-threatening social disease assaulting the male body and spirit in our nation. Yet most men do not use the word "patriarchy" in everyday life. Most men never think about patriarchy – what it means, how it is created and sustained. Many men in our nation would not be able to spell the word or pronounce it correctly. The word "patriarchy" just is not a part of their normal everyday thought or speech. Men who have heard and know the word usually associate it with women's liberation, with feminism, and therefore dismiss it as irrelevant to their own experiences. I have been standing at podiums talking about patriarchy for more than thirty years. It is a word I use daily, and men who hear me use it often ask me what I mean by it ...

Patriarchy is a political-social system that insists that males are inherently dominating, superior to everything and everyone deemed weak, especially females, and endowed with the right to dominate and rule over the weak and to maintain that dominance through various forms of psychological terrorism and violence ...

... Patriarchy demands of men that they become and remain emotional cripples. Since it is a system that denies men full access to their freedom of will, it is difficult for any man of any class to rebel against patriarchy, to be disloyal to the patriarchal parent, be that parent female or male ...

... Indeed, radical feminist critique of patriarchy has practically been silenced in our culture. It has become a subcultural discourse available only to well-educated elites. Even in those circles, using the word "patriarchy" is regarded as passé. Often in my lectures when I use the phrase "imperialist white-supremacist capitalist patriarchy" to describe our nation's political system, audiences laugh. No one has ever explained why accurately naming this system is funny …

… Until we can collectively acknowledge the damage patriarchy causes and the suffering it creates, we cannot address male pain. We cannot demand for men the right to be whole, to be givers and sustainers of life. Obviously some patriarchal men are reliable and even benevolent caretakers and providers, but still they are imprisoned by a system that undermines their mental health.

Patriarchy promotes insanity. It is at the root of the psychological ills troubling men in our nation. Nevertheless there is no mass concern for the plight of men …. (hooks, 2004)

BEAUTIFUL FAILURE

I refused to make a home of scarcity. The Daddies and I made an artwork out of scraps and cruelty. We wrote the play of love and cast ourselves as leads. We have been in training, rehearsing for the real thing. Sexual violence does satisfy, if not the need for love, the need for something. We had something. The Daddies gave me something precious that could rest in my hand while I waited.

At first I wanted the Daddies dead because the possibility of healing felt so remote. I wanted to kill my stepfather, silently wait for my father to die without ever risking the action of sitting close, holding his hand. I have re-written the play now so that he can phoenix up from the canyon into which I toss his body. He will see me differently and we can both rise up. It's painful to see how helpless the Daddies have been. When my stepfather rises up out of the canyon, he doesn't tell me that he'll protect me from everything. He tells me he'll work with me to diminish the forces that threaten us.

I can see how I have upheld the patriarchy and endangered my sons by taking the Daddies into my care, into my bed. I have allowed them to pour their pestilence into my little animal body while still looking at them with loving eyes. My steady gaze enabled their not speaking, not feeling, and not feeling their loss. I nodded and wept for them, as they wrapped the rope around my hands, held their cocks in their hands and squeezed. Pleasure and pain together. I opened for them so they wouldn't have to.

I am the sheep that comes down the chute for slaughter and when my throat is cut, I gently lick the blood from the butcher's arm before life leaves me. I see how I have made a place for the dominance and violence, not knowing how to do otherwise. I have known only how to construct love where I can make it, as it has been shown to me to make it. Giving up on masculinity was not an option for me. Some can renounce it, reject it, turn away from sons, turn away from the Daddies and say, "That is yours to fix. I will save myself. That is your problem now."

Should I stop loving, bear the pain of separation from the Daddies, reject my sons? No, this will not do. I have remained connected and that is the source of the art and industry that allows me now to imagine alternatives. Now that things have come this far, now that the blade is always gleaming in my peripheral vision, now that I know I cannot cure the Daddies of the sadness they carry. I cannot bear their weight and must fail.

Dear Daddy,

I fail joyfully now. I fail willingly. I cannot help you Daddy and I say this with love and longing for something new. You have to find your capacity to be responsible Daddy. Start with you. Responsibility for you, not me. This goes against all you've learned, I know. Responsibility is only possible if you know when to control and when to let go of ruling, trying, doing. Loosen your grip, Daddy, in order to get stronger. Your hand needs to open and close again to build muscle, grasp and release. You have had me in a firm grip for too long and this has weakened you.

Do you trust that every hole in the walls of our house can be repaired? Do you trust that every falling shingle can be put right? The weather may not wait, Daddy. You may not get your father's love. You have to grieve, find the pain that you wrapped around and around and around your fist until it was solid enough to force between my teeth and gag my mouth. You nearly stopped my breathing Daddy and you said it was for love, for pleasure. You found your pleasure in dominion.

You could not help but lie; I know that now. Not only did I ask you for those smooth jewels to caress my soft throat, you had no choice. Your mask-ulinity requires an iron face. Nothing in your boyish freedom would be lovable if you let it shine. Nothing in your supple body would be protected. The zipper-backed, gnashing-jaw dogs of convention would've torn you to shreds.

And what of the lie that both you and I would be unsafe if you were allowed to love? Both you and I and all of our beloved progeny would perish if you weren't able to kill on command? Daddy, my fierce protection of you has given lie to the statement that you are the triumphant protector and I would be prey. Daddy, these words between us now tell the story of our history – how we were once, and are still, prey to bigger animals, fiercer doctrines, hulking harbingers of doom that drape themselves across the sun, threatening. We are both needed to restore the balance between heavens and earth. We are both capable of this magic, this feat.

And where will the turn-on be, if not in your dominance, Daddy? I know you are wondering, not being able to fathom my slick yielding without your hardness, Daddy. I have wondered too. Maybe you have to trust that every damage can be repaired and that another's movement will not leave you behind. I am afraid of change too at times, Daddy. And it is inevitable, though we choose our ways. I will hold my fear to the roof of my mouth, like a seed germinating, waiting to be planted. My own light-seeking tendrils wait in dark stillness. You have taught me how to fear and do nothing. You have taught me how to hold fear and wait. Now I will hold fear as I act and change and move. I will forgive you our history and compassion will wash over me like milk.

Can we arrive in our bodies as the best of male and female in whatever ratios suit us most? Will our turn-on, love-drive, hot-flint joys evolve too? How can this growth, which we have wanted for so long (yet guarded so fiercely against) be an effortless yearning, rather than a forced march toward propriety? I will not abandon the animal lust of us, I promise you.

And I don't have to know now. I don't have to know to what I will be attracted in you when you grow up. I only fear the loss of that which I know to be pleasing, though damaging, pleasing though incomplete. My pleasing face is gone and I trust that others will see something there to love. What if I let you do the same, trusting that I will see something to love, to compel me, undulating, ripe with joy?

Love,
Kimberly

CHAPTER 34

START WITH SALT

Dear Daddies,

I have been your little girl, your whore, your slave and mother, jailor, mentor, wife. It doesn't matter how cute I am, how submissive or how rational and grown-up. It doesn't matter how hot I am, how smokin' red hot sexy I can be. I cannot save you. And here's the kicker: I can have a good life, but unless you choose to change, there's only so far I can go too, only so much of the world I can see without our two sets of eyes making one in sight.

What would it look like if you grew up too, Daddies? I have considered this question in so many ways, and sometimes I've tried to prompt you, force you, tie your hands and take you to the gangplank, but you don't walk. You don't jump. You are still and stoic with icy shoulders. I can hold your noses, but I can't make you drink the potion. I'm not sure it works because we haven't tried. You haven't, though I've seen you pondering the potion pot.

How can I help you when I'm still casting about trying to hook my own sunshine as well? All I can do is shine. And be kind. And forgive.

It's up to you, Daddies, to find out the details on your own.

I think you start with wonder. I think you start with love. Not just the wonder you feel at the softness of my yielding, but go ahead and begin there. Not just the wonder you feel at being able to bring me joy, but go ahead and be there. But don't stay there on the cushion of my innocence. I will always betray you. This is kind. This is forgiveness.

Start with what you feel, Daddies. The trees and the water and polar bears and the silk in your pocket. Start with what you feel. The stones and the birds and the music and the fine meal. Start with your own sweat. Start with your own tears.

Put the thimble full of tears by the bed. And in the morning, when the moisture's gone, salt the food.

© KONINKLIJKE BRILL NV, LEIDEN, 2019 | DOI:10.1163/9789004383562_034

Put the cup of sweat on the altar. Make an altar. Vow to self. Find the jug, the tub. Move and feel until they fill.

Learn to float and when you are lost in the sea of love, find your firmness. Solid as earth, hold together the roots you twine with other's stories, feelings, songs and wishes.

Learn to burn, and re-grow. Become the season turning, the crucible of transformation.

Become as vast as the sky.

I don't know the details, Daddies. Those are up to you.
I think it starts with salt though.
A little exertion.
A tear.

Standing by you,
Kimberly

DISCUSSION GUIDE

1. How does the word "Daddy" carry different meaning than the word "Father?" How are the two words used in public conversations, in intimate discussions and by whom?
2. Given that "Daddy" is a word that usually refers to men, how does the text de-center maleness from our understanding of "Daddy?" What does it mean to de-center maleness in this way?
3. How is "Who's your daddy?" both a statement of power and a joke, at the same time? (What does joking conceal or reveal about social norms and values in this instance?)
4. How have you heard the phrase "Who's your Daddy?" used in personal and community interactions, in sports, politics or advertising? What has changed about your understanding or use of this phrase in reading *The Daddies*?
5. The italicized sections of the book represent the voice of the "mythic girl." She is both the same as the narrator and also more than the narrator. How does this literary treatment enhance the story's ability to transcend personal storytelling?
6. The first section of the book includes childhood snapshots – moments when the importance of gendered hierarchy are being instilled in the main character. Can you remember moments from your own childhood that instilled the importance of gendered hierarchy?
7. There are two different chapters entitled "The First Time." Other than one being an account of incest and the other being a consensual sexual relationship between adults – how do the two scenes differ?
8. How are purity and ownership rituals, inherent in traditional marriage, romanticized? Why does this persist in modern culture, given their clear misogynist underpinnings?
9. How do voters look for and laud masculine traits, even in female political candidates?

10. How do interpersonal relationship rituals between men and women support incest culture? I.e., how is childlike appearance and behavior in women romanticized in mainstream culture and in interpersonal dialogue?
11. Is gender difference necessary for attraction?
12. How are women complicit in patriarchy and misogyny? (This complex question should be answerable in numerous ways, based on the text.)
13. The final chapters of the book imply that power relationships might be possible without oppression and without the necessity of gendered dynamics. Do you agree? Why and why not?
14. Do you find the final chapters of the book hopeful? Why and why not? How might it be possible in your own life to create and nurture non-violent forms of masculinity?
15. How and why are actual stories (and analyses) of sex and sexual interactions kept out of public and scholarly discourse? Who/ what is protected when sex is not discussed from a variety of perspectives?
16. How might it look to eradicate misogyny from your own thinking, choices, language and life? How might that influence the culture we collectively create if more people were to do this?

REFERENCES

Banerjee, N. (2008, May 19). Dancing the night away, with a higher purpose. *The New York Times*. Retrieved from http://www.nytimes.com/2008/05/19/us/19purity.html

Dark, K. (2016). *Out of the woods*. San Diego, CA: San Diego University Press.

Deming, B. (2004). Preface. In b. hooks (Ed.), *The will to change: Men, masculinity, and love* (pp. xi–xvii). New York, NY: Simon & Schuster.

Hardy, T. (2009). Working class incest survivor femme. In J. C. Burke (Ed.), *Visible: A femmethology* (Vol. 2, p. 160). Ypsilanti: Homofactus Press L.L.C.

hooks, b. (2004). *The will to change: Men, masculinity, and love*. New York, NY: Simon & Schuster.

Knox, S. (2008). The Ms. education of Shelby Knox [Web log post]. Retrieved from http://www.shelbyknox.wordpress.com/

Lakoff, G. (1996). *Moral politics: How liberals and conservatives think*. Chicago, IL: The University of Chicago Press.

Purity Balls [Television broadcast]. (2007). *The today show*. New York, NY: NBC. Retrieved from http://www.youtube.com/watch?v=uYdKfUbOdao#action=share

Rushing, J. H. (2010). *Erotic mentoring: Women's transformations in the university*. Walnut Creek: Left Coast Press.

Schneider, M. (2012). *Marilyn's last sessions*. Edinburgh: Canongate.

Stelter, B. (2011, April 28). CBS reporter recounts a 'merciless' assault. *The New York Times*, p. A13.

Sylver, S. (2014, September 24). *Ten years gone: Pedro Martinez calls the Yankees his daddy*. Retrieved from https://bosoxinjection.com/2014/09/24/ten-years-gone-pedro-martinez-calls-yankees-daddy/

Wilson, R., Wilson, L., & Lueders, B. (2001). *Celebrations of faith: Tying our children's heartstrings to the truth*. Colorado Springs, CO: Faith Parenting.

Winfrey, O. (2009, May 14). *Facing freedom*. Retrieved from http://www.oprah.com/oprahshow/freed-from-prison-after-killing-her-father/all

ABOUT THE AUTHOR

 **Kimberly Dark** is a writer, professor and raconteur working to reveal the hidden architecture of everyday life so that we all discover our influences and reclaim our power as social creators. She's performed stories and poetry at hundreds of venues worldwide and her essays appear in a wide range of scholarly and popular publications. She's the author of *Love and Errors* (Puna Press, 2018) and co-editor of *Ways of Being in Teaching* (Sense, 2017). She teaches in Sociology at Cal State, San Marcos and in the Cal State Summer Arts Program.

Printed in the United States
By Bookmasters